STREET
FOODS

STREET FOODS

HINNERK VON BARGEN

THE CULINARY INSTITUTE OF AMERICA

Photography by **Francesco Tonelli**

Culinary Institute
of America

WILEY

This book is printed on acid-free paper.

This edition published 2025

Copyright © 2016 by The Culinary Institute of America.
All rights reserved.

Cover and interior photography © 2016 by Francesco Tonelli, with the exception of the Preface and Chapter 1.

THE CULINARY INSTITUTE OF AMERICA

PRESIDENT	Dr. Tim Ryan '77, CMC
PROVOST	Mark Erickson '77, CMC
DIRECTOR OF PUBLISHING	Nathalie Fischer
SENIOR EDITORIAL PROJECT MANAGER	Margaret Wheeler '00
EDITORIAL ASSISTANT	Laura Monroe '12

Published by John Wiley & Sons, Inc., Hoboken, New Jersey

Published simultaneously in Canada

No part of this publication may be reproduced, stored in a retrieval system, or transmitted in any form or by any means, electronic, mechanical, photocopying, recording, scanning, or otherwise, except as permitted under Section 107 or 108 of the 1976 United States Copyright Act, without either the prior written permission of the Publisher, or authorization through payment of the appropriate per-copy fee to the Copyright Clearance Center, Inc., 222 Rosewood Drive, Danvers, MA 01923, 978-750-8400, fax 978-646-8600, or on the web at www.copyright.com. Requests to the Publisher for permission should be addressed to the Permissions Department, John Wiley & Sons, Inc., 111 River Street, Hoboken, NJ 07030, 201-748-6011, fax 201-748-6008, or online at www.wiley.com/go/permissions.

Evaluation copies are provided to qualified academics and professionals for review purposes only, for use in their courses during the next academic year. These copies are licensed and may not be sold or transferred to a third party. Upon completion of the review period, please return the evaluation copy to Wiley. Return instructions and a free-of-charge shipping label are available at www.wiley.com/go/returnlabel. Outside of the United States, please contact your local representative.

Limit of Liability/Disclaimer of Warranty: While the publisher and author have used their best efforts in preparing this book, they make no representations or warranties with respect to the accuracy or completeness of the contents of this book and specifically disclaim any implied warranties of merchantability or fitness for a particular purpose. No warranty may be created or extended by sales representatives or written sales materials. The advice and strategies contained herein may not be suitable for your situation. You should consult with a professional where appropriate. Neither the publisher nor author shall be liable for any loss of profit or any other commercial damages, including but not limited to special, incidental, consequential, or other damages.

For general information on our other products and services, or technical support, please contact our Customer Care Department within the United States at 800-762-2974, outside the United States at 317-572-3993, or fax 317-572-4002.

Wiley publishes in a variety of print and electronic formats. Some content that appears in print may not be available in electronic books. For more information about Wiley products, visit our website at www.wiley.com.

Cover and interior design by Wendy Lai

Library of Congress Cataloging-in-Publication Data:
Von Bargen, Hinnerk.
  Street foods / Hinnerk von Bargen [and] the Culinary Institute of America.
    pages cm
  Includes bibliographical references and index.
  ISBN 978-0-470-92864-6 (cloth : acid-free paper) |
  ISBN 9781394347780 (paperback)
  1. Street food. 2. International cooking.
I. Culinary Institute of America. II. Title.
  TX823.V67 2015
  641.59—dc23

2015003509

Printed in the United States of America
SKY10096265_011425

CONTENTS

Preface vi
Acknowledgments viii
About the Author ix

CHAPTER 1
What Is Street Food? 2

CHAPTER 2
Meat & Poultry 44

CHAPTER 3
Fish & Seafood 120

CHAPTER 4
Vegetables 184

CHAPTER 5
Grains, Legumes, Noodles, & Bread 252

CHAPTER 6
Sweets & Beverages 328

Glossary 382
Bibliography 392
Index 393

PREFACE

"Every day, somewhere on the globe, embers are readied to roast eggplants and peppers; cooks shape fresh pasta into little ears and long noodles; garlic and ginger sizzle as they hit the surface of hot woks; fish is sliced for ceviche; fresh tamales are carefully packed into steamers; tapas, mezze, and antipasti platters are stacked high; meats are skewered and rubbed with spice mixtures; old metal tables are wiped clean; and the lights are turned on in night markets from Chiang Mai to Marrakech anticipating hungry crowds. It's SHOWTIME in the world of food!"

— GREG DRESCHER

THESE WERE THE OPENING REMARKS OF GREG DRESCHER, vice president of strategic initiatives and industry leadership, at the 2009 Worlds of Flavor International Conference focusing on street food at The Culinary Institute of America's Greystone campus.

Street food, in the past often ignored, looked down upon, or even ridiculed by many culinary professionals, has moved into the epicurean spotlight. Operators of food trucks use the latest technology and social networking to inform their devout followers of upcoming specials and locations. Recreational and even business travelers are looking for exciting and original hawker centers instead of the hottest, newest fine-dining restaurant. And classical street foods and their creative interpretations have made their way onto the menus of critically acclaimed eateries. The playing field has been leveled; outdoor culinary professionals, who create, prepare, and serve exciting meals in casual settings, receive acknowledgment for their contributions, just like their star-studded restaurant counterparts.

Globalization, the media, international travel, and trade have broadened most people's culinary horizons; they have sparked a genuine desire to also explore street food beyond the local palate. Formerly unknown international classics such as bánh mì, pad thai, Turkish water börek, sincronizada, and falafel have become familiar and are met with comfort, and sometimes with the confident knowledge of where to find the best one.

Today, many dishes transcend geopolitical borders. Tacos filled with Korean beef and kimchi, Spam sushi, seafood hot dogs with creamy savoy cabbage, and Indian chai with tapioca bubbles are standing witness that chefs and customers alike are on the constant lookout for new ideas and inquisitively experimenting with novel combinations.

The objective of *Street Foods* is to offer a new look at food served out of trucks, booths, and mobile vending stations. The aim is to recodify established classics and introduce new creations. The almost 250 recipes are selected and sorted by main ingredient and serving style rather than by ethnicity or regional background. When the recipes were chosen and edited, authenticity was not always the main factor. In interviews, street-food vendors and international food-service experts made it very clear that concerns about food safety and practicality and the local tastes take priority over authenticity. All food vendors agreed, however, that just like quality and taste, the dish's culinary integrity should not be compromised. There are many versions and interpretations of a burger, a panino, falafel, and other street-food classics, but the key elements of these dishes need to be honored and maintained.

CHAPTER 1, WHAT IS STREET FOOD?, further explores these topics by establishing a working definition of street food and looking at the history of the evolution of street food. It outlines the categories of street foods that the recipes are divided into and tells the reader how to prepare, transport, and serve street food. Additionally, the chapter looks at the different flavor profiles for street foods from around the world by discussing the dishes, ingredients, and tools from the countries represented in the book.

Chapters 2 through 6 contain the recipes for the book and are organized by ingredient category, such as Meat and Poultry or Vegetables. Each of the recipe chapters contains additional text about techniques that are used and ingredient-specific information for creating street-food dishes.

CHAPTER 2, MEAT & POULTRY, discusses the fundamental cooking techniques for meat and how they can be adapted for an environment where street food is being prepared. There are also charts that identify the best types of meat for each cooking method.

CHAPTER 3, FISH & SEAFOOD, offers tips and charts on the best ways to cook fish and seafood.

CHAPTER 4, VEGETABLES, includes information about how to properly store vegetables and a table that breaks down the methods for vegetable cookery and the most appropriate vegetables for each method.

CHAPTER 5, GRAINS, LEGUMES, NOODLES, & BREAD, tackles a big segment of street foods in its coverage of grains, pasta, noodles, and bread. Each category has its own table that offers information about the characteristics and applications for preparation of each ingredient.

CHAPTER 6, SWEETS & BEVERAGES, gives the reader an overview of the street-food approach to sweets and drinks from around the world.

The recipes are written with a culinary professional or well-versed food enthusiast in mind, providing inspiration and guidance through the wonderful world of casual street-food dining.

SUPPLEMENTAL MATERIALS

Street Foods offers an **Instructor's Manual**, including a **Test Bank** to help instructors who are designing courses based around healthy menu items.

A password-protected Instructor Book Companion Web site (www.wiley.com/college/ CIA) provides access to the online **Instructor's Manual** and the text-specific teaching resources. The **PowerPoint lecture slides** are also available on the website for download.

ACKNOWLEDGMENTS

First and foremost, I would like to acknowledge my wife, Ming, and our daughter Melina, whose love, patience, and genuine passion for all things culinary kept on inspiring me. Your continuous sincere feedback has helped me to stay on the right track.

Additionally, I need to thank my parents, Erika and Gerhard, and my sister Caroline with her family, for their love and tolerant understanding toward my ideas. You planted the seeds to help me become the culinarian I am today.

The Culinary Institute of America, under the visionary leadership of Dr. Tim Ryan, deserves special recognition. This infinite, ever-growing pool of gastronomic expertise, resources, and inspiration has empowered me to develop and grow beyond my wildest dreams, eventually enabling me to author a book. Thank you for helping me to make a chef's dream come true.

Francesco Tonelli, your gift of translating my dishes and random thoughts into awe-inspiring pictures was a crucial building block in making this book what it is; the impressions you left are not going anywhere. These pictures also stand witness for the invaluable support from Leo Deoti e Silva and Derek Laughren during the photo shoot; I could not have cooked all the food without you.

Nathalie Fischer, Maggie Wheeler, Erin McDowell, and everybody else in the publishing department of The Culinary Institute of America: I cannot help but admire your expertise, dedication, and patience.

To my friend Chris Dunn and his wife, Nissa, culinary and articulate geniuses, thank you for your guidance through the world of written words and the best currywurst ever.

Of course, I have to thank my friends and colleagues all across the globe. I would love to name each one of you in appreciation for the active and passive mentoring, coaching, and priceless inspiration. So many have touched my life and career that I am afraid I cannot name them all without forgetting somebody. Special thanks, however, to a few of my friends: Chefs Robert Danhi, Parvinder Bali, Marco Brüschweiler, Dereck Brown, Elizabeth Johnson, and Iliana de la Vega. Each one of you is a walking and breathing encyclopedia. I am grateful for your generosity with your time, knowledge, and recipes. Our conversations have been eye-opening and encouraging.

Last but not least, I need to thank all the devoted culinarians who hit the road every day, rain or shine, and actually do the work. Researching for this book has helped me tolerate my weakness and simply give in to tasty snacks on the go. It is nice to have endless excuses to indulge in my favorite hobby—eating street food from all over the world.

Thank you to you all,
Hinnerk von Bargen

ABOUT THE AUTHOR

HINNERK VON BARGEN is a professor of culinary arts at The Culinary Institute of America, San Antonio, Texas. Since joining the CIA faculty in 1999, Chef von Bargen has been teaching various culinary arts courses in the associate's degree program and continuing education for culinary professionals at the college's campuses in Hyde Park and San Antonio. A Certified Hospitality Educator (CHE), Chef von Bargen holds a Master Chef certificate from the Hotel School in Hamburg, Germany. He completed two apprenticeships in his native Germany before beginning his professional career, which has included chef positions in hotels and restaurants in Germany, South Africa, and China.

Founded in 1946, **The Culinary Institute of America** is an independent, not-for-profit college offering associate's and bachelor's degrees with majors in culinary arts, baking and pastry arts, and culinary science, as well as certificate programs in culinary arts and wine and beverage studies. As the world's premier culinary college, the CIA provides thought leadership in the areas of health and wellness, sustainability, and world cuisines and cultures through research and conferences. The CIA has a network of 45,000 alumni that includes industry leaders such as Grant Achatz, Anthony Bourdain, Roy Choi, Cat Cora, Dan Coudreaut, Steve Ells, Johnny Iuzzini, Charlie Palmer, and Roy Yamaguchi. The CIA also offers courses for professionals and enthusiasts, as well as consulting services in support of innovation for the food-service and hospitality industry. The college has campuses in Hyde Park, New York; St. Helena, California; San Antonio, Texas; and Singapore.

Photography by Alessa Ammeter

CHAPTER 1

WHAT IS STREET FOOD?

treet food is a loosely coined expression to describe snacks or whole meals prepared and sold from a non-permanent structure, mainly for immediate consumption. Trucks or carts, small booths in public places, or floating markets are the most common venues.

Served swiftly on sticks; in bowls; on plates; or wrapped in flatbread, lettuce, or paper, street food is inexpensive, convenient, and portable, ideal for a mobile, on-the-go lifestyle or for a quick economical meal.

Different from fast food, street food is perceived to be based on local, seasonal, fresh, and minimally processed ingredients. Many street-food stands represent the local cuisine with its most common ingredients. Typically prepared by independent vendors who specialize in very few dishes, street food is seen as a true and authentic reflection of a culture and its cuisine. There might be some truth to that: A successful native vendor selling chicken and beef satays from his mobile grill in Kuala Lumpur has had his whole career and life to perfect and personalize it. On the other hand, there are many street-food favorites with little relation to the culinary classics of the locale. Introduced by the media, travelers, or migrants, these specialties have secured a definite place in the hearts and stomachs of the people. A popular street food in the Puebla region of Mexico is the *taco Árabe*, or "Arab-style taco," filled with meat sliced from an upright rotisserie that most would recognize as Gyros (see page 98) or shawarma. To this day a reflection of Middle Eastern cooking, it has over time given in to local interpretations. The traditional mutton has changed to pork, some vendors use tortillas instead of the traditional pita bread, and the yogurt or tahini sauce has been replaced with regional salsas. A comparable version, known as *taco al pastor*, made its way into Mexico City in the early 1970s and is now found all over Mexico.

Sometimes the introduction of a single ingredient has a massive impact on a street-food culture. Brought to Hawaii as part of U.S. military rations, Spam, a relatively inexpensive canned meat product, has left its mark on the islands. Hawaiian cuisine, known for its unique combination of East Asian, Polynesian, and European flavors and culinary practices, has embraced Spam in many ways. Omnipresent on restaurant menus as well as at street-food stands, it can be found paired with rice as a sushi variation, deep-fried like tempura, or as a simple grilled Spam steak.

Street food can be found anywhere sufficiently large groups of people have settled, but it is more widespread in less-developed countries. Small dwellings with very basic cooking spaces lead to an active life outside the home. Residents of industrialized regions, however, are rediscovering street food as part of a contemporary lifestyle and as an inexpensive opportunity to explore exotic and new food items, or simply to enjoy familiar comfort food.

Many cultures serve and consume street food as a snack or small meal for quick nourishment. In other regions, it is the main meal. Residents of East and Southeast Asia have embraced street food as a way of life; meals are often social events with friends, family, or even strangers who happen to share one of the communal tables. Singapore especially, with its unparalleled passion for food, has become a world-renowned gastronomic-travel destination for its risk-free street food. All small food vendors are located in hawker centers under the supervision of a public health inspector. These hawker centers are found everywhere, including in public housing developments, major subway stations, open-air pavilions, and climate-controlled shopping centers, where they are called food courts.

THE HISTORY OF STREET FOOD

Throughout history, food for the common people has been produced and consumed as a communal affair. Retreating to one's private quarters to eat a meal alone or in a very small group is a relatively recent development, found mostly in industrialized regions. Interestingly, many cultures struggle to understand the importance of privacy in the western world. In some other languages, the word *privacy* actually has a negative connotation, often associated with isolation or exclusion.

In the cities and towns of ancient civilizations, food was hawked in public places. The majority of urban dwellings during that time did not have a kitchen, and most food was purchased already prepared. Trajan's Market, inaugurated in Rome in 113 c.e., consisted of administrational offices and shops selling cheeses, fresh meats, wine, or prepared dishes. To ensure food safety and wholesomeness, the food distribution to and from this market was overseen by a sophisticated system of government-appointed health inspectors. Today, the ruins of this market are a major tourist attraction, often referred to as Rome's oldest shopping mall.

During medieval times, street food was sold at fairs, tournaments, and other large gatherings throughout settlements and cities. Peddlers used pushcarts to sell stews, porridges, and baked goods. Over time, food became more sophisticated, and with the onset of industrialization came the need to safely cater to the rapidly growing population of the expanding cities, giving rise to today's strict food-safety regulations.

In many cultures, settlements have commonly been built around a communal cooking place. In European villages of the past, this would have been a large brick oven. When the baker finished baking his bread, the residents would use the residual heat of this public oven to cook their stews or bake their cakes. Many traditional dishes have their origins in these collective kitchens. *Bäckeoffe*, literally translated as *baker's oven*, is an Alsatian meat stew cooked in an earthenware dish with a tight-fitting lid. Traditionally, the lid is sealed with bread dough before baking, to retain as much of the moisture as possible. In Brazilian cuisine, a similar technique is applied to a dish known as *barreado*, a meat and vegetable stew cooked slowly for up to 15 hours in a clay pot sealed with a manioc paste. The word *chowder* is derived from "cauldron," a big metal pot used to cook large amounts of soup or stew for a crowd.

Communal cooking and eating arrangements are still common practice in many less-developed regions. Helping to use resources effectively, such shared kitchens also serve as a meeting place and provide opportunities for the villagers to socialize, enjoy some small talk, and exchange news.

Collective kitchens and canteens have even been part of political movements. During China's Cultural Revolution of the 1960s and 1970s, some local governments called for the dismantling and elimination of all household kitchens. All meals for the residents of the towns or villages would be catered at public commons. The objective was to create a more proficiently working food supply as well as to boost the nation's steel production by melting all iron and steel gathered from the kitchens. Even though the initiative was abandoned very quickly, this segment of Chinese history left a distinct mark on the country's culinary landscape. Today known as Revolutionary Cuisine, this style, featuring dishes and recipes prepared with the simplest ingredients and methods, is looked back upon with some sense of nostalgia.

Our universal desire to explore and conquer has also contributed to the development and evolution of mobile catering. In military field-mess units or on ships, crowds of hungry soldiers, warriors, and sailors had to be fed with the simplest means. Over time, this food has evolved from a lucky meal of a freshly killed animal cooked over an open fire to nourishing rations prepared in well-equipped mobile field kitchens.

Today's variety of street food has expanded immensely; a pulled pork sandwich might be served in a steamed bun and feature Chinese BBQ. Crispy sliced French bread is offered with a variety of toppings as "bruschetta to go." And in an effort to combine good food with a show, a rendition of macaroni and cheese is browned with a massive blowtorch. The gloves are off; dishes that in the past would never have been associated with street food are now common fare on food trucks. As the competition grows, vendors are coming up with increasingly creative ideas. Culinarians continue to educate themselves to keep up with the ever-shifting culinary landscape.

The tables have turned. The business of peddling street food no longer suggests that other attempts have failed; undertaken with passion, ingenuity, and skill, it has progressed into an attractive career choice for culinary professionals and in some cases leads to a whole fleet of food trucks or a well-established storefront business.

PREPARING, TRANSPORTING, AND SERVING STREET FOOD

Hypothetically, anything can be served as street food. However, limited resources at the site, local and state food-safety regulations, and transportability concerns curb the diversity of mobile menus. Street food is simple: Produce, seafood, or meat tossed in a sauce or dressing, or quickly assembled wraps and sandwiches, are popular cold items.

Among hot dishes, soups, stews, braises, grain pilafs, and hot cereals are all characterized by their capability to be held hot for extended periods. Other hot foods include dishes that can be cooked with simple means, such as deep-fried, stir-fried, or grilled foods.

The casual atmosphere and environment of street food is one of the appealing aspects for many patrons. However, uncontrollable ambient temperatures require close monitoring of serving and holding temperatures. Approved food trucks are sufficiently equipped to fulfill current food-safety requirements. In less advanced settings with limited or no electricity, cold holding is accomplished with portable coolers and refreezable gel packs or ice blankets. Hot holding is most easily achieved with slow cookers, electric water baths, or sturdy pots on portable induction burners. In the absence of electricity, portable gas burners are an alternative for cooking, holding, or reheating. However, wind gusts might extinguish the flame, resulting in potential fire and safety hazards. And, depending on local regulations, the use of open flames might require the approval of the fire department.

Required permits and licenses for mobile food vending depend on local and state regulations. In most cases, a mobile vending permit from local authorities and a state food-manufacturing license need to be obtained. Additionally, an inspected and approved commercial pantry or kitchen is required for all preparatory work and storage of the food; in most cases, the vending site, the food truck, or a home kitchen do not qualify. When choosing a location for the food truck or vending site, zoning and parking restrictions need to be considered. Often, local regulations will not allow public vending in close proximity to restaurants or other food-service operations. In recent years, local zoning rules began to designate areas where food trucks could come together, comparable to a food court or hawker center. Often teasingly referred to as trailer parks, these privately managed locations offer public restrooms and sometimes an approved prep kitchen for hourly or daily rent for the food-truck operators.

CATEGORIES OF STREET FOOD

BOWL FOODS

Bowl foods have evolved from communal feeding situations in which everybody helped himself to a portion from a large pot of stew. Serving food in bowls is a quick way to satisfy the hunger of a large crowd of waiting guests. Most dishes served in bowls, such as BBQ Hominy Stew (page 289), Tomato-Braised Cauliflower (page 194), or Black Bean Soup (page 267) are held hot and can be swiftly served into a bowl or onto a plate. Dishes such as the Salad of Bean Starch Sheets (page 269) or Stir-Fried Shredded Flatbread (page 290) require some last-minute cooking or final assembly.

In advanced mobile food-service settings with the possibility of ware washing, reusable plastic or ceramic vessels are sometimes used. To lower the risk of cross contamination and breakage, however, most street-food operators prefer to serve their food on disposable serving ware.

FOODS ON A STICK

Foods on a stick have their origins with nomadic tribes or traveling warriors who would place their food onto swords or wild branches and cook over an open fire. Today, it is the convenience factor and the casual appeal that make these dishes so attractive to the customer. Many culinary cultures include diced meat, seafood, or vegetables threaded on wooden or metal skewers. In some cases, the meat or seafood is ground, allowing for the use of trimmings and less desirable cuts. Usually, the objective with skewered items is to cook them quickly with minimal equipment and energy. Traditional kebob or satay grills, which have no grill racks and are only about 6 in/18 cm wide, suspend the skewer a few inches above a small amount of hot charcoal. This way, the food cooks rapidly with minimal loss of heat. Additionally, the narrow grill allows enough space for the meat to cook over intense heat, creating bold seared and charred flavors without burning the wooden skewers. Some prominent examples are the Turkish Shish Kebob (page 88) and the Chicken Köfte Kebob (page 79).

Other savory foods served on sticks include Corn Dogs (page 103), Grilled Corn on the Cob (page 212), and the Pakora Fried Vegetable Skewer (page 214). Here, the skewer serves as a vehicle of serving and eating rather than as a cooking tool. Similarly, most popular sweet street foods on a stick are skewered for convenience of eating. Fried Bananas in Manioc Crust (page 357), ice pops, cotton candy, and fresh fruits dipped in a sugary glaze are some sweet favorites.

Skewers are made from a variety of materials. For its convenience, biodegradability, and sustainable production methods, bamboo is a popular choice among many mobile vendors. Metal skewers, commonly made from stainless steel, are valued for their durability, resistance to extreme heat on grills, and in some cases, their design. Their high price and food-safety concerns, on the other hand, often make them less suitable for mobile food-service environments.

BREAD, STUFFED FOODS, AND SANDWICHES

Parched or baked grains, in one form or another, have been a principal food source for millennia. The first breads were based on coarsely crushed grains and water; unleavened and dense, these cakes probably resembled dried-out cereals. Over time, these cakes developed into today's classical breads. Unleavened breads include Corn Tortillas (page 279) from Mexico and Chapati Bread (page 115) from India. Among the leavened breads, Caribbean Roti Bread with Guyanese Filling (page 102) and Pita Bread (page 111) from the Middle East are favorites.

In many regions, bread is served as the main item as part of a salad or it is accompanied by a dip, such as pita bread with Hummus (page 322) or baba ghanoush in the Middle East. In Singapore or Malaysia, the flaky Roti Prata (page 110) with curry gravy is a popular breakfast.

In many other instances, the bread is the vehicle for a filling or topping. Dishes like this include sandwiches, Mexican sincronizada, Bruschetta (pages 301–304), and many others.

FINGER FOODS

Finger foods, as the name suggests, are meant to be enjoyed without the help of any cutlery. For much of mankind's history, and in some cultures to this day, food has been eaten without utensils. In many cases, finger foods are thought of as small snacks, served as hors d'oeuvres, appetizers, or something to share rather than a main meal. Commonly two- or three-bite items that are crispy or dry on the outside, most finger foods can easily be held between the thumb and two fingers and can be enjoyed cleanly. Technically, sandwiches also fall under this category, but they generally represent a whole meal and are therefore not considered finger foods. Classical finger food examples are Chicken Flautas (page 99) from Mexico, French Fries (page 177), Vietnamese or Chinese Crispy Spring Rolls (pages 105 and 106), and fried Plantain Fritters (page 237) from Puerto Rico.

SWEETS AND BEVERAGES

Mostly eaten as a feel-good snack, reward, or refreshment, sweet street food is found all over the world. In most cultures, a family trip to the zoo, the beach, or amusement park is accompanied by something sweet, and not only for the little ones. Most parents also know that a good helping of ice cream, a candied apple, or cotton candy can expedite the drying of children's tears or help to mediate young siblings' squabbles. Sweets are simply the sometimes guilty pleasures we all like to indulge in from time to time.

Frequently, sweet street foods are part of a celebration or regional or seasonal event. Beignets (page 358) or funnel cakes seem to be compulsory snacks at county fairs in the United States. At Christmas fairs in Europe, especially Germany and Austria, Quark Fritters (page 360) are an omnipresent snack.

Many cultures serve hot sweet dishes for breakfast. In Thailand, Black Rice Pudding with Coconut Milk and Dried Mango (page 343) is a much-appreciated boost of energy during the morning hours. And in China, Spicy or Sweet Soft Tofu (page 280) and Plain or curdled Soy Milk (page 275) are popular breakfast dishes.

Many cultures have distinct beverages, traditionally served on the go. American children dream of raising some funds with a lemonade stand. In the Middle East and Central and South Asia, yogurt drinks are very popular; Indian cuisine is famous for its Mango Lassi (page 365), a sweet mango smoothie. Slightly salted yogurt drinks, known as salty lassi in India or *Ayran* in Turkey, serve as thirst quenchers on blistering hot days, with benefits comparable to isotonic sports drinks.

Alcoholic beverages such as mulled hard cider or red wine, served outdoors during cold winter months, are designed to help people to stay warm. A hot Tea Punch (page 378), known as Jagertee in Austria, is popular among hikers and skiers after a cold winter day in the Alpine woods, as it truly helps to warm up the body.

INTERNATIONAL FLAVOR PRINCIPLES

The world of street food has changed and continues to evolve at a rapid pace. Today, street food is as international as its patrons and vendors. The public's knowledge and awareness of good food is growing, and the competition is inspiring, but also fierce.

To retain customers who return for specific dishes, successful vendors work hard to maintain the integrity and high quality of established menu items. To attract patrons looking for an innovative quick meal, regular limited-time offers with international dishes or new creations inspired by foreign cuisines can be implemented on the menu.

Taking a close look at world cuisines and their global flavor principles helps to find options that keep the establishment exciting. Different flavors, ingredients, techniques, or dishes can be identified. Paramount to success of a cross-cultural menu design is the respect of the culture and its cuisine. A superficial approach with copied and untested recipes might turn fusion cuisine into confused food, not likely to result in successful menu offerings. Moreover, new dishes and techniques, when they are intertwined with existing menu items, need to be chosen wisely to avoid compromising the brand identity of the business.

There are countless cuisines from which to choose. Foods from China, Japan, Korea, Vietnam, and Thailand enjoy worldwide recognition and can offer interesting applications on a menu. The cuisines of the Middle East and North Africa, strongly influenced by Arab culture and the Muslim religion, present a completely different array of street foods. In the western hemisphere, the new-world cuisines of the Americas offer classical and innovative international foods in North America and exciting vibrancy in Central and South America. Chefs in Europe have also embraced many influences from abroad and interwoven them with their well-established and time-honored cuisines. This section will take a look at flavor principles and techniques of popular world cuisines and will try to communicate a basic understanding of their culinary cultures.

EAST AND SOUTH ASIA

Asia represents an enormous landmass with very diverse people, cultures, and cuisines. Differing from the rest of the world, many of the cultures and cuisines have developed over centuries with limited influence from the outside. However, when cultural exchange does occur, newly introduced ingredients and techniques are often embraced and assimilated.

In Asia, street food is usually not sold from an isolated vendor, but rather it is found in busy bazaars, night markets, or in organized hawker centers. Interestingly, many people in Asia like to differentiate between street food and food sold on the streets. Traditional street foods include snacks and small dishes for immediate consumption. Just as often, however, people buy whole dishes or components of a meal from vendors on the street to eat at home with the family or at work.

Photography by Terrence McCarthy

International Flavor Principles 11

Common Tools in **East and South Asia**

The wok is probably one of the most identifiable culinary tools of Asia. Known under different names in many regions, this ubiquitous all-purpose cooking vessel can be used to execute almost every cooking technique. The cooking range for a wok is just as unique. Designed to suspend the wok over the heat source, it provides instantly available high heat while limiting energy loss, thereby creating a sustainable use of energy for food preparation.

Japanese cuisine, known for its sophisticated elegance, is also famous for a variety of specialized tools. These include ceramic graters to turn radishes or wasabi into a very fine paste. Interestingly, these graters helped to inspire the line of tools we know today as Microplanes. Other specialized utensils include bamboo mats to roll sushi and drop lids to ensure that a simmering or poaching item is fully submerged in its cooking liquid. Japanese knives, highly coveted all over the world, further illustrate this refined approach to all things culinary. Unlike chefs from other Asian countries who are famous for their ability to cut everything with a cleaver, Japanese chefs have specific knives for most tasks.

An upright cylindrical oven, oftentimes built directly into the ground, can be found in many regions of south and central Asia. Known as a tandoor in India, it is commonly constructed with thick hearth walls. Fired with wood, charcoal, gas, or, in remote regions, with dried cow dung, a tandoor is capable of reaching temperatures of up to 900°F/482°C—perfect to roast skewered meats and vegetables, and to bake flatbreads. Despite this high heat output, a tandoor is designed to limit the loss of energy.

The omnipresence of rice in Southeast Asia has led to the design of many unique tools for its preparation. Rice noodles, for example, are made by forcing a rice-water slurry through a perforated metal disk into boiling water. The resulting strands of rice noodles are ready to use. Alternatively, a paste from raw rice and water is steamed into thin sheets and cut into desired shapes or ribbon-style noodles. Sweet potato noodles or noodles based on mung bean starch are made with comparable methods. A conical, tightly woven bamboo steamer with a corresponding pot is a unique tool from Thailand to steam glutinous rice.

China

Chinese street food is as diverse as China itself with its vastly varying landscapes, climate zones, and population made up of more than fifty ethnic groups. Many meals are enjoyed outside the home in small restaurants or street stands. In urban areas, it is very common for people to gather in public places at dawn for calisthenics. At that time, cargo bicycles or small mopeds often pass by to offer breakfast items such as Curdled Soy Milk with Fried Crullers (page 276) and salted vegetables or steamed buns.

The climate of northern China is suitable for growing wheat. Rice, while popular, often plays a secondary role on northern tables. Noodles, flatbreads, steamed breads, and dumplings are more common fare. Reflections of this can be found in the Stir-Fried

Shredded Flatbread (page 290) or the Salad of Bean Starch Sheets (page 269). Typical northern flavors include pungent sweet and sour dishes and subtler, delicately seasoned foods highlighting the ingredient's natural flavor. Found all over China, but especially typical for this region, is the use of garlic, ginger, and scallions. The proximity of Mongolia and its rule over China from 1279 to 1368 introduced dishes such as hot pot and Mongolian barbecue into northern China.

In the coastal east around Shanghai, a warmer, more humid climate promotes the cultivation of rice, making it the region's most popular staple. Soy sauce and sugar are omnipresent flavor components, resulting in many sweet and salty dishes, often with a generous amount of sauce; this approach is illustrated by the Braised Pork Belly with Dried Mustard Greens and Lily Buds in Fermented Tofu Sauce (page 93). The cuisine of the landlocked Sichuan region in the central west of China is known for its generous use of chiles and Sichaun peppercorns, resulting in fiery hot dishes with a popular flavor profile known as *Ma-La*, literally translating into "numb and spicy." The Spicy Tofu with Mushrooms (page 202) exemplifies that flavor.

Food from the south of China, known as Cantonese cuisine, is subtle, with flavorings and techniques that highlight the food's natural flavor. Famous for dim sum, Cantonese cuisine has a broad variety of steamed or fried snacks, such as Pan-Steamed Cilantro and Pork Dumplings (page 309).

TABLE 1.1 Typical Ingredients in a Chinese Kitchen

CONDIMENTS	HERBS/SPICES	PRODUCE	PROTEIN	STARCHES/LEGUMES
White and dark rice wine vinegar	Five-spice	Mushrooms	Wheat gluten	All-purpose flour
Light and dark soy sauce	Cilantro	Eggplant	Tofu	Dumpling wrappers
Sesame oil	White pepper	Leafy green vegetables	Beef	Mung beans, soybeans
Hoisin sauce	Sichuan pepper	Bean sprouts	Chicken	Noodles based on wheat, rice, mung beans, or sweet potatoes
Shaoxing wine	Ginger	Water lily buds	Organ meats	Refined starches from water chestnuts, mung beans, corn, potatoes
Chili bean paste Chili oil Dry chili paste Fresh chili paste	Garlic	Cabbages	Pork	Bean starch sheets
Oyster sauce	Star anise	Scallions	Seafood in coastal regions	Short- and long-grain rice

Japan

Japanese cuisine is characterized by its elegant simplicity; it aims to enhance and highlight the essential qualities of food. Spicy food is relatively uncommon. Sansho, a relative to the Chinese Sichuan pepper; and the Japanese seven-spice (also known as *shichimi togarashi*), a mixture of cayenne pepper, sansho, black and white sesame seeds, dried orange peel, ground ginger, and nori seaweed, are the only sources for some piquancy. In general, all aromas are clear and easily recognizable. Common flavors include light soy sauce as the all-purpose seasoning, mirin as the most common sweetener, and miso in soups or dressings.

As an island nation, Japan consumes large amounts of seafood and sea vegetation. Rice is a staple, and every meal revolves around it. In addition to rice, noodles based on wheat, buckwheat, sweet potato starch, or rice are very popular. In fact, Japan has among the highest noodle consumption per capita. Street food is not quite as popular and common as in other East Asian countries; most meals are consumed at home or in restaurants. The younger generation, on the other hand, embraces the comfort food served from small stands and street-side restaurants. Iconic dishes include Chicken Yakitori (page 82), a char-grilled and glazed chicken skewer. Most vendors offer variations featuring all parts of the chicken, from liver, gizzard, heart, and wings to the thigh and breast. Popular Japanese street-food variations include the famous ramen noodles, which are based on the Chinese la mian, hand-pulled noodles served in an aromatic broth, and other noodle dishes, including the nontraditional but popular Curry Udon Noodles (page 294). Among sweet snacks, taiyaki, a fish-shaped sweet cake filled with sweetened adzuki beans, can be found on the streets of Japan as well as Korea.

TABLE 1.2 Typical Ingredients in a Japanese Kitchen

CONDIMENTS	HERBS/SPICES	PRODUCE	PROTEIN	STARCHES/LEGUMES
Light soy sauce	Bonito flakes	Shitake mushrooms	Savory fish cakes	Ramen, somen, udon, and soba noodles
Sake	Sesame seeds	Leeks	Seafood	Short-grain rice
Mirin	Sansho	Daikon radish	Pork	Rice cakes
Gingko nuts	Dry mustard	Napa cabbage	Chicken	Soybeans
White rice vinegar	Ginger	Scallions	Beef	Mung beans
Wasabi	Kinome	Sea vegetation	Tofu	
Sesame oil	Seven-spice	Watercress		
Miso paste	Kelp	Persimmons		

Korea

The cuisine of the Korean peninsula has created many interesting ways to take advantage of the ocean's bounty. Seafood and maritime vegetation such as seaweed, kelp, and algae can be found on many tables. An anchovy extract, comparable to the Southeast Asian fish sauce, is an all-purpose seasoning almost as common as soy sauce. A unique aspect of Korea, compared to other northeast Asian cuisines, is the popularity of hot red chiles. Mostly used dried and omnipresent in every pantry, they are used to add a significant punch to stews, soups, salads, and, of course, kimchi, the ubiquitous spicy fermented vegetable accompanying every meal from breakfast to dinner. A popular Korean tableside condiment and cooking ingredient is *koju jiang* or gochujang. Made from red chiles, fermented rice, and soybeans, its status on Korean tables can be compared to the popularity of ketchup in the United States.

Highlighted on many menus as a featured ingredient, beef is the most popular meat in Korea; the intensely flavored oxtail and short ribs are the most coveted and expensive cuts. Pork, historically looked down upon and only consumed by lower classes of society, has gained momentum in recent decades. Now found on many tables and prepared in interesting ways, like Spicy Kimchi Stew with Pork (page 63), it is still often a secondary ingredient, playing a supporting role. Wheat was introduced to Korea only in the recent past and does not play a very prominent role. Because of this, Korean noodles are made from a variety of alternative starches and flours. The most common ingredients are sweet potatoes, corn, potatoes, rice, buckwheat, and mung beans. Stir-Fried Glass Noodles (page 297) is a popular dish that uses noodles made from sweet potato starch. Mung beans are common in

TABLE 1.3 Typical Ingredients in a Korean Kitchen

CONDIMENTS	HERBS/SPICES	PRODUCE	PROTEIN	STARCHES/LEGUMES
Light soy sauce	Anchovy extract	Fresh green chiles	Beef	Noodles based on rice, wheat, buckwheat, or sweet potatoes
White rice vinegar	Ginger	Scallions	Seafood	Pearl barley
Sesame oil	Garlic	Napa cabbage	Chicken	Short-grain rice
Kimchi	Chives	Mung beans	Tofu	Buckwheat
Red pepper paste (gochujang)	Dried red pepper powder	Radishes, turnips	Pork	Refined starches based on mung beans and sweet potatoes
Mirin	Mugwort	Sea vegetation		Millet
Fermented soybean paste		Dried vegetables		Mung beans

International Flavor Principles **15**

many Korean pantries as well. Their starch is used to produce bean threads, crystal-clear thin noodles with an interesting, slippery texture, often used in salads or soups. Mung beans are also used in rice, vegetable, and seafood dishes, like Chinese Mung Bean and Rice Crêpes (page 306). In general, street food in Korea is comfort food, convenient and fulfilling, served in friendly environments.

Vietnam

Vietnam is famous for its street food; because it is less regulated than in other countries, many experts feel it is true street food. In many countries, street food is often sold from an open window or wall in a storefront or a stall. In Vietnam, however, vendors roam the streets with their offerings. Typically offering only one item, they have spent their life and career refining and perfecting the perfect roasted pork belly, the fantastic bowl of pho, or the most flavorful rich coffee. Common cooking techniques of Vietnamese street food are coal grilling, deep-frying, and steaming.

The cuisine of Vietnam is known for its light and fresh appeal, with fresh herbs often offered whole, ripped coarsely, and added to the food at the last moment. Compared to other Southeast Asian cuisines, Vietnamese food is not inherently spicy; hot condiments are offered separately and added to achieve a personalized level of spiciness. A unique aspect of Vietnamese cuisine is the layering of flavors and textures, and many dishes are assembled at the last moment, often to the customer's specification or by the diner himself, like in the Vietnamese Grilled Shrimp Cake on Sugarcane (page 152).

The characteristics of Vietnamese cuisine vary from region to region. In the south, the pungency of fish sauce is dominant, and generous helpings of herbs are used to accentuate many dishes. Rice, a very important aspect of Vietnamese culture, is especially popular in the south.

Influenced by the imperial city of Hue, the cuisine of central Vietnam is considered to be more sophisticated, and a fair amount of herbs accompany a large choice of vegetarian dishes. Fish sauce as well as shrimp paste are standard seasonings, and chile spice is used more frequently. Rice noodles are also very popular in central Vietnam.

In the north, food is simpler, with not quite as many herbs; it is less sweet than in other regions, and not very spicy. Beef is a popular meat in this region, which is the origin of the world-famous Vietnamese noodle soup pho.

Thailand

With the two countries in close proximity to each other, the cuisines of Thailand and Vietnam are comparable. Year-round availability of a seemingly endless supply of fresh produce flavored with fresh herbs and a generous helping of hot red chiles give the foods of Thailand a bright and crisp appeal. Just as in Vietnamese cuisine, flavors are prominent and easily recognizable. In the south of Thailand, beef, goat, and seafood

Photography by Terrence McCarthy

International Flavor Principles 17

TABLE 1.4 Typical Ingredients in a Thai or Vietnamese Kitchen

CONDIMENTS	HERBS/SPICES	PRODUCE	PROTEIN	STARCHES/LEGUMES
Fish sauce	Basil	Bamboo shoots	Seafood	Bean thread and rice noodles
Curry paste	Mint	Cucumber	Pork	Rice paper
Shrimp paste	Saw-leaf herb (known as culantro in Latin America)	Bean sprouts	Chicken	Long-grain and sticky rice
Chiles	Lemongrass	Limes	Duck	Mung beans
Palm sugar	Ginger	Scallions	Beef	Red rice
Light soy sauce	Galangal	Shallots		
Coconut	Cilantro	Leafy green vegetables		
Hoisin sauce	Kaffir limes and leaves	Tamarind		
Fresh or roasted chili paste	Cilantro	Lotus roots		

are popular. In general, southern food is spicier, with a distinct Muslim influence coming from Malaysia. In the north of Thailand, food tends to be somewhat less spicy. Instead of chiles, green peppercorns, often added as whole sprigs to the food, are used to provide the coveted zing.

Noodles, most commonly made from rice flour, are among the most popular street foods in Thailand. Often served on the petals of banana blossoms, regional varieties of pad thai can be found all over the country. Most street food is grilled, stir-fried, deep-fried, or simmered. Skewered grilled meat like a satay or Beef Skewers with Green Chili Sauce (page 85) are good illustrations of how meat is served from mobile vending stations in Thailand. Som tam, a very spicy green papaya salad made to order, is often served accompanying grilled meats.

EASTERN MEDITERRANEAN AND NORTH AFRICA

Gastronomic customs of the Middle East have been influenced by trade with other Mediterranean nations, as well as the Silk Route trade with Central and East Asia. The expansion of Arab culture from the Levant over the Maghreb to parts of Spain during medieval times had a substantial impact on the societal and cultural makeup of the region. The introduction of new crops, along with innovative agricultural techniques and irrigation systems, transformed the arid plains of North Africa into fertile farmland. After the Renaissance, the exploration and colonization of Africa and the New World by European powers brought yet another great variety of new produce and techniques to the region's cuisine.

Common Tools in **the Eastern Mediterranean and North Africa**

Living and thriving in an area with little easily accessible water and fuel, the people of the Middle East and North Africa have developed tools and techniques to conserve these invaluable resources. Couscous, a culinary staple from the Maghreb, is a direct reflection of this approach. Couscous is made by mixing hard-wheat semolina with small amounts of water into a gritty mixture. This mixture is then rubbed between the hands to achieve a coarse, almost cornmeal-like consistency. After drying, the small couscous pebbles are steamed in a pot with a perforated bottom, which is tightly clamped over a different pot with simmering stew. This contraption, known as a couscousière, employs the steam of the simmering stew beneath to cook the couscous, eliminating the need for any additional water or energy.

Tagines, ceramic pots from Morocco and Tunisia, are another ingenious tool to conserve resources. For a tagine, all ingredients are cooked very slowly in the iconic earthenware pot with its conical lid. The low heat applied allows for cooking in the item's own juices without the need for any additional liquid.

Narrow kebob grills for cooking skewered meat, fish, or seafood rapidly over intense heat have also been developed out of the need to conserve energy.

Greece

Greece, a predominantly Christian country with a long history, is known for its generous use of vegetables, legumes, and grains. Meat is consumed in relatively small amounts, with lamb as the most popular and pork not uncommon. Dairy, especially yogurt, cheese, and goat's milk, is an important part of the Greek diet. Greek food is flavored simply; the most common aromatics include olive oil, lemon, garlic, and oregano.

TABLE 1.5 Typical Ingredients in a Greek or Turkish Kitchen

CONDIMENTS	HERBS/SPICES	PRODUCE	PROTEIN	STARCHES/LEGUMES
Olive oil	Sumac	Tomatoes	Lamb	Grains
Pomegranate molasses	Parsley	Lemons	Sheep's milk cheese	Bulgur
Chili pastes	Garlic	Walnuts	Seafood	Rice
Eggplant spreads	Mint	Quinces	Yogurt	Potatoes
Olives	Oregano	Figs	Beef	Wheat
Tzatziki	Cumin	Pomegranates	Chicken	Phyllo dough
Pickled vegetables	Paprika	Cucumbers	Pork (*Greece only*)	Bread
		Leafy greens		

International Flavor Principles **19**

Turkey

Turkey, the land link between the Levant, Central Asia, and Europe, has a cuisine that can be simply described as fresh. Food is often served as a large variety on small plates. Often cooked pilaf-style and served as a side dish, or as a main dish with other ingredients, grains such as rice and bulgur are found all over Turkey. Common flavors include mint, parsley, paprika, and cumin. Sumac, a sour berry, is used to provide acid to many dishes.

Middle East

The cuisine of the Arab Levant, made up of Egypt, Israel, Lebanon, Syria, Iraq, Saudi Arabia, and Jordan, is a fusion of many traditional foods. The hot and arid climate of the region

Photography by Terrence McCarthy

inspired foods pickled with salt and vinegar. Grilled meats, served with fresh or marinated vegetables, are very popular and often served mezze-style on small plates accompanied by a large array of condiments, like Hummus (page 322), Tabbouleh (page 327), or baba ghanoush.

TABLE 1.6 Typical Ingredients in a Middle Eastern Kitchen

CONDIMENTS	HERBS/SPICES	PRODUCE	PROTEIN	STARCHES/LEGUMES
Olive oil	Coriander	Lemons	Camel	Whole wheat
Sesame paste	Parsley	Pomegranates	Lamb	Chickpeas
Za'atar	Sumac	Eggplant	Mutton	Bulgur
Pomegranate molasses	Thyme	Pistachios	Goat	Rice
Sesame seeds	Cumin	Grapes	Dairy	Bread
Legume pastes	Cilantro	Quinces		Lentils

North Africa

North African cuisines are famous for tagines, couscous, preserved lemons, and mint tea. Common flavors of the region include ginger, hot peppers, and cumin. Spices are often combined into very aromatic spice mixtures. See Table 1.15 for information about international spice blends.

TABLE 1.7 Typical Ingredients in a North African Kitchen

CONDIMENTS	HERBS/SPICES	PRODUCE	PROTEIN	STARCHES/LEGUMES
Orange flower water	Mint	Citrus fruits	Lamb	Couscous
Olive oil	Hot peppers	Dates	Pigeon	Lentils
Rose water	Coriander	Nuts	Beef	Semolina
Dried fruit	Parsley	Almonds	Mutton	Wheat flour
Preserved lemons	Cilantro	Apricots	Chicken	Rice
Harissa	Cumin	Olives	Seafood in coastal regions	Bread
Honey	Caraway seeds	Tomatoes	Cheese	Millet
	Paprika	Garlic		

International Flavor Principles 21

In the eastern and southern Mediterranean, many related street foods can be found in several countries under different names. Tzatziki (page 112), a Greek condiment based on yogurt, garlic, and cucumbers, is known as caçik in Turkey, and comparable variations are found in many other places. A popular method in many areas is roasting highly seasoned slabs of meat on an upright rotisserie. While it cooks beside the fire, the meat is carved thinly with a long sharp knife and served with a regionally specific flatbread and condiments. In Greece, it is called Gyros (page 98), and pork is often the choice of meat. In Islamic countries, where the dish is known as *shawarma* in Arabic or *döner kebab* in Turkish-speaking regions, beef and lamb are used due to religious restrictions on pork.

Middle Eastern and North African cuisines are known for a variety of energy-saving cooking methods. Grilling diced meat on skewers directly over a flame helps to significantly reduce the cooking time. As a result, shish kebobs, char-grilled skewered lamb or beef with onions, garlic, and tomatoes, are a popular street food found all over the Middle East and North Africa. In coastal areas, kebobs with fish or seafood are widely available. Chicken Köfte Kebobs (page 79), skewered and grilled ground meat mixed with spices, aromatic vegetables, and soaked stale bread, are also popular. Common flavorings for kebobs include lemon juice, olive oil, parsley, cumin, and coriander, with many regional variations.

Falafel (page 317), chickpea fritters served with tahini sauce, tomatoes, and cucumbers in pita bread, is a popular quick-service food in Israel and adjacent countries. Instead of cooking the chickpeas for a long time until they are soft, they are simply soaked in water for a day or two before they are ground and shaped into patties and quickly deep-fried. In Egypt, where it is often stuffed with seasoned ground beef, falafel is known as tacmiyya. Other popular legume dishes include Hummus (page 322), a chickpea and sesame purée from the Middle East, and leblebi, a spiced chickpea stew from Tunisia.

Popular snacks of the eastern and southern Mediterranean include savory stuffed pastries known as Turkish Water Börek (page 284), briwat, samboussek, spanakopita, and katmar. Regional varieties are stuffed with mixtures of cheese, vegetables, meat, or seafood and are baked, griddled, or fried.

EUROPE

The cuisines of Europe developed over centuries with limited foreign influence. New ingredients, often introduced from the New World or colonies abroad, commonly came without guidance on original cooking methods. Assimilated into the culinary culture, these ingredients facilitated the conception of new dishes with a distinct spirit of the local cuisine. Case in point is curry powder, created in the United Kingdom by colonists returning from the Indian protectorate. Missing and craving the spicy and flavorful foods from abroad, they would often enhance the local food with a sprinkle of Indian spices. Soon after, variations of this spice mix became known as curry powder; in India, comparable spice mixes are known

Photography by Terrence McCarthy

International Flavor Principles 23

as masala. The word *curry* might have been derived from *kari*, the Tamil word for "sauce," or from *karahi*, Hindi for a ubiquitous all-purpose cooking vessel in Indian kitchens. Curry powder has made its way into many cuisines. The famous German Currywurst (page 54) gets a generous sprinkle of the blend after being doused in a spiced ketchup or tomato sauce.

Globalization and migration patterns of the twentieth century have altered the food scene all over Europe. Most travelers agree that London is rightfully famous for its authentic Indian food; a true step forward from curry powder–sprinkled rations. Berlin, with the largest concentration of Turks outside Turkey, is known for phenomenal Turkish food; döner kebab is actually Germany's most popular street food. And on the streets of France, sandwiches filled with a spicy North African merguez sausage, harissa paste, and French Fries (page 177) are a coveted snack on the go.

Photography by Terrence McCarthy

Common Tools in **Europe**

Many regions of Europe are famous for their vast and dense forests. The resulting abundance of high-quality firewood led to the development of wood-fired ovens to bake crusty breads. Over time, these relatively simple ovens evolved into sophisticated appliances with precise temperature-control mechanisms. The ability to manage the heat accurately, has, in turn, allowed for the development and production of delicate cakes and pastries. Initially, these were only affordable for nobles and royalty. After their introduction to the middle classes, however, the rising demand for pastries and cakes generated a completely new profession, the pastry chef. The oven became such an essential part of European cuisines that it evolved from a communal cooking tool into a standard appliance found in almost every modern household kitchen.

Not only baking depends on an oven. Over time, European chefs have refined the art of roasting and learned to understand its science. An oven has become an essential tool to gently cook large cuts of meat or whole animals. To this day, the traditional "Sunday roast," cooked to perfection with a delectable crust and a juicy interior, is still a highly anticipated family event.

In many cuisines, most cooking vessels are designed to execute a variety of methods, limiting the amount of pans necessary to do the job. A pot room in a well-equipped European kitchen, however, is filled with a wide assortment of different skillets, pots, and pans. Oftentimes they are made from a range of materials, varying in size and shape to perfectly suit a very specific cooking technique.

Spain

Traditional street foods in Europe vary from region to region. Spanish tapas, snacks served on small plates accompanied by a glass of sherry, have helped this cuisine gain

TABLE 1.8 Typical Ingredients in a Spanish Kitchen

CONDIMENTS	HERBS/SPICES	PRODUCE	PROTEIN	STARCHES/LEGUMES
Olives	Garlic	Nuts	Pork	Calasparra rice
Anchovies	Pimentón	Peppers	Serrano ham	Chickpeas
Olive oil	Onions	Eggplant	Cheese	Potatoes
Garlic	Saffron	Squash	Rabbit	Noodles
Sherry (wine and vinegar)	Smoked paprika	Quinces	Salt cod	Wheat
Capers	Parsley	Fennel	Seafood	Bread
Aïoli	Cilantro	Tomatoes	Game	

Photography by Terrence McCarthy

world recognition. In many places, the word *tapas* has actually become synonymous with this eating style, regardless of the cuisine. The cuisine of Spain is a culinary amalgam of Spain's key regions. It is straightforward and free of finicky presentations—simple comfort food for the people. Olives are probably one of the most typical ingredients; the omnipresent olive oil can even be found in desserts and other sweet preparations. Other important components of Spanish cookery include fresh garlic, fresh and dried peppers, rice, wheat, and tomatoes. The common use of nuts, chickpeas, saffron, and many other spices has its roots in the Moors' rule of Spain from the eighth to the thirteenth centuries.

France

The food of the French people is quite different from the haute cuisine of their culinary grandmasters. As diverse as the population, the cooking and ingredients are influenced by the *terroir* of the individual regions and by immigration. Long coastlines in Brittany and Normandy in the north provide a large variety of seafood, as well as the famous salt meadow lamb. Dairy is an integral component, and the apple orchards in Normandy helped create apple cider and Calvados.

Influences from neighboring Germany helped create the culinary culture of Alsace and Lorraine with its celebrated choucroute garnie, Riesling wines, and quiches, like the Leek Quiche (page 225). Southern France, with its Mediterranean climate, has a cuisine all its own. Dominated by strong flavors, like olives, garlic, herbs, and tomatoes, the foods of Provence and Languedoc are perfect partners for the bold wines of that region.

TABLE 1.9 Typical Ingredients in a French Kitchen

CONDIMENTS	HERBS/SPICES	PRODUCE	PROTEIN	STARCHES/LEGUMES
Anchovies	Artichokes	Apples	Duck	Bread
Harissa	Parsley	Asparagus	Charcuterie	All-purpose and bread flour
Olives	Chives	Wild greens	Game	Pasta
Garlic	Chervil	Tomatoes	Chicken	Potatoes
Wine	Rosemary	Leeks	Goose	White beans
Mustard	Tarragon	Green beans	Seafood	Rice
Capers	Thyme	Green peas	Dairy	Semolina
Vinegar	Oregano	Fennel	Eggs	

Crêpes, possibly the most iconic street food of France, originated in Brittany and were classically made from buckwheat flour, like in the Buckwheat Crêpes (page 352). Today these paper-thin pancakes are found all over the country, prepared freshly with fillings from ham and cheese to fruit compotes, spreads, or nut butters. Other popular snacks on the go include waffles, like the Crispy Chocolate Waffles with Mint Syrup and Whipped Cream (page 335), French Fries (page 177) served in paper cones with mayonnaise or ketchup, and portable sandwiches.

Italy

In Italy, eating is an integral part of life. The culinary arts are taken seriously, and traditional dishes, recipes, and methods are honored, respected, and preserved. Food is prepared and served sincerely, without much fluff. Simple but perfectly executed is a good way to describe the traditional cuisine. Fast food, while known, is not popular; even for street food, most people prefer to take a brief rest and sit down for a few moments to enjoy an espresso, a freshly fried arancini, or a gelato. The foods of Italy vary regionally. Northern Italy is famous for the locally grown rice, great wines, and truffles. In the alpine regions, dairy, and consequently beef and veal, is an integral part of the cuisine. Butter is a common cooking fat; olive oil, known and used all over Italy, is more popular in warmer regions. In general, the food of the north is richer, more elaborate, and more complex than the cuisines of the south. *Cucina povera*, which means "poor cuisine," is often used to describe the rustic foods of central and southern Italy. The phrase describes a minimalist approach where chefs transform inexpensive and straightforward foods into great meals. Skillfully prepared, *cucina povera* shines through its simplicity, the quality of its elements, and the chef's esteem for the ingredients.

TABLE 1.10 Typical Ingredients in an Italian Kitchen

CONDIMENTS	HERBS/SPICES	PRODUCE	PROTEIN	STARCHES/LEGUMES
Anchovies	Basil	Nuts	Salami	Polenta meal
Crushed red peppers	Parsley	Tomatoes	Tuna	White beans
Olive oil	Oregano	Garlic	Prosciutto	Arborio rice
Capers and caperberries	Dried chiles	Artichokes	Sausages	Durum, 00, all-purpose, and semolina flour
Olives	Fennel seeds	Fennel	Veal	Potatoes
Balsamic vinegar	Garlic	Greens	Cheese	Chickpea flour
Vinegar	Nutmeg	Corn	Seafood	Crusty bread
Wine	Rosemary	Beans	Dairy	Pasta

Photography by Terrence McCarthy

International Flavor Principles 29

TABLE 1.11 Typical Ingredients in a Northeastern European Kitchen

CONDIMENTS	HERBS/SPICES	PRODUCE	PROTEIN	STARCHES/LEGUMES
Pickled vegetables	Parsley	Beets	Cured meats	Rye bread
Vinegar	Chives	Onions	Cured seafood	Potatoes
Lard	Dill	Cabbage	Cold cuts	Pasta
Mustard	Allspice	Apples	Dairy	All-purpose and rye flour
Mayonnaise	Caraway seeds	Turnips	Pork	Barley
Honey	Juniper berries	Carrots	Eggs	Whole-grain bread
Sauerkraut	Bay leaves	Leeks	Duck	Buckwheat
Horseradish	Cloves	Pears	Goose	Oats

Northeastern Europe

Long coastlines, moderate summers, cold winters, and Viking influences from Scandinavia have influenced the cuisines of North-Central Europe, now becoming very popular as Nordic cuisines. Rye, oats, potatoes, root vegetables, cabbages, and tubers are as integral to the menu as are meat and seafood. Traditional aromatics include caraway seed, black pepper, and juniper. Established street foods of the region include grilled, sautéed, or simmered sausages; sandwiches with pickled fish; and seafood and potato pancakes. Warmer summers and cold winters, with a guarantee of snow in the southern regions of Central Europe, have shaped a different cuisine. Cultural influences from the Roman and Ottoman Empires have added a great layer of complexity to the cuisines of southern Germany, Austria, Hungary, and Switzerland. In these mainly landlocked regions, freshwater fish is more popular than ocean fish, and the cultivation of wheat due to the warmer climate is illustrated by the popularity of dumplings based on wheat flour and semolina. Sausages are equally popular, but are commonly offered in a greater variety. Other iconic street foods include pretzels, crêpes, and fried doughnuts known as pfannkuchen or Berliners.

THE AMERICAS

The United States

The cuisine of the United States has had an unjust reputation for being composed of fast food and restaurant chains. In fact, past and present immigration to the United States has created a culinary diversity found in few other places around the world. European-style

Common Tools of **the Americas**

The cuisines of the Americas continue to be shaped and inspired by epicurean cultures from all over the world. As a result, tools found in American kitchens are a direct reflection of the demographic makeup of a region. Outdoor smokers and grills, to produce coveted barbecue, are found in almost every household in the southern and southwestern United States. Skillet frying, a widespread method in the Deep South of the United States, is done best in the popular cast-iron cookware.

Tortilla presses, to shape perfect corn tortillas, can be found in many Mexican households as well as restaurants. These tortillas are commonly cooked on a comal, a round skillet/griddle traditionally made from earthenware. Nowadays, nonstick comals or those made from cast iron have become more popular.

A unique tool found in the cuisines of the Caribbean is a tostonera, a hinged wooden press to make tostones, plantain fritters, popular in Puerto Rico.

foods of the Northeast and Midwest give way to the soul food of the South, with its fried green tomatoes, pulled pork, and braised greens. On a westbound trip from Louisiana, Cajun and Creole fare, represented by crawfish étouffée and gumbo, gradually becomes Texan barbecue and Tex-Mex cuisine, with its strong Mexican influence. Florida is known for exciting Caribbean food, and on the West Coast, cross-cultural food is a common find on the street and in restaurants. Attempting to pigeonhole the cuisine of the United States is an exercise in futility; every region has its own culinary landscape, with distinct marks left by new and established residents. In addition to regional cuisines, native American cooking methods—like grilling on a cedar plank, the nixtamalization of corn, or fry bread—are being rediscovered and promoted to reconstruct pre-Columbian food or to intertwine them with current cuisine to form culinary novelties.

The evolution of the U.S. food scene has also had a tremendous impact on the country's street food. The nation's fast-paced lifestyle, paired with a newly found passion for well-prepared food, has been the perfect breeding ground for remarkable fare on the boulevard. All-time favorites like hot dogs, soft pretzels, and hoagies can now be found beside eclectic food like Korean barbecue, gourmet s'mores, hand-cut French Fries (page 177), or a bowl of pho. Every customer has his own preferred vendor and street-food hot spot; many people agree, however, that the current hubs are New York City; Austin, Texas; Portland, Oregon; Philadelphia, Pennsylvania; and Chicago, Illinois, where vendors sometimes squabble over the most desirable location for the cart or food truck. Some areas in those cities are known for lunchtime gatherings of vendor communities, where the quality and diversity of the food effortlessly stands its ground in comparison to the famous hawker centers and food courts in Singapore. These regional cuisines are often identified and characterized by typical ingredients found in household as well as in commercial kitchens. The following table is designed to illustrate the diversity of all the U.S. regional cuisines.

International Flavor Principles

TABLE 1.12 Typical Ingredients in the Regional Kitchens of the United States

MIDWESTERN STATES

CONDIMENTS	HERBS/SPICES	PRODUCE	PROTEIN	STARCHES/LEGUMES
Mustard	Parsley	Morels	Beef	Wheat
Ketchup	Black pepper	Celery	Pork	Cornmeal
Mayonnaise	Chives	Carrots	Freshwater fish	Wild rice
Ranch dressing	Horseradish	Turnips	Chicken	Potatoes
Dill pickles	Chives	Concord grapes	Game	Rye bread

NORTHEASTERN STATES

CONDIMENTS	HERBS/SPICES	PRODUCE	PROTEIN	STARCHES/LEGUMES
Mustard	Parsley	Corn	Beef	Rice
Ketchup	Black pepper	Eggplant	Pork	Pasta
Mayonnaise	Basil	Beans	Chicken	Potatoes
Molasses	Horseradish	Tomatoes	Game	Rye bread
Dill pickles	Chives	Apples	Seafood (fresh and preserved)	Wheat
Maple syrup	Brown sugar	Cranberries	Freshwater fish	Cornmeal

SOUTHERN STATES

CONDIMENTS	HERBS/SPICES	PRODUCE	PROTEIN	STARCHES/LEGUMES
Dark roux	Filé powder	Peanuts	Virginia ham	Rice
Hot sauce	Honey	Sweet potatoes	Ham hocks	Cornmeal
Buttermilk	Garlic powder	Okra	Crawfish	Wheat
Spicy brown mustard	Cayenne pepper	Cooking greens	Trout	Biscuits
Regular mustard	Paprika	Black-eyed peas	Catfish	Hominy grits
Peanut butter	Oregano	Peaches	Shrimp	Corn fritters
Barbecue sauce	Garlic	Sweet onions	Liver	

TABLE 1.12 (*continued*)

SOUTHWESTERN STATES

CONDIMENTS	HERBS/SPICES	PRODUCE	PROTEIN	STARCHES/LEGUMES
Barbecue sauce	Dried chiles	Cactus paddles	Quail	Corn masa
Honey	Cilantro	Squash	Game	Cornmeal
Salsas	Epazote	Peppers	Beef	Dried beans
Hot sauce	Mexican oregano	Tomatoes	Pork	Wheat
Ketchup	Chili powder	Jícama	Freshwater fish	Tortillas
Vinegar	Pepper	Avocado	Seafood	Pozole
Lime juice	Garlic	Pecans	Organ meats	Rice

NORTHWESTERN STATES

CONDIMENTS	HERBS/SPICES	PRODUCE	PROTEIN	STARCHES/LEGUMES
Ketchup	Ginger	Mushrooms	Pacific salmon	Pasta
Mustard	Galangal	Fiddlehead ferns	Game	Rice
Soy sauce	Garlic	Avocado	Crabs	Wheat
Fish sauce	Basil	Fennel	Geoduck clams	Bread
Olive oil	Curry powder and paste	Grapes	Pork	Tortillas
Vinegar	Cilantro	Citrus	Beef	Potatoes
Sesame oil	Chiles	Berries	Chicken	Beans

CENTRAL AND SOUTH AMERICA

Immigration from all over the world has shaped the unique cultures of Latin America. The cuisines, famous for their exciting vibrancy, are a perfect blend of indigenous culinary traditions with ingredients and methods introduced by immigrants. Pork, one of the most popular meats, was unknown in the Americas in pre-Columbian times. Prior to colonization of an area or an island, Spanish explorers released pigs in the area to provide fresh meat for later settlers.

International Flavor Principles **33**

TABLE 1.13 Typical Ingredients in a Caribbean Kitchen

CONDIMENTS	HERBS/SPICES	PRODUCE	PROTEIN	STARCHES/LEGUMES
Pickled chiles	Allspice	Bread fruit	Salt cod	Yucca
Jerk seasoning	Ginger	Papaya	Rock lobster	Arrowroot
Papaya slaw	Tamarind	Star fruit	Conch	Plantains
Chutneys	Chiles	Okra	Goat	Yellow split peas
Hot sauce	Curry powder	Bananas	Seafood	Sweet potatoes
Vinegar	Habanero chiles	Guavas	Pork	Rice
Lime juice	Cilantro	Callaloo	Chicken	Beans

Caribbean

The popularity of curries in Caribbean cuisines also illustrates the influence of immigration. After the abolition of slavery, the region was in desperate need of skilled low-paid workers. To fill this void, British colonists organized the migration of native East Indians to the Caribbean territories. Known as curry to the British settlers, all the flavorful Indian stews and their adaptations became an integral part of Caribbean cooking.

Peru

Peru, the birthplace of potatoes, is also famous for the inventive use of seafood. Inspired by Japanese immigrants, *causa*—made from mashed potatoes, lime juice, and often fish or seafood—is one of the region's most popular dishes. Typically served as a roll, it bears a strong resemblance to the Japanese maki sushi. Ceviche, raw marinated fish or seafood popular in many regions of Latin America, is strongly represented in Peru. For this dish, known in Peru as tiradito, raw fish is sliced thinly and arranged on a plate. Unlike seviche, tiradito is not marinated; it is served with a dressing called *leche de tigre*, meaning "tiger's milk." This dressing is made from lime juice, raw fish scraps, bonito flakes, peppers, and other aromatics.

Brazil

The cuisines of Brazil, the largest country in South America, are as diverse as its people. Churrasco, a cowboy-style barbecue created by cattle-herding horsemen of the country's south, enjoys great popularity in the whole country. Along the southern coastline of Bahia, the food reflects a rich and tropical cuisine with African influences. Common ingredients include coconut milk, malagueta peppers, dried shrimp, okra, and dende oil. The cuisines of the Amazon reflect the richness of the region. Rare fish, exotic plants, and super fruits, like açai berries, acerola, and passion fruit, provide a rewarding playground for creative chefs. The arid regions northeast of the Amazon offer the perfect *terroir* for salted or sun-dried meats. Various flours, made from fermented or unfermented manioc, known as farinhas, are another important staple.

In Brazil, many street foods are often referred to as *salgadinhos*, literally translated as "little salty ones." Most Brazilians enjoy food from street-side cafés, where they can socialize with a drink in hand; it is relatively uncommon to eat these snacks on the run. Popular street-food snacks include *pao de quejo* (page 314), small baked cheese rolls made from tapioca flour. Pasties, bolinhos, or empanadas, like the Tuna and Goat Cheese Empanadas (page 156), are baked or fried turnovers or dumplings that feature a variety of stuffings and are popular quick snacks. On the beaches of Rio de Janeiro, omnipresent are booths offering the Caipirinha (page 367), Brazil's famous cocktail made from lime juice and cachaça, a liquor made from fermented sugarcane juice.

More and more chefs and culinary professionals have begun to recognize the potential that the cuisines of Latin America have to offer. Amazonian cuisines have often been called the final frontier for chefs, and authentic dishes and creative interpretations can be found in restaurants across the globe.

Mexico

Added to UNESCO's list of intangible cultural heritage in 2010, the cuisines of Mexico are recognized by most culinary professionals as a major player among the world cuisines. Mexican food, with its long history, has evolved around maize, beans, and chiles. Field corn often undergoes a special treatment known as nixtamalization. For this process, a common practice even before the European discovery of the Americas, the kernels are briefly boiled and soaked in a calcium hydroxide solution. Once fully hydrated, the corn is ground into a paste. Known as masa, this paste is used to produce Corn Tortillas (page 279), Sweet Tamales (page 346), and other specialties. Significant other ingredients include tomatillos, tomatoes, cheese, and aromatics, such as cilantro, cumin, lime, and epazote, a very aromatic herb often employed as a digestive aid. Mexican street food has a long history; returning Spanish conquistadors reported with amazement on the variety of the foods sold in Mexican markets. Today, the street food of Mexico is known as *antojitos*, or "little whim," and is often described as spicy, colorful, vibrant, and fresh. Most Mexicans agree that layering of textures is a very important aspect. Tacos; tortillas with different fillings, like Tacos with Poblano Peppers in Cream (page 221) or Grilled Fish Tacos (page 159); as well as Mexican sandwiches known as tortas, are characterized by an array of flavors and textures. Tamales, steamed masa cakes wrapped in cornhusks or banana leaves, are also popular examples of a layered sensory experience. Other popular Mexican street foods include Pan-Fried Quesadillas (page 217), burritos, and Grilled Corn on the Cob (page 212), known as *elotes asodos*.

International Flavor Principles **35**

Photography by Terrence McCarthy

TABLE 1.14 Typical Ingredients in a Mexican Kitchen

CONDIMENTS	HERBS/SPICES	PRODUCE	PROTEIN	STARCHES/LEGUMES
Olives	Cumin	Limes	Cheese	Dried beans
Dried chiles	Pumpkin seeds	Tomatoes	Goat	Rice
Salsas	Epazote	Corn	Sour cream	Corn masa
Guacamole	Cilantro	Jícama	Pork	Tortillas
Capers	Garlic	Squash blossoms	Seafood	Noodles
Lime juice	Mexican oregano	White onions	Beef	Plantains
Pomegranates		Avocado		

Just like anywhere, the foods of Mexico change from region to region. A nomadic life style in pre-Columbian times created a simple cuisine in the north. Wheat, introduced by Spanish explorers, made flour tortillas a popular choice. Complex sauce preparations, such as the famous moles, illustrate a higher level of refinement of Mexico's southern cuisines. A greater variety of chiles is available there, and black beans are more popular than the pinto beans from the north. The culinary hub of Mexico has always been and still is the capital. The streets and shops of Mexico City offer products from all over Mexico and the world; inquisitive culinary minds with even the most unique craving can be satisfied in Mexico City.

TABLE 1.15 Herbs

Whether they are the featured flavor or employed to support the theme of a dish, herbs add a generous layer of complexity. Ideally they are used fresh; in many cases, drying will compromise their fresh flavor. This is especially true for tender herbs such as basil, parsley, and chives or similar. Resinous herbs like rosemary, thyme, and oregano are a little more forgiving and retain their flavor better during the drying process. In order to get the biggest epicurean benefit, it is important to add them to the dish at the right time during the cooking process. As a rule of thumb, resinous herbs should be added at the beginning; their flavors will actually benefit from cooking. The flavor of tender herbs, however, tends to dissipate during cooking; hence they should be added at the very end of the preparation.

The following table shows a variety of herbs commonly used in many cultures.

COMMON HERBS AND THEIR USES

TYPE	DESCRIPTION	COMMON CULINARY USES
Basil	Small to large, oval, pointed leaves; green or purple; pungent; varieties include opal, lemon, and Thai basil; also available dried	Flavoring for sauces, dressings, infused oils, and vinegars; pesto sauces; popular in Mediterranean cooking
Bay leaf	Smooth, oval leaves; green, aromatic; most commonly available dried	Flavoring for soups, stews, stocks, sauces, and grain dishes

(*continued*)

International Flavor Principles **37**

TABLE 1.15 (*continued*)

COMMON HERBS AND THEIR USES

TYPE	DESCRIPTION	COMMON CULINARY USES
Chervil	Small, curly leaves; green; delicate texture; anise flavor; also available dried	Component of fines herbes; garnish
Chives	Long, thin; bright green; mild onion flavor	Flavoring for salads and cream cheese garnish; component of fines herbes
Cilantro/coriander	Similar shape to flat-leaf parsley; green; delicate leaves; fresh, clean flavor	Flavoring for salsa and uncooked sauces. Leaves and stems should be used and should not be chopped too finely.
Curry leaves	Small to medium size; pointed oval; dark green; mild, aromatic flavor	Flavoring for stir-fries and curries
Dill	Long, feather-like leaves; green; distinct flavor; also available dried	Flavoring for salads, sauces, stews, and braises
Lemongrass	Long blades with rough surface; pale yellow-green	Flavoring for soups, stocks, stir-fries, and steamed preparations
Marjoram	Small, oval leaves; pale green; mild, similar flavor to oregano; commonly available dried	Flavoring for lamb and vegetable dishes
Mint	Pointed, textured leaves; pale green to bright green; leaf size and strength varies with type; varieties include peppermint, spearmint, and chocolate mint	Flavoring for sweet dishes, sauces, and beverages; garnish for desserts; mint jelly is an accompaniment to lamb
Oregano	Small, oval leaves; pale green; pungent flavor; Mexican and Mediterranean varieties are available; commonly available dried	Flavoring for tomato-based dishes
Parsley	Curly or flat leaves; pointed, scalloped edges; bright green; clean tasting; flat-leaf parsley is also known as Italian parsley; commonly available dried	Flavoring for sauces, stocks, soups, dressings; component of fines herbes; garnish; used in bouquet garni and sachet d'épices
Rosemary	Pine needle–shaped leaves, woody stem; grayish, deep green color; strong pine aroma and flavor; commonly available dried	Flavoring for grilled foods (lamb) and marinades; popular in Mediterranean cuisine; branch-like stems are used as skewers
Sage	Thin, oval, velvety leaves; grayish green color; musty flavor; varieties include pineapple sage; commonly available dried, both crumbled and ground	Flavoring for stuffings, sausages, and stews
Savory	Oblong leaves; dark green; soft, fuzzy texture; commonly available dried	Flavoring for pâtés, stuffing; used to make poultry seasoning

38 CHAPTER 1 What Is Street Food?

TABLE 1.15 (*continued*)

COMMON HERBS AND THEIR USES

TYPE	DESCRIPTION	COMMON CULINARY USES
Thyme	Very small leaves; woody stem; deep green color; varieties include garden thyme, lemon thyme, and wild thyme; commonly available dried	Flavoring for soups, stocks, stews, braises, and roasted items; used in bouquet garni and sachet d'épices
Tarragon	Thin, pointed leaves; dark green; delicate texture; anise flavor; commonly available dried	Flavoring for béarnaise sauce; component of fines herbes

TABLE 1.16 Spices

The pungency and aroma of spices is coveted in almost all culinary cultures. Many societies have even incorporated them into proverbs, as in "the spice of life."

Just like herbs, spices add an interesting layer of complexity but can also overwhelm the flavor of a dish if not used carefully.

Below is a table of spices commonly used in many cuisines.

COMMON SPICES AND THEIR USES

TYPE	DESCRIPTION	COMMON CULINARY USES
Allspice	Dried, unripened, pea-size berry of the small evergreen pimiento tree; dark reddish brown; tastes like cinnamon, nutmeg, and cloves; available whole or ground	Braises, fish, pickles, desserts, pâtés
Annatto	Dried small achiote seeds; deep red; nearly flavorless; imparts yellowish orange color to foods; available whole	Popular in Latin American and Caribbean cooking; stews, soups, and sauces
Anise	Dried ripe fruit of herb *Pimpinellaanisum*; similar flavor to fennel seeds; light brown; sweet, spicy, licorice taste and aroma	Popular in Southeast Asian cooking; savory dishes, desserts, baked goods, and liqueurs
Caraway	Dried fruit of aromatic caraway plant; member of the parsley family; resembles small seeds; brown; delicate flavor similar to, but sweeter than, anise seeds	Popular in Austrian, German, and Hungarian cuisines; rye bread, pork, cabbage, soups, stews, some cheese, baked goods, and liqueur (kümmel)
Cardamom	Dried unripened fruit; member of the ginger family; small seeds enclosed in green, black, or bleached white cranberry-size pods; strong aroma; sweet, spicy flavor; available as a whole pod, seeds, or ground	Curries, baked goods, and pickles
Cayenne	Dried ripened fruit pod of *Capsicum frutescens*; bright red; hot, spicy; available fresh or dried	Sauces, soups, meat, fish, and poultry
Celery	Dried seed of a wild celery (lovage); strong flavor; available whole or ground	Salads, coleslaw, salad dressings, soups, stews, tomatoes, and baked goods

(*continued*)

International Flavor Principles   **39**

TABLE 1.16 (*continued*)

COMMON SPICES AND THEIR USES

TYPE	DESCRIPTION	COMMON CULINARY USES
Cinnamon	Dried inner bark of a tropical tree; reddish brown; available in sticks or ground	Baked goods, curries, dessert sauces, beverages, and stews
Cloves	Dried unopened flower of the tropical evergreen clove tree; reddish brown; spike shaped; sweet, pungent flavor; available whole or ground	Stocks, sauces, braises, marinades, curries, pickles, desserts, and baked goods
Coriander	Dried ripe fruit of the cilantro plant; small, tannish brown seeds; unique citrus-like flavor; available whole or ground	Popular in Asian, Indian, and Middle Eastern cuisines; curries, forcemeats, pickles, and baked goods
Cumin	Dried fruit of plant in the parsley family; small, crescent-shaped seeds; three colors: amber, black, and white; nutty flavor; available whole or ground	Popular in Indian, Mexican, and Middle Eastern cuisines; curries and chili
Dill	Dried fruit of the herb *Anethumgraveolens*; member of the parsley family; small, tan seeds; strong, pungent flavor; available whole	Popular in northern and eastern European cuisines; pickles, sauerkraut, cheeses, breads, and salad dressings
Filé powder	Dried leaves of the sassafras tree; woodsy flavor, similar to root beer; available ground	Popular in Creole cuisine; gumbos
Ginger	Plant from tropical and subtropical regions; tan, knobby root; fibrous; sweet, peppery flavor; spicy aroma; available fresh, candied, pickled, or ground	Popular in Asian and Indian cuisines; curries, braises, and baked goods
Horseradish	Large white root; member of the mustard family; sharp, intense flavor; pungent aroma; available dried or fresh	Sauces, condiments, egg salad, potatoes, and beets
Juniper berries	Small dried berry; dark blue; slightly bitter; must crush before using to release flavor	Marinades, braises, meats/game, sauerkraut, gin, liqueurs, and teas
Mace	Membrane covering of the nutmeg seed; bright red when fresh; yellowish orange when dried; strong nutmeg taste and aroma; available whole or ground	Forcemeats, pork, fish, spinach and other vegetables, pickles, desserts, and baked goods
Mustard	Seeds from plants within the cabbage family; three types: the traditional white/yellow (smaller; less pungent flavor), brown, and black (larger; pungent, hot flavor); available whole or powdered	Pickles, meats, sauces, cheese, eggs, and prepared mustard
Nutmeg	Large seed of a fruit that grows on a tropical evergreen; small egg shape; dark brown; sweet, spicy flavor and aroma; available whole or ground	Sauces, soups, veal, chicken, aspics, vegetables, desserts, baked goods, and eggnog

TABLE 1.16 *(continued)*

COMMON SPICES AND THEIR USES

TYPE	DESCRIPTION	COMMON CULINARY USES
Paprika	Dried ground pods of sweet red peppers; many varieties; superior from Hungary; colors range from orange-red to deep red; mild to intense flavor and aroma; available ground	Popular in Hungarian cuisine; braises, stews, goulashes, sauces, and garnishes
Saffron	Tiny dried stigmas of the violet flowers of *Crocus sativus*; thread-like; yellow-orange; 14,000 stigmas per 1 ounce of saffron; expensive due to labor-intensive process; available ground or as threads	Popular in paella, bouillabaisse, and risotto Milanese; poultry, seafood, rice pilafs, sauces, soups, and baked goods
Star anise	Dried, 8- to 12-pointed pod from Chinese evergreen, member of the magnolia family; star shaped; dark brown; intense licorice flavor and aroma; use sparingly; available whole or ground	Popular in Asian dishes; pork, duck, baked goods, teas, and liqueurs
Sumac	Dried flower bud of a shrub grown in North Africa and the Middle East; tart citrus flavor; available ground	Popular in Middle Eastern and Arab cuisines. Sprinkled on rice or hummus to provide a tart lemony flavor.
Turmeric	Root of the tropical plant *Curcuma longa*, related to ginger; shape similar to ginger; bright yellow; intense spicy flavor; available fresh or ground	Popular in Indian and Middle Eastern cuisines; curries, sauces, mustard, pickles, and rice

TABLE 1.17 International Spice Blends

Flavor profiles are an identifying aspect of most culinary cultures. These frequently occurring conjunctions of flavoring ingredients within a cuisine can conveniently be re-created with traditional and oftentimes commercially available spice blends. The following table shows several of the more identifiable blends from around the world along with their uses.

HERB AND SPICE BLENDS

MIXTURE	ORIGIN	USED FOR	FORM	COMPONENTS
Baharat	Middle East	Widely used to flavor all types of dishes, particularly soups and stews	Whole spices are ground together	Cloves, nutmeg, cinnamon, coriander, black pepper, paprika
Berberé	North Africa	Cure for meats, added to condiments and stews	Ingredients are mixed together, then simmered prior to use	Chiles, cardamom, cumin, black pepper, fenugreek, allspice, ginger, cloves, coriander

(continued)

International Flavor Principles **41**

TABLE 1.17 (*continued*)

HERB AND SPICE BLENDS

MIXTURE	ORIGIN	USED FOR	FORM	COMPONENTS
Rempah	Indonesia Malaysia	Used to flavor rendangs and gulais, spicy dishes served with sauce	Ingredients are puréed into a fine paste and then fried in oil before remaining ingredients of dish are added	Shallots, ginger, turmeric, chiles, spices
Cajun blackening spices	Louisiana, United States	Used to coat fish or meat prior to grilling or pan searing	Ground raw spices	Mustard seeds, cumin, paprika, cayenne pepper, black pepper
Crab or shrimp boil	Chesapeake Bay, United States	Thrown in water used for boiling crab or shrimp	Ground raw spices	Peppercorns, mustard seeds, coriander, salt, cloves, ginger, ground bay leaves
Curry powder	Worldwide, based on Indian cooking	Used to flavor thin, soupy sauces	Freshly ground spices are sautéed in oil at beginning of cooking process	Curry leaves, turmeric, chiles, coriander, black pepper, and sometimes cumin, ginger, fenugreek, cinnamon, cloves, nutmeg
Five-spice powder	China	Used as flavoring in wide variety of Chinese dishes	Whole spices are ground into a raw powder	Anise, fennel seeds, cloves, cinnamon, peppercorns
Green curry paste	Thailand	Used as flavoring in green curries	Ingredients are ground together in mortar and pestle to form a wet paste	Green Thai bird chiles, lemongrass, kaffir lime zest, galangal, shrimp paste, coriander, cumin, white peppercorns
Garam masala	Northern India	Usually added at end of cooking to complete seasoning	Spices are roasted whole, then ground into a powder	Cinnamon, cardamom, cloves, cumin seeds, coriander, black peppercorns
Herbs de Provence	Provence, France	Used with roasted or grilled meat or poultry	Minced fresh or dried herbs	Thyme, summer savory, lavender, rosemary, and sometimes fennel fronds, basil, oregano, or sage
Harissa	Northwest Africa	Used as paste on meats and other items	Dried chiles (hot and mild) are stemmed, seeded, and broken up; soaked in cold water and drained; ground to a paste	Hot red chiles, garlic, coriander seeds, caraway seeds, olive oil

TABLE 1.17 (*continued*)

HERB AND SPICE BLENDS

MIXTURE	ORIGIN	USED FOR	FORM	COMPONENTS
Massaman paste	Thailand	Flavoring used in Thai massaman curries	Ingredients are ground together in mortar and pestle to form a wet paste	Red Thai bird chiles, coriander, cumin, cinnamon, cloves, star anise, cardamom, white peppercorns
Panch phoron (Indian five-spice mix)	Eastern India—Bengal	All-purpose flavoring for vegetable dishes	Ingredients are sautéed in hot oil prior to cooking	Whole cumin seeds, fennel seeds, fenugreek, black mustard seeds
Pickling spices	Europe	Used as flavoring in pickles and certain liquids	Raw whole spices	Mustard seeds, cloves, coriander seeds, mace, black peppercorns, allspice, ginger, chiles
Quatre-épices	France	Most often used in pâtés	Spices are combined and then ground into a powder	Pepper, nutmeg, cloves, ginger, and sometimes cinnamon
Ras al hanout	Morocco	All-purpose flavoring powder	Whole spices are ground together	Allspice, cloves, cumin, cardamom, chiles, ginger, peppercorns, mace, turmeric, caraway seeds
Recado	Yucatán Peninsula, Mexico	Rubbed on food prior to cooking; also used as all-purpose flavoring for sauces and stews	Spices are pounded to a paste in combination with vinegar, garlic, and herbs	Achiote, cloves, black pepper, chiles, allspice, cinnamon
Tabil	Tunisia, Morocco	Used in salads, stews, and couscous	Spices are combined and then ground into a powder	Coriander, caraway, garlic powder, red hot pepper, curry powder
Za'atar	Middle East	Used as flavoring for meats, vegetables, and bread	Ingredients are ground into a powder	Sumac, thyme, sesame seeds, marjoram, oregano, salt

International Flavor Principles **43**

CHAPTER 2

MEAT & POULTRY

Dietary restrictions aside, meat has always been an integral part of the human diet. Nourishing and wholesome, it is a good source of valuable protein, vitamins, and minerals, as well as of essential amino and fatty acids. Red meat and organ meat are especially rich in minerals, vitamin E, and B-complex vitamins. Pork is known for its high content of vitamin B1, and poultry is a good source of lean protein. As part of a well-balanced diet, consuming meat in moderate amounts helps to provide many essential nutrients.

HISTORY OF MEAT PREPARATION AND CONSUMPTION

In pre-agricultural societies, the consumption of meat was mostly a group event, conducted by distinct rituals and accompanied by celebration. Eating meat was a relatively infrequent occurrence. Hunts were not always successful, and more often than not, the hunters returned empty-handed. Pursuing and killing an animal with the primitive weapons of the time was risky; in addition to competing predators and scavengers, the prey itself could inflict severe, potentially lethal injuries during its struggle. A successful hunt, therefore, resulted in a feast, where the kill was shared with the whole group, the hunters were honored, and tribute was paid to the creature for surrendering its life. Preservation of meat was relatively uncommon during that period, since the almost immediate consumption of the whole animal by the group made it unnecessary.

Agricultural civilizations often slaughter animals to honor significant events, such as the arrival of a special guest, a successful harvest, or religious occasions. Every culture has a unique set of rules dictating how to kill the animal and prepare the flesh. Over time, domestic societies developed a desire for a steady protein supply, inspiring many ways to use every part of the animal, as well as ways to preserve it by salting, drying, curing, and smoking. European cuisines are famous for their charcuterie traditions with countless variations of preserved meats and sausages. In North America, dried beef jerky helped to nourish explorers during their long and often uncertain journeys. The cuisines of East Asia, even though not famous for it, actually offer a variety of preserved meat products, commonly used in small amounts to flavor vegetable and rice dishes. Today, preservation of the meat is generally not the prime concern; we simply enjoy the distinctly salty and sometimes smoky flavor of skillfully preserved meats.

MEAT COOKERY AND COOKING METHODS

In any food-service setting, meat is a high-cost item and most often a featured element. Therefore, its skillful preparation is as important as the meat's quality. Even the most highly priced cuts of meat from the best animals will taste underwhelming if prepared incompetently and with a lack of respect. On the other hand, the less expensive cuts of meat, chosen wisely and prepared with expertise, can be employed to create impressive dishes, encouraging customers to return. See Table 2.1 for recommended cooking methods for different cuts of meats.

Aiming to create the best nutritional value and the most gratifying taste experience, culinary cultures all over the world have devised distinct cooking methods for the different parts of the animal. Known as *terroir*, local conditions such as climate, geography, and culture impact the interpretation and execution of these methods, creating regional variations.

GRILLING

Executable with relatively simple means, grilled food can be found at street-food stands the world over. The method relies on an intense heat fueled by gas, wood, charcoal, and, on rare occasions, electricity. Design and execution of the method differ. Skewered pieces of meat are often suspended a few inches directly above the flame, where they are turned repeatedly to ensure even cooking. Portion-size or larger pieces of meat might be grilled on metal or ceramic rods above the heat, creating the coveted grill marks. The characteristic exterior browning and rich flavor are results of the Maillard reaction, a chemical reaction between the meat's proteins and carbohydrates. Proper seasoning will enhance this reaction. Rubbing salt into the meat until it dissolves draws water-soluble proteins to the surface, where they are exposed to the intense heat of the grill. The importance of a well-seared, charred exterior must not be underestimated; the juiciest steak or kebob will not win over a new guest if the flavor is lacking due to inadequate browning.

Marinating is a popular way to add interesting flavors and enhance the appearance of grilled food. Bought commercially or made in-house, marinades can be used to create unique signature dishes. However, marinades containing sugar or other natural sweeteners need to be handled cautiously. The high heat of the grill can cause the marinade to burn before the meat has reached its proper doneness, though this can be avoided by adjusting the intensity and proximity of the heat. Alternatively, the marinade can be applied when the meat is nearly cooked. With this method, the food benefits from the proper searing and the marinade can be allowed to caramelize as needed.

TABLE 2.1 Cooking Methods and Suitable Cuts of Meat

METHOD	BEEF	PORK	LAMB	POULTRY
Grilling Sautéing Frying *Suitable mostly for the meat of young animals*	Loin Tenderloin Top sirloin Rib section Shoulder tender Shoulder top blade, thinly sliced Flank steak Skirt steak Hanger steak	Loin Tenderloin Butt, shoulder Belly, thinly sliced	Loin Rack Tenderloin Shoulder Leg	Breast Legs
Roasting	Loin Tenderloin Top sirloin Shoulder tender Shoulder top blade	Loin Tenderloin Butt, shoulder Belly Ham Ribs	Loin Rack Shoulder Neck Ribs	Whole birds
Slow-Roasting/Smoking/Barbecue	Loin Tenderloin Top sirloin Shoulder tender Shoulder top blade Round Brisket Shoulder clod Short ribs	Loin Tenderloin Butt, shoulder Belly Ham Ribs Hocks	Loin Rack Shoulder Neck Ribs	Whole birds
Braising/Stewing	Round Brisket Shoulder clod Shank Tail Short ribs Cheeks	Butt, shoulder Belly Ham Hocks	Shoulder Neck Ribs Shank	Whole birds, commonly cut into sections

Some culinarians believe that marinades, especially acidic ones, tenderize tough proteins. This is not true; acids actually have the opposite effect. Comparing sashimi, tender sliced raw fish, and the much firmer ceviche, raw fish marinated with lime juice, illustrates that. In some recipes, commercially available meat tenderizers or certain produce, like ginger, papaya, pineapple, or kiwi, are advertised as a solution for tough meat. The enzymes they contain supposedly help to tenderize meat. Unfortunately, the texture they create is undesirably grainy and mushy. Most of the naturally tough cuts of meat are simply not suitable for the grill, and they benefit instead from slow roasting, braising, stewing, or simmering. Good candidates for the grill are portion-size legs and breasts from young poultry, as well as steaks from the loin, tenderloin, and certain parts of the shoulder. Flank steaks or skirt steaks, even though a little less tender and larger than a portion, are also popular on the grill. They are commonly grilled to medium doneness, and when carved thinly right at the moment of service, they can be a delicious example of properly grilled meat. See page 48 for a table of cuts of meat and their most appropriate cooking methods.

FRYING

Fried foods, such as French Fries (page 177), fried chicken, and tempura, are well liked all over the world, and variations can be found in almost any cuisine. Each year, food stands at carnivals and county fairs boast the newest fried innovations.

In addition to being widely regarded as comfort food, fried food appeals through the attractive texture contrast between a crunchy, well-browned exterior and a juicy, flavorful interior. The amazing popularity of fried food can be illustrated with the classic southern fried chicken; this humble dish has created a demand big enough to sustain several multi-national quick-service restaurant chains focusing on this preparation.

Fried foods cook partially or completely submerged in hot oil. To achieve the desirable crunch, most items, with the exception of fried doughs or starchy vegetables, are coated with a breading, batter, or crust before frying. In addition to providing texture, this coating protects the item from the high heat, allowing it to cook relatively slowly, resulting in a moist interior. As a quick cooking method, frying is not suitable for tough cuts of meat or poultry. Naturally tender cuts of meat, seafood, and certain vegetables are well suited for frying. See page 48 for a table of cuts of meat and appropriate cooking methods.

Deep-frying, common in mobile vending settings, uses enough oil to allow the item to swim freely. Pan-fried items, on the other hand, are cooked in significantly less fat, usually only submerged by half.

Maintaining the proper temperature, ideally with a temperature-controlled fryer, is a crucial element in proper frying. For most dishes, the oil is kept between 350°F/177°C and 375°F/191°C to achieve the ideal texture and color. For some specialized dishes, the temperature may vary.

Most chefs choose specialized fryer shortenings for their neutral flavors, high smoke points, and long shelf lives. Distinctly flavored oils like olive oil, roasted peanut oil, mustard oil, or rendered animal fats such as lard or duck fat are popular choices for specialized businesses. Potentially a selling point, the use of a special fat or oil needs to be clearly advertised on the menu to justify the higher price, as well as to create customer awareness in case of any dietary restrictions.

With any fat, proper maintenance will help to avoid deterioration and extend usability. Limiting exposure to excessive heat, straining frequently to remove burnt particles, and keeping salt or spices from falling into the fat will help to extend the oil's useful life.

SAUTÉING, STIR-FRYING

Sautéing cooks naturally tender cuts of meat, fish, or seafood rapidly in a small amount of fat in a hot skillet. Traditionally, the pan drippings are deglazed with a flavorful liquid for an accompanying sauce. In an effort to create an appealing, flavorful exterior, meat, fish, and seafood are seared as one of the initial steps. The temperature required for searing varies. White meat is commonly exposed to a lower temperature than red meat to achieve a golden brown but not too dark exterior. Thin cuts are seared hotter than thick steaks to guarantee appropriate browning once they reached the desired doneness. And last, skin-on poultry or fish is seared, skin side down, over relatively low heat to ensure a very crispy skin and tender flesh. Duck breast, with its fatty skin, is seared at a very low heat to render as much of the fat as possible and ensure crispiness. Searing, contrary to popular belief, does not seal in the meat's juices; the objective of searing is to achieve an attractive exterior color and texture with the resulting strong flavor, as well as to generate pan drippings as a base for the sauce.

In a process strongly resembling stir-frying, sautéed vegetables are cut into attractive, bite-size pieces before they are cooked under constant motion in a skillet or a wok. In mobile food-service situations, limited space often dictates the replacement of skillets and woks with a stationary flattop griddle. Cooking meat on these surfaces also results in a flavorful *fond*, which should not be wasted. Because it is difficult to deglaze a griddle with liquid, the drippings can be captured by cooking sliced, high-moisture vegetables like onions, peppers, and mushrooms in the drippings after the meat is done.

For an efficient service during peak business hours, many sautéed items can be either partially or fully cooked ahead and held warm or finished in an oven as needed.

ROASTING, SLOW ROASTING, BARBECUE

Roasting, likely one of the oldest cooking methods, has been part of the human diet since long before fireproof cookware and grills were invented. For thousands of years, meat was cooked over direct flames, but as man learned to control fire, these methods evolved to cooking with indirect heat. Food would be placed near the open flame or on rocks that were placed in the fire. This discovery broadened the diet vastly; many previously indigestible or hazardous foods could now be made palatable by placing them for the right amount of time in the right proximity to the fire. Over time, this crude method has evolved into roasting as it is known today.

Relying exclusively on radiant heat transfer, roasting cooks the food gradually, slowly enough that large cuts of meat or even whole animals can be prepared without burning or drying out. The temperature varies depending on the item. Skin-on poultry is commonly roasted at a relatively high temperature to ensure a crispy skin; for larger birds, the temperature is lowered to make sure the bird does not brown excessively before it is cooked through. Roasted meat is commonly seared intensely to ensure a well-browned and flavorful exterior. The remainder of the cooking should happen at a relatively low temperature to ensure that the desired doneness is achieved throughout. Roasting at low enough temperatures will actually tenderize tough cuts of meat like ribs, beef brisket, or the whole animal. When the food is cooked over a wood fire, with the addition of smoke, this method is known as barbecue.

Roasting vegetables, on the other hand, is accomplished by cutting the produce into bite-size pieces before roasting them at a very high heat. Whole roasted vegetables are often referred to as "baked," like baked potato or baked squash.

Rotisserie, or spit roasting, is a popular variation. Stacked thick slices of meat, animal parts, whole birds, or whole animals are roasted on a slowly turning skewer. Steadily rotating above or beside the heat, the meat cooks very evenly with an appealing color and juicy interior. In some instances, a pan lined with thick slices of bread is kept underneath the meat to catch dripping juices. Upon service, the soaked bread is served as the meat's accompaniment. Traditionally a celebratory meal, spit roasting has a strong visual impact that makes it especially popular for open-air and street-food settings.

BRAISING, STEWING

With their distinct comfort-food appeal, braised or stewed dishes are gaining popularity among street-food vendors. Omnipresent and popular in every cuisine, well-prepared stews of meat, seafood, or vegetables can awaken nostalgic food memories. The bold flavors are a direct result of the ingredients and methods. The well-exercised muscles used in this method are rich in proteins and connective tissue, helping to generate the coveted savor and texture of the meat and the sauce. For flavor and color enhancement, the main item is oftentimes seared or sweated before it is slowly simmered in a flavorful liquid until it is very tender. This liquid, the base for the sauce of the final dish, is kept at a particular level, enough to ensure even cooking, but not more than necessary to avoid diluting the flavors. Fish, with its inherent natural tenderness, is rarely braised, though some recipes suggest braising fish, not to tenderize it but simply to create distinct characteristics.

The ability to hold braised or stewed food hot for a long time without significant loss of quality makes these preparations especially fitting for a mobile vending environment. Almost all dishes can be entirely prepared ahead in a commercial kitchen, then easily transported to the site and reheated.

Meat Cookery and Cooking Methods **51**

POACHING, SIMMERING, BOILING, STEAMING

Gently poached or steamed fish, boiled dinners, and similar dishes have only recently become more prominent on the street-food scene. Unjustly, this food is often perceived to be bland and boring. Traditionally, such dishes are found regionally, at the main item's point of origin, like boiled lobster and steamed clams in New England or a crawfish boil in Louisiana.

Designed to draw attention to the main item's natural flavors, moist-heat cooking requires skillful execution and impeccable-quality ingredients. For example, poaching, cooking in a flavorful liquid between 145°F/63°C and 185°F/85°C, depends strongly on temperature control. When rapidly boiled, a naturally tender piece of fish or meat will shrink tremendously and become dry and rubbery. Poaching at the right temperature in a well-seasoned liquid, however, will result in a good yield and a moist and tender dish. When the temperature of the liquid is maintained at only a few degrees above the required final internal temperature, the risk of overcooking and drying out is eliminated. Recent improvements in equipment, especially induction burners, have made precise cooking a much easier task.

Generous seasoning is crucial to counteract the limited flavor interaction between the main item and the liquid because of the short cooking time and low temperature. Many accomplished chefs, especially in coastal regions, even go as far as to poach their fish in purified ocean water. However, if the poaching liquid is meant to be part of the final dish, as in shallow poaching, or if the item is served in its broth, seasoning should be kept at a reasonable level.

Steamed food, cooked without ever coming in contact with the water, needs to be seasoned directly. Using strongly flavored liquids such as stocks, broths, or wine to steam food, as some recipes suggest, will not impart much flavor. Most of the aromas will evaporate away or concentrate in the liquid beneath the food. Preparing an accompanying sauce from these liquids is a more effective way to use their flavor.

Based on classic preparations such as duck or tuna confit, poaching in a flavorful fat has also become very popular. Commonly, the item is cured or marinated before poaching to ensure a flavorful result. Using a method known as reverse searing, steaks are poached in olive oil or butter until the desired doneness is achieved and then seared on a hot grill or in a hot skillet at the moment of service.

Recent advances in technology and the desire to reinterpret classical cooking methods have introduced new tools to the culinary world. Immersion thermocirculators, with their ability to precisely control the temperature of a liquid, have made their way out of labs and into kitchens and even some food trucks. Sous vide cooking, a technique requiring this tool, has become very popular and widespread in the culinary industry. Translating to "under vacuum," the French term *sous vide* is used to describe a cooking method where an item, vacuum sealed in a plastic bag, is cooked at precise, often very low, temperatures to achieve a distinct texture and flavor profile. Perfect for mass-producing dishes in advance, reheating at service, or hot-holding for extended periods, this method is receiving a lot of attention, especially among companies with a central kitchen catering several mobile vending locations.

Meat dishes will always be present on the world's street-food stage. While many of us will always appreciate a well-prepared classic burger, kebob, or gyro, guests are also looking for fresh and innovative dishes. These dishes, prepared with care, will help to contribute to the evolution of cuisine and keep food exciting.

CURRYWURST

Currywurst, created in 1949 at a street-food booth in Berlin, is one of the most iconic fast-food snacks in Germany. It is prepared at street-food stands by pouring seasoned curry ketchup over a grilled and sliced bratwurst, or by sprinkling plain ketchup with curry powder, and serving it with soft bread or French fries. This recipe was provided by Chef Chris Dunn, a freelance food writer in San Antonio, Texas, who has done extensive research on currywurst.

YIELD: 8 PORTIONS

10 oz/284 g minced onions	3 oz/85 g brown sugar
1 fl oz/30 mL vegetable oil	2 fl oz/60 mL cider vinegar
1 oz/28 g curry powder	½ oz/14 g Dijon mustard
1 tbsp/7 g paprika	Salt, as needed
14 oz/397 g canned tomatoes with juice, chopped	Cayenne, as needed
⅔ cup/160 mL ketchup	8 bratwurst

1. For the sauce, sweat the onions in the vegetable oil over moderate heat until very tender, 5 to 10 minutes. Add the curry powder and the paprika and continue to cook gently until fragrant, about 30 seconds.

2. Add the tomatoes, ketchup, sugar, vinegar, and mustard. Bring to a boil, and simmer gently for about 30 minutes.

3. Purée in a blender until very smooth and the consistency of medium to heavy nappé. Adjust viscosity and season as needed with salt and cayenne.

4. Cook the bratwurst in a skillet, on a griddle, or on a grill until golden brown on all sides, fully cooked, and heated through, about 5 minutes.

5. Pour the curry sauce on top and sprinkle with more curry powder as desired.

RED HOMINY AND MEAT STEW

YIELD: 8 PORTIONS

1 lb/454 g boneless pork shoulder

4 oz/113 g sliced onions

2 garlic cloves, crushed

Salt, as needed

½ chicken (about 1 lb 8 oz/680 g)

4 guajillo chiles, seeds, stems, and ribs removed

2 chiles de árbol, seeds, stems, and ribs removed

1 oz/28 g lard

1 lb/454 g cooked hominy

1 tsp/1 g Mexican oregano

1 tsp/1 g dried marjoram

Ground black pepper, as needed

Garnishes

4 oz/113 g very finely shredded green cabbage

1 tbsp/3 g Mexican oregano

1 tbsp/3 g dried marjoram

3 oz/85 g thinly sliced white onions

3 oz/85 g thinly sliced red radishes

2 limes, quartered

1. Combine the pork, onions, garlic, and water to cover by 1 in/3 cm. Bring to a boil, and then reduce the heat to simmer gently for 30 minutes, skimming frequently. Adjust seasoning with salt as needed.

2. Add the chicken and simmer until all the meat is tender, about 45 minutes. Add water as needed to keep covered by ½ in/1 cm.

3. When done, take the meat from the broth and remove all the fat, bones, and gristle. Pull it into bite-size pieces and set aside. Strain the broth and set aside.

4. In a dry skillet, toast the chiles until fragrant, and then soak them in water for 15 minutes. Purée the soaked chiles in a blender until smooth. Add water as necessary to facilitate blending.

5. In a large rondeau over medium heat, fry the chile purée in the lard for about 3 minutes.

6. Add the meat, broth, hominy, oregano, and marjoram. Simmer for 8 to 10 minutes. Adjust seasoning with salt and pepper.

7. Serve in bowls and offer all the garnishes separately.

RED COOKED PORK BELLY

Tofu knots are dried sheets of tofu skin shaped into a knot. They are often served as a textural component in Chinese dishes. As they cook along with the food, they take on all the flavors of the dish. Dark soy sauce is thicker and significantly darker than regular soy sauce. With added molasses and a longer aging period, it has a much richer flavor. It is often used to drastically alter the flavor and color of the dish.

YIELD: 8 PORTIONS

4 oz/113 g dried tofu knots	2 tbsp/30 mL Shaoxing wine or sherry
3 lb/1.36 kg fresh pork belly, skin on, large dice	½ cup/120 mL light soy sauce, not low-sodium
2 oz/57 g brown sugar	3 tbsp/45 mL dark soy sauce
1 oz/28 g sliced ginger	3 star anise
2 green onions, cut into 1-in/3-cm pieces	Water, as needed
	Steamed rice, as needed

1. Soak the tofu knots in hot water for 30 minutes.
2. In a stockpot or small rondeau, sweat the pork belly, without oil, over medium heat for 1 minute. Add the brown sugar and continue sweating until aromatic, about 1 minute. Add the ginger and green onions and cook until aromatic, about 1 minute more.
3. Add the Shaoxing wine, light and dark soy sauces, star anise, and enough water to just barely submerge the meat. Cover tightly with a lid and simmer over very low heat for about 1 hour.
4. Add the tofu knots and continue to cook for another 30 minutes, until everything is tender. Add more liquid throughout cooking as necessary.
5. Serve pork belly on top of steamed rice in deep bowls.

CHEF'S NOTE — Shaoxing wine is a common rice wine used mostly for cooking in Chinese cuisine. It has a flavor resembling sherry, which can be used as a substitute.

BEEF CHEEKS AND TRIPE WITH SPANISH CHORIZO

YIELD: 8 TAPAS PORTIONS

1 lb/454 g beef or calf tripe	2 garlic cloves, minced
Salt, as needed	1 tbsp/7 g Spanish paprika
1 lb/454 g beef cheeks	1 cup/240 mL white wine
8 oz/227 g small-dice Spanish chorizo	1 bay leaf
2 fl oz/60 mL extra-virgin olive oil	Coarsely ground black pepper, as needed
6 oz/170 g minced onions	1 tbsp/3 g coarsely chopped parsley
	Crusty bread (optional)

1. Wash the tripe in cold water until the water runs clear. In a bowl, rub the tripe with salt and allow to sit for about 1 hour. Wash again, and cut into 1-in/3-cm dice.

2. Cut the beef cheeks into 1-in/3-cm pieces.

3. In a stockpot or similar pot, submerge the tripe and cheeks with cold water and add salt as needed. Bring to a boil, and simmer gently until everything is tender, about 2 hours.

4. In a rondeau or similar pot, render the chorizo in the olive oil. Add the onions and cook on low heat until translucent, 2 to 3 minutes. Add the garlic and paprika and continue to sweat until fragrant, about 30 seconds. Add the cooked tripe and cheeks and mix well.

5. Add the white wine and bay leaf and reduce until fully evaporated; then add enough of the tripe and cheeks' cooking liquid to barely submerge.

6. Simmer gently for about 30 minutes. Adjust seasoning with salt and a generous amount of black pepper.

7. Add the parsley and serve with crusty bread on the side.

HAINANESE CHICKEN RICE

YIELD: 8 PORTIONS

2 chickens (about 3 lb/1.36 kg)

1 oz/28 g peeled and crushed ginger

5 garlic cloves, peeled

2 leek stalks, washed and cut in half

Salt, as needed

Chicken Rice

5 shallots, minced

2 garlic cloves, minced

2 fl oz/60 mL fat from chicken broth

1 qt/960 mL long-grain rice

1½ qt/1.44 L chicken broth from simmering chicken

Salt, as needed

1 oz/28 g coarsely chopped cilantro

Soy Dipping Sauce (page 107)

Chili Dipping Sauce (page 107)

1. Place the chickens, ginger, garlic, and leeks in a stockpot and add enough well-salted boiling water to submerge the chicken by 1 in/3 cm. Return the water to a boil, turn the heat down, and cook the chicken at a temperature not exceeding 185°F/85°C.

2. About 15 minutes into the cooking, turn the chickens. Skim the fat off the broth and retain it for cooking the rice.

3. Once the chicken is done, remove it, drain liquid from the body cavity, and place in cold water to cool down. Retain the broth for cooking the rice.

4. For the rice, sweat the shallots and garlic in the chicken fat until fragrant, about 1 minute. Add the rice and sweat for 1 minute. Add the chicken broth and season with salt.

5. Bring to a boil over high heat, stirring frequently, and lower to a gentle simmer. Stop stirring, cover tightly, and continue cooking over very low heat or in a 350°F/177°C oven for about 20 minutes.

6. Bone the chicken, and carve it into bite-size pieces. Serve the chicken at room temperature (see Chef's Notes for important food-safety information) on the cooked rice with the cilantro, accompanied by the dipping sauces.

CHEF'S NOTES

Never hold chicken for more than 4 hours at room temperature. Ideally, chickens will be prepared continuously throughout the day to ensure freshness.

Brilliant in its simplicity, this dish, originating from the southern Chinese island of Hainan, is probably one of the most iconic dishes in Singaporean cuisine. The key to success is to cook the chicken ever so gently in well-salted water in order to retain all its juices. To achieve the strongest possible chicken flavor, keep all of the fat from skimming the broth and use it to cook the rice.

SPICY KIMCHI STEW WITH PORK

The importance of kimchi, which accompanies nearly every Korean meal, cannot be overestimated. This traditional condiment is made by fermenting vegetables, such as napa cabbage, radishes, or cucumbers, with chiles, ginger, green onions, garlic, and oftentimes anchovies. Ripe and fully fermented kimchi is added to give this popular Korean stew a richer flavor.

YIELD: 8 PORTIONS

10 oz/284 g large-dice onions	1 lb 8 oz/680 g cabbage kimchi, cut into bite-size pieces
1 fl oz/30 mL vegetable oil	
2 garlic cloves, sliced	1½ qt/1.44 L white chicken or beef stock
1 lb 8 oz/680 g thinly sliced pork shoulder	1 lb/454 g large-dice soft tofu
	Salt, as needed
1 fl oz/30 mL gochujang (Korean hot pepper paste)	2 green onions, sliced
	1 jalapeño, thinly sliced
2 tsp/2 g dried ground Korean chile	

1. In a rondeau or similar pot over medium heat, sweat the onions in the oil until softened, for about 5 minutes. Add the garlic and continue to sweat until fragrant, about 30 seconds.

2. Add the pork and cook until the meat turns opaque. Add the gochujang and ground Korean chile and cook for another 30 seconds.

3. Add the kimchi and just enough white stock to barely submerge. Bring to a boil, and simmer gently for 20 minutes.

4. Add the tofu, stirring very carefully in order not to break it apart. Continue to simmer very gently for 10 minutes, until the meat is tender. Adjust seasoning as necessary.

5. To serve, ladle the stew into a deep bowl and garnish with sliced green onions and jalapeño.

MIXED VEGETABLES AND BEEF WITH RICE (BIBIMBAP)

Bibimbap is an iconic Korean dish that is served decoratively arranged in a bowl. The guest will mix everything together with a spoon and add the Korean hot pepper paste according to his or her personal preference.

YIELD: 8 PORTIONS

Beef Marinade

2 fl oz/60 mL light soy sauce, not low-sodium

1 tbsp/15 mL mirin

4 green onions, minced

6 garlic cloves, minced

1½ tsp/4 g minced ginger

1 tbsp/9 g sesame seeds, toasted and crushed

1 tsp/5 mL sesame oil

2 lb/907 g beef skirt steak, thinly sliced parallel to the grain

8 oz/227 g sliced shiitake mushroom caps

8 oz/227 g julienne daikon

8 oz/227 g julienne carrots

8 eggs

8 portions steamed medium-grain rice, hot

½ head green leaf lettuce, cut into chiffonade

8 oz/227 g julienne European cucumber

8 fl oz/240 mL gochujang (Korean hot pepper paste)

1. Combine the soy sauce, mirin, green onions, garlic, ginger, sesame seeds, and sesame oil to form a marinade.

2. Combine the beef with the marinade and allow to marinate for 1 hour.

3. At service, stir-fry the mushrooms until cooked through, 3 to 4 minutes. Add the daikon and carrots, and continue cooking until they begin to tenderize, 4 to 5 minutes. Adjust seasoning and hold warm.

4. Drain the meat from its marinade, and stir-fry until just barely cooked, 2 to 3 minutes.

5. Fry the eggs sunny side up. While they are frying, place each portion of rice in a hot, deep bowl. Place the stir-fried beef and the vegetables on top of the rice. Place the lettuce and cucumber julienne beside it in the bowl. Top each portion with a fried egg and serve with the gochujang.

CHEF'S NOTE | Korean hot pepper paste (gochujang) is an indispensable Korean condiment that cannot be substituted with any other pepper paste. Made from ground dried red chile, glutinous rice, and fermented soybeans, it is used as a tableside condiment, a marinade, or a flavoring in soups and stews.

BEEF CURED WITH LIME AND ONIONS

YIELD: 8 PORTIONS

Marinade

1 red onion, sliced paper thin against the grain

¾ cup/180 mL lime juice

1 tbsp/10 g Vietnamese chili-garlic paste

2 fl oz/60 mL fish sauce

5 garlic cloves, minced

2 tbsp/25 g sugar

3 lb/1.36 kg beef, shoulder top blade or similar cut

2 fl oz/60 mL vegetable oil as needed for searing

8 oz/227 g bean sprouts

8 oz/227 g roasted peanuts, crushed

4 green onions, sliced

1 oz/28 g coarsely chopped cilantro

1 head green leaf lettuce

1. Combine the onion, lime juice, chili-garlic paste, fish sauce, garlic, and sugar to form a marinade.

2. Slice the beef into strips about 2 in/5 cm in girth and sear in a skillet or on a grill until well browned on all sides, 1 to 2 minutes.

3. After the beef has cooled, slice it paper thin with a sharp knife, combine with the marinade, and allow to sit for a maximum of 10 to 15 minutes.

4. At service, add the bean sprouts, peanuts, green onions, and cilantro and adjust seasoning if necessary. Provide lettuce leaves for the guest to prepare beef wraps.

POTATO GNOCCHI WITH DUCK STEW

YIELD: 8 PORTIONS

2 lb/907 g russet potatoes	Ground black pepper, as needed
4 egg yolks	Grated nutmeg, as needed
12 oz/340 g bread flour	Duck Leg Stew (page 70)
Salt, as needed	

1. For the gnocchi, bake the potatoes in a 400°F/204°C oven until cooked through, 30 to 45 minutes.

2. Cut the potatoes in half lengthwise and force each potato, flesh side down, through a medium-size wire rack into a hotel pan; the skins will stay behind on the wire rack.

3. Purée the potatoes with a food mill or ricer while still hot. Spread the potatoes on a sheet pan to cool and dry.

4. Once the potatoes are cool, add the egg yolks, flour, salt, black pepper, and nutmeg. Knead quickly, adding more flour if necessary to make a soft, smooth dough.

5. Roll the dough into logs of about 2 in/5 cm in diameter. Slice the logs into 2-in/5-cm pieces. Roll each piece over the tines of a fork or on a gnocchi board to achieve a rippled texture.

6. At service, cook the gnocchi in 1 gallon/3.79 L of well-salted, gently simmering water until they float at the surface, 3 to 5 minutes.

7. Toss in the Duck Leg Stew before serving.

DUCK LEG STEW

YIELD: 8 PORTIONS

3 duck legs (1½ to 2 lbs/680 to 907 g)	2 tbsp/35 g tomato paste
Salt, as needed	1½ cups/360 mL red wine
Ground black pepper, as needed	¼ cup/60 mL chicken stock
2 oz/57 g minced pancetta	2 rosemary sprigs
4 oz/113 g small-dice onions	3 thyme sprigs
1 tbsp/9 g minced garlic	3 bay leaves
4 oz/113 g small-dice celery	2 oz/57 g butter
4 oz/113 g small-dice carrots	3 oz/85 g grated Parmesan cheese
4 oz/113 g paysanne-cut leeks	¼ cup/12 g chopped parsley

1. Season the duck legs with salt and pepper as needed. On a sheet pan, sear the duck legs in a very hot oven until well browned on all sides, 10 to 15 minutes. Once the duck legs are well browned, remove them and reserve.

2. Drain the excess fat from the sheet pan into a rondeau or similar pot and deglaze the sheet pan with a small amount of water to capture the pan drippings. In the drained duck fat, cook the pancetta over medium heat until crispy, about 1 minute.

3. Add the onions and sweat over medium heat until tender, 1 to 2 minutes. Add the garlic, celery, carrots, and leeks and continue to sweat gently until aromatic, about 1 minute more. Add the tomato paste and cook until the paste turns rusty brown and smells sweet, 1 to 2 minutes.

4. Add the red wine and reduce to *au sec*, about 15 minutes.

5. Add the duck legs to the pot and add chicken stock to cover by 1 in/3 cm. Add the rosemary, thyme, and bay leaves. Adjust seasoning. Simmer slowly until the duck legs are tender, about 1 hour.

6. Once the duck legs are tender, remove from the sauce and set aside to cool. Remove all herbs from the sauce and, if necessary, reduce to a light nappé.

7. Take the meat off the bone, pull into bite-size pieces, and return it to the sauce.

8. At service, toss the hot gnocchi in the duck ragout. Add the butter and heat through.

9. Add Parmesan cheese and parsley, and adjust seasoning as needed.

MENUDO

YIELD: 8 PORTIONS

2 lb/907 g beef tripe
Juice of 2 limes
2 tbsp/20 g salt
1 white onion, peeled and halved
3 garlic cloves, peeled
4 ancho chiles
2 guajillo chiles
1 tsp/3 g cumin seeds

Garnishes

1 white onion
2 tbsp/6 g Mexican oregano
½ cup/120 mL coarsely chopped cilantro
4 limes, cut in half

1. Wash the tripe in cold water until the water runs clear. In a bowl, rub the tripe with the lime juice and salt and allow to sit for about 1 hour. Wash again, dry the tripe, and cut into 1-in/3-cm dice.

2. Place the tripe in a stockpot, cover with water, bring to a boil, and simmer gently for 10 minutes. Drain the cooking liquid and discard.

3. Return the tripe to the pot, add the onion and garlic, cover with water, and simmer gently until the tripe is very tender, for up to 3 hours. Adjust seasoning with salt and add water throughout the cooking as necessary to keep the tripe submerged. Once the tripe is tender, discard the onion halves and garlic cloves.

4. Stem and seed the ancho and guajillo chiles and gently dry-roast them in a skillet or a comal until their color begins to change, about 1 minute. Transfer the chiles to a bowl and cover with some of the tripe's hot cooking liquid for 10 to 15 minutes.

5. In a blender, purée the chiles with the cumin seeds until very smooth. Add some tripe broth as needed to facilitate the blending.

6. Add the puréed chiles to the tripe and continue to simmer for another 15 minutes. Adjust seasoning as needed, and serve with the garnishes on the side.

CHEF'S NOTE

Menudo, the aromatic tripe stew from Mexico, is a popular comfort food, traditionally served at weekend family events. A dish with the same name can also be found in the Philippines, evidence for the strong Spanish and Mexican influences on that country's culinary landscape. In the Philippines, however, menudo is a pork stew with liver, peas, potatoes, carrots, and, sometimes, garbanzo beans.

BEEF RENDANG

Often inappropriately referred to as dry curry, rendang is an iconic dish of Southeast Asia. Popular in Indonesia, Malaysia, and Singapore, it is often made with beef, but it can also be made with other meats or starchy vegetables. A key to success with this dish is to cook the beef until the sauce is completely dry and the fat begins to render.

YIELD: 8 PORTIONS

Rempah

3 guajillo chiles, stems and seeds removed

3 kaffir lime leaves

1 tsp/2 g cracked black peppercorns

½ oz/14 g thinly sliced peeled galangal

¼ cup/48 mL ground turmeric

5 garlic cloves

5 shallots, sliced

3 stalks lemongrass, coarsely chopped

3 macadamia nuts

2 fl oz/60 mL vegetable oil

3 lb/1.36 kg beef shoulder, cut into 1½-in/4-cm cubes

Salt, as needed

3 cups/720 mL coconut milk

Juice of 3 limes

Steamed rice, as needed

1. Soak the chiles in water for about 10 minutes.

2. In blender, combine the chiles, lime leaves, peppercorns, galangal, turmeric, garlic, shallots, lemongrass, and macadamia nuts. Purée until smooth. Use water to facilitate blending only if necessary.

3. In a rondeau or wok, sweat the rempah in 1 fl oz/30 mL oil over moderate heat until the fat begins to separate from the solids and the rempah is aromatic, 8 to 10 minutes.

4. Season the beef with salt, add to the rempah along with the remaining oil, and continue to sweat gently over medium heat until the beef is cooked on all sides, about 5 minutes.

5. Add the coconut milk, and cook until the meat is tender and a "dry sauce" is created, 45 to 60 minutes. If the sauce has reduced to almost a paste consistency but the meat is not tender yet, add more water and continue cooking as needed.

6. Once the beef is tender and the sauce is reduced to a paste, add the lime juice, and continue to cook for 1 minute more. Adjust seasoning with salt if needed.

7. Serve over steamed rice.

(continued) →

CHEF'S NOTE *Rempah* is the Malay word for "spice pastes." Many Malaysian and Indonesian dishes begin with a rempah. Depending on the dish, a small or large variety of spices and aromatic vegetables, usually raw, are pounded in a mortar or puréed in a blender. Mostly used for braised dishes, the rempah is then slowly fried in oil until the fat separates from the solids.

Add water to facilitate the blending of the rempah to form a smooth paste.

Transfer the mixture to a wok.

Cook the paste in the oil over medium heat.

The finished paste will be dry in appearance and oil will begin to release from the mixture.

74 CHAPTER 2   Meat & Poultry

CURRY CHICKEN

YIELD: 8 PORTIONS

2 whole chickens, cut into 8 or 10 pieces

Salt, as needed

Rempah

2 tbsp/24 mL coriander seeds

1½ tbsp/18 mL cumin seeds

2 tsp/8 mL fennel seeds

One 2-in/5-cm cinnamon stick

8 shallots, coarsely chopped

6 Fresno chiles, seeded, or similar chiles

1 tbsp/12 mL coarsely chopped ginger

8 garlic cloves

2 tbsp/24 mL ground turmeric

4 fl oz/120 mL vegetable oil

1 qt/960 mL coconut milk

3 stalks lemongrass, cut into 1-in/3-cm pieces, bruised

Roti Prata (page 110) (optional)

Steamed rice (optional)

1. Season the chicken pieces generously with salt and reserve.

2. To prepare the rempah, toast the coriander, cumin, fennel, and cinnamon in a dry skillet over moderate heat until fragrant, about 1 minute. Grind into a fine powder using a spice mill or grinder. Combine with the shallots, chiles, ginger, garlic, and turmeric in a blender and process to a fine paste. Add water as necessary to facilitate blending.

3. In a wok or rondeau, sweat the rempah in the oil over moderate heat until the solids separate from the fat and the rempah is very fragrant, 10 to 15 minutes. Add the chicken pieces and continue to cook until they are evenly coated with the spice paste.

4. Add the coconut milk and lemongrass, and bring to a boil. Establish a simmer, and simmer until tender, 30 to 40 minutes. Adjust seasoning with salt as needed. Serve with Roti Prata or steamed rice.

CHICKEN THIGHS WITH GREEN OLIVES

YIELD: 8 PORTIONS

2 lb/907 g bone-in chicken legs and thighs

Salt, as needed

Ground black pepper, as needed

1 fl oz/30 mL extra-virgin olive oil

1 lb/454 g large-dice onions

1 oz/28 g minced garlic

1 tsp/4 mL ground ginger

1 tsp/4 mL ground cumin

1 tbsp/12 mL sweet paprika

1 pinch whole saffron

3 cups/720 mL chicken stock

1 lb/454 g green olives, pitted and cracked

½ cup/120 mL chopped flat-leaf parsley

½ cup/120 mL coarsely chopped cilantro

½ fl oz/15 mL lemon juice

Pita Bread (page 111)

1. Season the chicken with salt and pepper. In a rondeau or similar pot over medium heat, sear the chicken in the olive oil until well browned, 5 to 8 minutes. Remove the chicken from the pan and set aside.

2. In the pan drippings, sweat the onions over moderate heat until very tender, about 10 minutes. Add the garlic, ginger, cumin, paprika, and saffron. Cook over low heat for 1 minute, until fragrant.

3. Return the chicken pieces to the pot and add chicken stock to submerge by 1 in/3 cm. Add the olives and adjust seasoning as needed. Simmer until the chicken is tender, 30 to 45 minutes.

4. Once the chicken is tender, add the parsley and cilantro, and adjust seasoning with the lemon juice and salt.

5. Serve with Pita Bread on the side.

GRILLED PORK SKEWERS

YIELD: 8 PORTIONS

Marinade

1 cup/240 mL extra-virgin olive oil

4 oz/113 g coarsely cut onions

4 garlic cloves, peeled

1 chipotle chile in adobo

1 oz/28 g brown sugar

1½ fl oz/45 mL light soy sauce, not low-sodium

1 tsp/4 mL achiote paste

½ oz/14 g cilantro

3 lb/1.36 kg pork loin, cut into 1-in/3-cm dice

Salt, as needed

8 bamboo skewers, 8 in/20 cm

1. Combine the oil, onions, garlic, chipotle, sugar, soy sauce, achiote, and cilantro in a blender and purée until the mixture forms a smooth marinade.

2. Season the pork with salt. Combine it with the marinade, and allow to marinate for about 1 hour.

3. Thread the pork onto bamboo skewers, and grill until well charred and cooked to an internal temperature of 145°F/63°C, 4 to 5 minutes.

4. Serve 1 skewer per portion.

CHICKEN KÖFTE KEBOB

YIELD: 8 PORTIONS

Ground Chicken

3 lb/1.36 kg skinless, boneless chicken thighs, diced

4 oz/113 g diced dried bread

3 garlic cloves, peeled

2 oz/57 g strained yogurt

1 oz/28 g chopped flat-leaf parsley

Salt, as needed

Ground black pepper, as needed

Red pepper flakes, as needed

8 flat metal skewers, ½-in/1-cm wide

Pomegranate molasses, as needed

Tzatziki, or Caçik (page 112)

Pita Bread (page 111)

1. Combine the chicken with the bread, garlic, yogurt, parsley, salt, pepper, and red pepper flakes, and grind everything through the medium disk of a meat grinder.

2. Form the ground chicken mixture into thin cylinders and place onto skewers.

3. Grill over moderate heat until browned evenly on all sides and cooked to an internal temperature of 165°F/74°C, 4 to 5 minutes.

4. During the last minute on the grill, brush with pomegranate molasses and allow to cook until caramelized.

5. Serve with Tzatziki and Pita Bread (see Chef's Note).

CHEF'S NOTE | It is common practice in much of the Middle East and South Asia to purchase whole pieces of meat and ask the butcher to grind it together with additional ingredients such as bread, spices, and flavorful vegetables. This dish can be served on a plate with the sauce and pita bread on the side, or the köfte can be taken off the skewer after cooking and served inside the pita pocket with the sauce drizzled on top.

MALAYSIAN CHICKEN SATAY

YIELD: 8 PORTIONS (24 SKEWERS)

Chicken Marinade

5 stalks lemongrass, trimmed and roughly chopped

3 garlic cloves, peeled

1 tbsp sliced galangal

½ cup/120 mL water

3 lb/1.36 kg boneless, skinless chicken thighs

Salt, as needed

3 oz/85 g sugar

3 oz/85 g ground roasted peanuts

1 oz/28 g ground turmeric

24 bamboo skewers, 8 in/20 cm, as needed

Peanut Sauce (page 113), as needed

Red Onion Relish (page 113), as needed

1. Purée the lemongrass, garlic, galangal, and water in a blender. Set aside ¼ cup/60 mL of the mixture to use for the Peanut Sauce.

2. Cut the chicken thighs into strips measuring 3 to 4 in/8 to 10 cm, season with salt, and thoroughly combine with the marinade.

3. Add the sugar, peanuts, and turmeric and combine thoroughly.

4. Thread the chicken onto skewers, and allow to marinate, refrigerated, for 4 to 5 hours. Grill the satays directly over charcoal until cooked through, 1 to 2 minutes.

5. Serve with the Peanut Sauce and Red Onion Relish on the side.

CHEF'S NOTE

Satays are a street-food staple found on almost every corner in Southeast Asia. Varying in length but only 4 to 5 in/10 to 13 cm wide, a satay grill is a unique gadget. The meat is suspended only a few inches above the hot coals without exposing the skewer to the flames. This allows the meat to cook at very intense temperatures without burning the wooden skewers. Additionally, these grills are easy to transport and quite energy efficient, making them popular in many culinary cultures all over Asia.

CHAPTER 2   Meat & Poultry

JERK CHICKEN SKEWERS

Jerk, a Jamaican specialty, refers to a spicy dry rub or wet marinade as well as the method of cooking the marinated meat over a direct flame, allowing the surface to char well. Traditionally, oil barrels cut in half lengthwise, hinged and with holes drilled for ventilation, are used to cook or "jerk" meat.

YIELD: 8 PORTIONS

Spice Mix

1 tbsp/12 mL ground allspice

5 garlic cloves, peeled

1 tbsp/12 mL thyme

10 fl oz/300 mL malt vinegar

1½ oz/43 g minced green onions

1 tsp/2 g grated nutmeg

1 tsp/2 g ground cinnamon

½ tsp/1 g ground cloves

1 Scotch Bonnet chile, seeded

2 tbsp/30 mL dark rum

3 lb/1.36 kg boneless, skinless chicken thighs, cut into large dice

Salt, as needed

8 bamboo skewers, 8 in/20 cm

1. In a blender, purée the allspice, garlic, thyme, vinegar, green onions, nutmeg, cinnamon, cloves, chile, and rum until smooth, adding water as needed to facilitate the blending.

2. Season the chicken with salt, combine with the spice paste, and allow to marinate for 2 hours.

3. Soak the wooden skewers in water for 30 minutes. Thread the chicken onto the skewers.

4. Wipe off excess marinade and grill the chicken over medium-high to high heat, basting as needed until well charred and cooked to an internal temperature of 165°F/74°C, 3 to 5 minutes.

CHICKEN YAKITORI

YIELD: 8 PORTIONS

8 bamboo skewers, 8 in/20 cm

1 lb/454 g chicken livers, cut into ¾-in/2-cm pieces

2 lb/907 g boneless, skinless chicken thighs, cut into ¾-in/2-cm pieces

8 green onions, cut into ¾-in/2-cm pieces

Yakitori Sauce

12 fl oz/360 mL sake

5 fl oz/150 mL mirin

2 oz/57 g sugar

1 fl oz/30 mL dark soy sauce

5 fl oz/150 mL light soy sauce, not low-sodium

Ground sansho pepper, as needed

Japanese seven-spice, as needed

1. Soak the bamboo skewers.

2. Skewer the chicken livers, chicken thighs, and green onions alternately onto the skewers.

3. For the sauce, combine the sake, mirin, sugar, soy sauces, sansho, and seven-spice and allow it to simmer until it has reduced by a one-quarter, 5 to 10 minutes.

4. Grill the skewers until they are cooked to an internal temperature of 165°F/74°C, about 5 minutes.

5. During the last minute on the grill, brush the yakitori sauce onto the skewers and allow to caramelize slightly.

6. Remove from the grill, and sprinkle with sansho pepper and Japanese seven-spice.

CHEF'S NOTES

Sansho pepper is the Japanese counterpart to Sichuan pepper. Available in most East Asian groceries in the United States, sansho is commonly sold ground.

Japanese seven-spice, or *shichimi togarashi*, is one of the most popular tableside condiments in Japan, and considering the low level of spiciness in most Japanese dishes, the heat level of seven-spice is quite surprising. It is made from coarsely ground red peppers, sansho, orange peel, ginger, white and black sesame seeds, and nori seaweed.

SCHASCHLIK

Classically, schaschlik is a grilled meat skewer found all over Central and Western Asia. The word is derived from *shish*, the Turkish word for "skewer." This version, a pork kebob braised in an aromatic tomato sauce, is an extremely popular street-food snack found at street-food booths all over Germany.

YIELD: 8 PORTIONS

Sauce

8 oz/227 g minced onions

1 fl oz/30 mL vegetable oil

3 garlic cloves, minced

1 tsp/5 mL red pepper flakes

2 tbsp/30 mL sweet paprika

1 tbsp/15 mL curry powder

1 pint/480 mL crushed tomatoes

1 pint/480 mL ketchup

1 oz/28 g brown sugar

1 tbsp/15 mL Worcestershire sauce

2 tsp/10 mL Tabasco sauce

1½ tsp/2 g chopped oregano

Salt, as needed

Ground black pepper, as needed

2 lb 8 oz/1.13 kg boneless pork butt

1 onion (about 12 oz/340 g)

2 red peppers (about 12 oz/340 g)

12 oz/340 g sliced bacon

8 bamboo skewers, 8 in/20 cm

Salt, as needed

Ground black pepper, as needed

1. To make the sauce, sweat the onions in the vegetable oil over very moderate heat in a rondeau or similar pan until very tender and slightly caramelized, about 15 minutes. Add the garlic and sweat until aromatic, about 30 seconds. Add the red pepper flakes, paprika, and curry powder and cook until fragrant.

2. Add the tomatoes, ketchup, sugar, Worcestershire, Tabasco, oregano, salt, and pepper, bring to a boil, and simmer very slowly for about 30 minutes.

3. Purée the sauce in a blender until very smooth, and add water as needed to achieve a light nappé. Adjust seasoning and set aside.

4. For the schaschlik, cut the meat, onion, peppers, and bacon into 1-in/3-cm dice and skewer, alternating.

5. Season the meat with salt and pepper and sear in a rondeau over high heat until well browned on all sides, 5 to 10 minutes.

6. Add the sauce, bring to a gentle boil, and simmer very gently for 45 minutes or until the meat is very tender. Add water as needed to adjust viscosity of the sauce. Adjust seasoning if necessary.

7. Serve covered with a generous amount of sauce.

BEEF SKEWERS WITH GREEN CHILI SAUCE

YIELD: 8 PORTIONS

8 bamboo skewers, 8 in/20 cm

3 lb/1.36 kg beef sirloin or similar meat, diced

2 fl oz/60 mL light soy sauce, not low-sodium

1 tbsp/15 mL finely chopped palm sugar

6 cilantro roots, finely chopped

2 tbsp/30 mL coriander seeds

1 tbsp/15 mL white peppercorns

1 tbsp/15 mL minced galangal

4 stalks lemongrass, minced

Green Chili Sauce

2 tbsp/30 mL minced Thai bird chiles

1 tbsp/15 mL sliced garlic

Salt, as needed

1 tbsp/15 mL finely chopped palm sugar

½ cup/120 mL coarsely chopped cilantro

1 fl oz/30 mL fish sauce

Juice of 1 lime

1. Soak the bamboo skewers.

2. Cut the beef into ½-in/1-cm dice, mix with the soy sauce and palm sugar, and allow to marinate for about 2 hours.

3. Using a mortar and pestle, pound the cilantro roots, coriander seeds, white peppercorns, galangal, and lemongrass into a coarse paste.

4. Skewer the meat, rub with the paste, and reserve.

5. For the chili sauce, pound the chiles, garlic, salt, palm sugar, and cilantro in a mortar and pestle. Add the fish sauce and lime juice, adjust seasoning, and set aside. For larger amounts, a blender can be used.

6. Grill the beef skewers over very high heat until cooked through, 3 to 4 minutes.

7. Serve each skewer on a plate with the green chili sauce on the side.

GRILLED LAMB KEBOBS WITH WALNUT-HERB SAUCE

YIELD: 8 PORTIONS

3 lb/1.36 kg lamb shoulder, cut into ¾-in/2-cm dice

Salt, as needed

Ground black pepper, as needed

2 fl oz/60 mL olive oil

1½ tsp/4 g crushed garlic

¾ tsp/1.5 g ground cumin

½ tsp/1 g red pepper flakes

½ tsp/1 g ground allspice

8 flat metal skewers, ½ in/1 cm wide

Pita Bread (page 111)

Walnut-Herb Sauce (page 114)

1. Season the lamb with salt and pepper and combine with the oil, garlic, cumin, red pepper flakes, and allspice. Allow to marinate for 1 hour, and put the meat onto skewers.

2. Grill the kebobs over high heat until the meat is well charred on all sides, 4 to 5 minutes.

3. Serve with the Pita Bread and Walnut-Herb Sauce (see Chef's Note).

| CHEF'S NOTE | This is a handheld food that can be served on a plate with the walnut sauce, or the lamb can be removed from the skewer, served inside a pita pocket, and drizzled with the sauce. |

TURKISH SHISH KEBOB

YIELD: 8 PORTIONS

Marinade

1 lb/454 g large-dice yellow onions

4 garlic cloves, peeled

2 lb/907 g lean lamb shoulder or leg, cut into 1-in/3-cm dice

8 oz/227 g raw lamb fat, cut into 1-in/3-cm dice

Salt, as needed

Ground black pepper, as needed

2 fl oz/60 mL extra-virgin olive oil, plus as needed

8 flat metal skewers, ½ in/1 cm wide

1 lb/454 g cored and halved roma tomatoes

2 green peppers (about 12 oz/340 g), quartered, seeded, and deveined

1. For the marinade, purée the onions and garlic in a blender and drain through a cheesecloth or coffee filter to catch the juice. Discard the solids.

2. Place the lamb shoulder and lamb fat in a bowl, and season with salt and pepper.

3. Add the onion juice and olive oil to the meat and combine thoroughly. Allow the meat to marinate for about 2 hours.

4. Skewer the lamb and lamb fat onto the metal skewers, placing a piece of fat after each 3 pieces of meat.

5. Grill the lamb skewers over very high heat until well charred on all sides, 4 to 5 minutes, brushing frequently with the marinade.

6. Toss the tomatoes and peppers in olive oil and season with salt and pepper. Grill both vegetables until well charred on all sides, 3 to 4 minutes.

7. Serve with grilled tomatoes and peppers on the side.

CHICKEN TIKKA

Literally meaning "bits or pieces" of chicken, chicken tikka is a very popular dish in Indian and Pakistani cooking. In many regions, it is cooked in a tandoor, an extremely hot, vertical clay oven. In the region of Punjab, however, it is commonly cooked over red-hot charcoal.

YIELD: 8 PORTIONS

3 lb/1.36 kg skinless, boneless chicken thighs, cut into 1-in/3-cm dice

Salt, as needed

Ground black pepper, as needed

Juice of 1 lemon

2 fl oz/60 mL ghee

1 tbsp/6 g sweet paprika

1½ tsp/3 g ground Korean chili pepper

2 tsp/4 g ground cumin

1 tsp/2 g ground ginger

2 tsp/4 g ground turmeric

2 tsp/4 g ground coriander

4 oz/113 g small-dice onions

½ oz/14 g sliced garlic

1 cup/240 mL strained yogurt

8 flat metal skewers, ½ in/1 cm wide

Chapati Bread (page 115)

Cilantro-Cashew Chutney (page 116)

1. Season the chicken with salt, pepper, and lemon juice.
2. In a saucepan or similar pan, heat the ghee. Add the paprika, chili pepper, cumin, ginger, turmeric, and coriander and cook until aromatic, about 1 minute.
3. Add the onions and cook over medium heat until the onions are very tender, about 10 minutes. Add the garlic and continue to sweat for about 1 minute.
4. Purée the onion-spice mix in a blender, adding small amounts of yogurt as needed to facilitate the blending.
5. Combine the spice purée with the diced chicken, mix well, and add the remainder of the yogurt. Allow to marinate for about 1 hour.
6. Skewer the chicken pieces and grill until cooked through and well charred, 5 to 6 minutes.
7. Serve with Chapati Bread and Cilantro-Cashew Chutney.

CHEF'S NOTES

Ghee is a general-purpose cooking fat used in northern Indian and Pakistani cooking. It is made by simmering whole butter until all its water is evaporated and the milk solids turn brown. In order to avoid burning, it must be strained immediately.

Garam masala, literally meaning "warming spices," is a combination of spices originating in Indian cuisine. Common components are black pepper, cardamom, cinnamon, clove, and cumin seeds.

ITALIAN SAUSAGE DOG

YIELD: 8 PORTIONS

8 Italian sausages (about 4 oz/113 g each)

3 fl oz/90 mL extra-virgin olive oil

1 lb/454 g sliced onions

1 lb/454 g sliced roasted red peppers

½ cup/120 mL ketchup

½ tsp/1 g dried oregano

3 fl oz/90 mL water

1 oz/28 g light brown sugar

Salt, as needed

Ground black pepper, as needed

8 hoagie rolls, not too soft

5 oz/142 g basil pesto

4 oz/113 g grated mozzarella cheese

1. In a medium-hot skillet, sear the Italian sausages in the olive oil until well browned on all sides, 2 to 3 minutes. Remove the sausages from the pan and set aside.

2. In the same skillet, sweat the onions over moderate heat for about 10 minutes, until tender and slightly caramelized.

3. Add the roasted peppers, ketchup, oregano, water, and sugar. Adjust seasoning with salt and pepper.

4. Return the sausages to the pan and cover with a lid. Over low heat, cook for about 5 minutes, until the sausage is cooked through.

5. Spread the hoagie rolls with basil pesto and toast at 350°F/177°C until lightly crispy. Place the cooked sausage in the hoagie roll and cover with the onion and pepper mix. Sprinkle with mozzarella cheese and serve.

BRAISED PORK KNUCKLE BUN

YIELD: 8 PORTIONS (24 BUNS)

5 lb 8 oz/2.5 kg fresh pork knuckle, preferably hind leg, skin on, bone in	6½ fl oz/195 mL light soy sauce, not low-sodium
2 oz/57 g sliced ginger	2 fl oz/60 mL dark soy sauce
5 garlic cloves, sliced	2 tbsp/25 g sugar
3 green onions	Salt, as needed
8 whole star anise	24 steamed lotus buns
¼ tsp/0.5 g whole Sichuan peppercorns	2 oz/57 g coarsely chopped cilantro
1½ fl oz/45 mL Shaoxing wine or sherry	

1. Inspect the pork knuckle for any remaining bristles and remove as necessary. Place the pork knuckle into an appropriate-size pot and add enough water to cover the pork halfway. Bring to a boil over high heat, removing any scum as needed.

2. Add the ginger, garlic, green onions, star anise, Sichuan peppercorns, Shaoxing, soy sauces, and sugar. Adjust seasoning as needed.

3. Cover tightly with a lid and simmer gently until the pork knuckle is tender enough that the bone comes off easily; this may take 2 to 3 hours. During the cooking, turn the knuckle frequently to ensure even cooking and replace cooking liquid as needed.

4. Once tender, remove the pork knuckle from the liquid, remove the bone, and set aside.

5. Strain the cooking liquid and reduce over medium heat to maple syrup consistency, about 10 minutes; reserve.

6. Chop the meat and skin finely and add enough of the reduced cooking liquid to evenly coat the meat.

7. At service, stuff each steamed bun with meat and a generous amount of cilantro.

BRAISED PORK BELLY WITH DRIED MUSTARD GREENS AND LILY BUDS IN FERMENTED TOFU SAUCE

YIELD: 8 PORTIONS (24 BUNS)

3 lb/1.36 kg pork belly, skin on	4 whole star anise
2 oz/57 g dried mustard greens	Salt, as needed
4 oz/113 g dried lily buds	¼ cup/60 mL dark soy sauce
7 oz/198 g red fermented tofu, puréed	½ cup/120 mL soy sauce
½ oz/14 g sliced ginger	1½ oz/43 g brown sugar
1 green onion	24 steamed lotus buns

1. Inspect the pork belly for any remaining bristles and remove as necessary.

2. Soak the mustard greens and lily buds separately in water overnight.

3. Meanwhile, place the pork belly into an appropriate-size rondeau or similar pan and add the ginger, green onion, star anise, soy sauces, tofu, and sugar. Add enough water to submerge the pork belly by two thirds. Bring to a boil, cover with a lid, and simmer gently for 1 hour.

4. Place the pot in an ice bath or blast chiller, and allow the pork belly to cool in the cooking liquid. Once the pork belly is cool, cut into slices about ¼ in/6 mm thick and 3 in/8 cm wide.

5. Remove any tough parts of the soaked lily buds and mustard greens and cut into bite-size pieces. Combine the lily buds and mustard greens and place in an ovenproof dish. Place the pork belly on top and pour the cooking liquid over it. Cover tightly with aluminum foil and bake at 350°F/177°C until the pork belly is tender, 1 to 2 hours. Adjust seasoning with salt as needed.

6. At service, place about 2 oz/57 g of the pork belly inside each steamed bun and top with lily buds and mustard greens. Serve immediately.

CHEF'S NOTES

Red fermented tofu is a preserved tofu inoculated with special yeast cultures to achieve a flavor resembling washed rind cheese.

Dried lily buds are the unopened flowers of day lilies. With a slightly crunchy and at the same time chewy texture and an earthy flavor, they are often featured in dishes like mu xu pork and hot and sour soup.

Known as *mei cai*, dried mustard greens are a common side dish in southeastern China. They are leafy greens that are steeped in a mixture of salt, sugar, and soy sauce for a few hours and then allowed to air-dry.

Steamed lotus buns are buns with a folded shape that resembles Parker House rolls.

JAMAICAN BEEF PATTIES

YIELD: 8 PORTIONS

1 lb 12 oz/794 g all-purpose flour	2 lb/907 g 85% lean ground beef
1½ tsp/3 g ground turmeric	8 oz/227 g diced tomatoes
½ oz/14 g salt	1 tbsp/6 g minced thyme
1½ tsp/6 g baking powder	1 tbsp/6 g ground cumin
12 oz/340 g butter, softened	1½ tsp/3 g ground allspice
10 oz/284 g minced onions	Salt, as needed
4 garlic cloves, minced	Ground black pepper, as needed
½ tsp/2 g minced seeded Scotch Bonnet chile	12 fl oz/340 mL chicken stock
	1 oz/28 g coarsely cut cilantro
1½ fl oz/45 mL olive oil	3 eggs, beaten

1. Combine the flour, turmeric, salt, and baking powder. Add the butter and mix well. Add enough cold water to form a soft dough, 8 to 10 fl oz/240 to 300 mL. Wrap the dough in plastic and refrigerate for 1 hour.

2. In a skillet, sweat the onions, garlic, and chile in the olive oil until they are tender, about 2 minutes.

3. Add the beef, tomatoes, thyme, cumin, allspice, salt, and pepper. Cook over high heat until the beef is fully cooked, 2 to 3 minutes.

4. Add the stock and continue to cook until all liquid has evaporated, 5 to 10 minutes. Add the cilantro and allow to cool. Once cool, adjust seasoning as needed.

5. Roll the dough ¼ in/6 mm thick and cut into 8-in/20-cm circles. Place 2 tablespoons of the beef stuffing onto each dough circle. Brush the edges of the dough with beaten eggs. Fold the dough over and crimp the edge with a fork. Brush the top of the patties with beaten eggs.

6. Bake the patties in a 400°F/204°C oven until they are golden brown, 15 to 20 minutes. Serve each patty immediately, on a plate or wrapped in sandwich paper.

HAM AND CHEESE STACKED QUESADILLAS

YIELD: 8 PORTIONS

16 flour tortillas, 8 in/20 cm	1 lb/454 g cooked or baked ham, sliced
1 lb 8 oz/680 g queso Chihuahua or similar cheese	Raw Tomatillo and Avocado Salsa (page 118)

1. Place 8 tortillas on a flat surface. Using half of the cheese, make a thin layer on top of each tortilla.

2. Cover with a layer of the ham, making sure to completely cover the cheese.

3. Top with an even layer of the remaining cheese.

4. Cover each one with the remaining tortillas.

5. Cook the quesadillas on a griddle over medium heat, pressing down gently as they cook until the tortillas are crispy with some brown spots and the filling is warm with melted cheese, 3 to 4 minutes.

6. Serve warm with Raw Tomatillo and Avocado Salsa.

REUBEN SANDWICH

Popular on the streets of New York City, the Reuben sandwich has become a staple on street-vendor menus as well as in many diner-style restaurants.

YIELD: 8 PORTIONS

3 lb/1.36 kg raw corned beef brisket	16 slices Swiss cheese
16 slices rye bread	Sauerkraut for Reuben Sandwich (page 117)
Russian Dressing (page 117)	4 oz/113 g clarified butter

1. Cook the corned beef until fork-tender, about 3 hours. Split off the deckle, trim all excess fat, and submerge in ice water to cool without drying out.

2. Once cool, thinly slice the corned beef on a deli slicer.

3. To assemble the sandwiches, lay out all slices of the rye bread and spread the Russian Dressing on top. Place a slice of cheese onto 8 of the bread slices, then place 1 or 2 slices of corned beef onto the cheese to cover. Place 2 tbsp/30 mL of the sauerkraut onto the corned beef and spread evenly. Place 1 or 2 more slices of corned beef onto the sauerkraut to cover, and top with another slice of cheese. Top with the remaining 8 slices of bread and press down slightly.

4. Cook the sandwiches over moderate heat on a buttered griddle until well browned and crispy on both sides and heated through, 5 to 8 minutes.

CHEF'S NOTE — The key to success for a good Reuben is to keep the sauerkraut in the center of the sandwich, as it otherwise causes the bread to become soggy. Additionally, the sauerkraut needs to be well cooked to provide a pleasant mouthfeel. It is important to maintain a ratio of equal parts corned beef to sauerkraut; it is the combination of both that makes this sandwich so special. The bread should be a sturdy, slightly stale rye bread, ideally from the day before; it provides a more stable shell.

GYROS

Contrary to popular belief, gyros were originally made with pork. Versions with lamb or beef are made, but they are not very popular in Greece. Other cultures have comparable dishes. Known as döner kebab in Turkey or shawarma in the Middle East, these versions commonly use beef or lamb as prescribed by the common religion. The famous Mexican tacos al pastor is a similar preparation inspired by Lebanese immigrants in Mexico.

YIELD: 8 PORTIONS

3 lb/1.36 kg boneless pork butt	1 tbsp/9 g minced garlic
¾ oz/21 g salt	Tzatziki, or Caçik (page 112)
1 fl oz/30 mL white wine vinegar	½ sweet onion, thinly sliced
1½ tbsp/9 g sweet paprika	2 tomatoes, diced
1½ tsp/3 g ground black pepper	Pita Bread (page 111)
1½ tsp/3 g minced oregano	

1. Slice the meat into thin equal-size steaks and pound them to a ¼-in/6-mm thickness. Combine the meat with the salt, vinegar, paprika, pepper, oregano, and garlic and mix well. Allow to marinate under refrigeration for 2 hours.

2. Stack the sliced meat evenly on the skewer of an upright rotisserie, avoiding any gaps. Fold the slices of meat as necessary to prevent pieces hanging over. Creating a tubular shape will help ensure even cooking.

3. Cook the meat at about 375°F/191°C until well browned on the outside, 30 to 40 minutes.

4. With a long slicer or an electric knife, carve thin slivers of the meat.

5. Place Tzatziki, onion slices, and tomatoes onto each whole Pita Bread and top with meat. Fold the pita in half and serve.

CHEF'S NOTE | The amount of this recipe is designed for a small, home-style, upright rotisserie. For a commercial-size upright rotisserie, the amount needs to be increased according to the manufacturer's instructions. Should you not have an upright rotisserie, the meat can also be grilled after slicing and marinating to achieve a comparable result.

CHICKEN FLAUTAS

YIELD: 8 PORTIONS

2 garlic cloves, peeled	Salt, as needed
1 lb/454 g quartered roma tomatoes	16 corn tortillas
12 oz/340 g coarsely chopped white onions	½ cup/120 mL Mexican Cream (page 119)
Vegetable oil, as needed	1 cup/240 mL finely shredded romaine lettuce
1 lb/454 g poached and shredded chicken breast	Raw Tomatillo and Avocado Salsa (page 118)
	¼ cup/60 mL finely crumbled queso fresco

1. In a blender, purée the garlic, tomatoes, and onions.

2. In a skillet, cook the tomato mixture in 1 tbsp/15 mL oil for about 10 minutes over moderate heat, until it begins to get thick.

3. Combine with the shredded chicken, adjust seasoning with salt, and set aside to cool.

4. To soften the corn tortillas, dip them in oil at about 110°F/43°C.

5. On a kitchen towel, fill the softened tortillas with the chicken-tomato mixture, roll them, and secure them with a toothpick.

6. Pan fry the flautas at about 350°F/177°C until they are crispy on all sides, 2 to 3 minutes. Drain on a wire rack and gently blot with paper towels.

7. Arrange flautas on a plate, drizzle with the Mexican Cream, and top with lettuce, salsa, and crumbled queso fresco.

CHEF'S NOTE

Flautas, also known as *taquitos*, can be found in many food stands all over the southwestern United States as well as in many quick-service restaurants. Flautas can be stuffed with a variety of ingredients, including beef, chicken, pork, potatoes, or other vegetables.

CURRY GOAT WITH GREEN PAPAYA SLAW

YIELD: 8 PORTIONS

5 lb 8 oz/2.25 kg whole goat shoulder

Salt, as needed

Ground black pepper, as needed

2 oz/60 mL vegetable oil

2 tbsp/12 g toasted curry powder

2 qt/1.92 L brown veal stock

1 sprig thyme

1 Scotch Bonnet chile, seeded and minced

1 lb/454 g medium-dice seeded plum tomatoes

5 green onions, sliced ½ in/1 cm thick

1 fl oz/30 mL lime juice

Garnish

3 green onions, thinly sliced

Green Papaya Slaw (page 118)

Caribbean Roti Bread (page 102)

1. Season the goat shoulder with salt and pepper. In a rondeau over high heat, sear the goat in the hot vegetable oil, browning on all sides, 5 to 10 minutes.

2. Remove the goat shoulder and sweat the curry powder in the pan drippings. Add the brown veal stock, thyme, and chile. Return the goat shoulder to the pot and bring to a boil. Cover tightly with a lid and simmer very slowly until the goat shoulder is very tender, about 1 to 2 hours, adding liquid as needed to cook the goat evenly.

3. Once tender, remove the goat shoulder and pull the meat into bite-size pieces.

4. Strain the braising liquid, and cook over medium-high heat until it has reduced by half, about 15 minutes.

5. Once the liquid is reduced, add the shredded goat shoulder and simmer for 10 minutes. Adjust seasoning as needed.

6. At service, add the tomatoes, green onions, and lime juice. Bring to a simmer one more time, and adjust seasoning as needed.

7. Serve with the Green Papaya Slaw in a piece of Roti Bread.

CARIBBEAN ROTI BREAD WITH GUYANESE FILLING

YIELD: ABOUT 8 PORTIONS

Guyanese Filling

4 oz/113 g yellow split peas

1 tbsp/6 g ground cumin

2 garlic cloves, minced

Salt, as needed

Ground black pepper, as needed

Roti Bread

12 oz/340 g all-purpose flour

1 tbsp/10 g salt

1 tbsp/12 g baking powder

3 oz/85 g lard or butter

¾ cup/180 mL water

Vegetable oil, as needed, for cooking

1. For the Guyanese filling, cook the yellow split peas in gently simmering water until they are halfway cooked and begin to appear crumbly. Drain and allow to cool.

2. Combine the cooked peas with the cumin and garlic in a food processor and process until slightly crumbly. Taste and adjust seasoning.

3. For the roti, combine the flour, salt, and baking powder with 2 oz/57 g of the lard and mix to a mealy texture.

4. Add the water and knead until a smooth dough is achieved; add more flour as needed. Portion into 8 equal-size balls and allow them to rest for about 30 minutes, covered with plastic wrap.

5. On a lightly floured work surface, roll the dough balls into ⅛-in/3-mm disks and spread with 1 tsp of the remaining lard and some Guyanese filling.

6. Roll the dough disks like a jelly roll. Take one end of the "jelly roll" and roll it to resemble a snail shell; allow the dough to rest for 10 minutes.

7. Flatten the dough and roll into ¼-in/6-mm circles. Cook the roti on an oiled hot griddle or in an oiled cast-iron skillet over medium-high heat until well browned and crispy on both sides, 2 to 3 minutes.

CHEF'S NOTE

For this flatbread, also known as *dalpuri roti*, it is absolutely crucial to cook the yellow split peas only halfway before they are ground with the spices, to produce a crumbly mixture. Fully cooked peas would be mushy and sticky and would not provide the desired textural contrast. The idea of serving undercooked legumes may seem somewhat peculiar. They are fully done, however, once the bread is cooked on the griddle.

CORN DOG

YIELD: 8 PORTIONS

Batter

9 oz/255 g self-rising cornmeal	8 straight frankfurters
1 egg	8 bamboo skewers, 8 in/20 cm
8 fl oz/240 mL buttermilk	All-purpose flour, as needed
1 tsp/4 mL salt	Vegetable oil, for frying
2 oz/57 g grated aged Cheddar cheese	Tomato Ketchup (page 114)

1. For the batter, combine the cornmeal, egg, buttermilk, salt, and cheese and mix until smooth.
2. Skewer the frankfurters, allowing at least 4 in/10 cm of the skewer to protrude.
3. Dip the frankfurter into the flour and shake off all excess.
4. Dip the frankfurter into the corn batter and deep-fry in oil at 350°F/177°C until well browned, 2 to 3 minutes.
5. Serve immediately with the ketchup.

SERRANO HAM AND MANCHEGO CROQUETTES

YIELD: 8 TAPAS-SIZE PORTIONS

2 fl oz/60 mL extra-virgin olive oil

2 oz/57 g all-purpose flour, plus as needed

2 cups/480 mL hot milk

3 oz/85 g finely cut Serrano ham

2 oz/57 g grated manchego cheese

Salt, as needed

Ground black pepper, as needed

2 eggs, beaten

Bread crumbs, as needed

Olive oil, as needed, for frying

1. In a saucepan, combine the olive oil and flour, and cook over medium-low heat to make a blond roux, 5 to 8 minutes.

2. Add the milk and bring to a boil, stirring constantly. Simmer gently for 10 minutes.

3. Add the ham and cheese and adjust seasoning as needed.

4. Spread the ham mixture approximately ½ in/1 cm thick onto an oiled sheet pan. Cover with plastic wrap and refrigerate for at least 4 hours.

5. Cut the mixture into the desired shapes. Dredge each piece in flour, shaking off any excess. Dip each piece in the beaten eggs, and dredge in bread crumbs until evenly coated. Refrigerate until service.

6. Deep-fry each piece in 350°F/177°C olive oil until golden brown, 3 to 4 minutes. Serve immediately.

VIETNAMESE CRISPY SPRING ROLLS

YIELD: 8 PORTIONS (16 SMALL SPRING ROLLS)

Filling

1 oz/28 g bean thread noodles

1 oz/28 g dried wood ear mushrooms, soaked overnight, cut into fine chiffonade

1 carrot, peeled, finely grated

2 oz/57 g very finely minced shallots

3 green onions, thinly sliced

1 egg

1 fl oz/30 mL Vietnamese fish sauce

2 garlic cloves, minced

2 tsp/10 g sugar

½ tsp/1 g ground white pepper

8 oz/227 g lump crabmeat

8 oz/227 g ground pork

16 thin rice papers, 8 in/20 cm in diameter

Vegetable oil, for frying

Accompaniments

Vietnamese Dipping Sauce (page 178)

1 head iceberg lettuce, leaves separated

1. Soak the bean thread noodles in about 2 cups of boiling water until they are tender.

2. Combine the mushrooms, carrot, shallots, green onions, egg, fish sauce, garlic, sugar, white pepper, crabmeat, and pork with the noodles in a mixing bowl. Cook a test batch and adjust seasoning as needed.

3. Soak each sheet of rice paper individually in water, and place on a damp towel on the work surface. Place about 2 tbsp/30 mL of filling on the lower area of the wrapper. Using your fingers, mold the filling into a cylinder 2 in/5 cm long and ½ in/1 cm wide. Fold the two sides of the wrapper in and roll to enclose as tightly as possible. Complete all other rolls.

4. Deep-fry the spring rolls at 350°F/177°C until crispy, 3 to 4 minutes.

5. Serve immediately with Vietnamese Dipping Sauce. Provide the lettuce leaves at service so that the guests can wrap the spring roll in lettuce after they dip it into the sauce.

CHEF'S NOTE

Vietnamese spring rolls, not to be confused with salad rolls or summer rolls, differ from Chinese spring rolls in that they are wrapped in rice paper and the filling is made from ground raw meat and seafood, which cooks as the spring roll is deep-fried. Additionally, Vietnamese spring rolls are wrapped in lettuce by the diner before eating, a testament to the importance of layering flavors and textures in Vietnamese cooking. It is crucial to use the thin rice paper for these spring rolls. Should it not be available, please use lumpiah wrappers or something similar. The rolling technique is the same, but the roll needs to be sealed with a water-and-flour slurry.

CHINESE CRISPY SPRING ROLLS

YIELD: 8 PORTIONS (16 SPRING ROLLS)

Filling

1½ tsp/4 g minced ginger

4 green onions, finely minced

1 fl oz/30 mL vegetable oil

8 oz/227 g raw pork butt, finely shredded

1 oz/28 g wood ear mushrooms

4 oz/113 g shiitake mushrooms, stems removed, sliced

1 lb/454 g shredded Chinese cabbage

1 fl oz/30 mL light soy sauce, not low-sodium

1 tbsp/15 mL sesame oil

Salt, as needed

Ground white pepper, as needed

Cornstarch slurry, as needed

8 oz/227 g bean sprouts

16 spring roll sheets

1 cup/120 g all-purpose flour

1 cup/240 mL water

Vegetable oil, for deep-frying

Soy Dipping Sauce (page 107)

1. For the filling, sweat the ginger and finely minced green onions in the vegetable oil in a wok over high heat until aromatic, about 10 seconds.

2. Add the pork and stir-fry until it is opaque, about 30 seconds.

3. Add the mushrooms and cabbage and stir-fry until all the vegetables are tender but still have a slight bite, 1 to 2 minutes.

4. Add the soy sauce and sesame oil and adjust seasoning with salt and white pepper. Continue to cook until almost all the liquid has evaporated. Adjust viscosity with the cornstarch slurry; the mixture should be slightly cohesive.

5. Add the bean sprouts and toss to combine. Remove from the heat and allow the mixture to cool.

6. To roll the spring rolls, place a spring roll wrapper in front of you on a dry work surface. Combine the flour with the water into a paste and spread along the sides of the wrapper as a glue before rolling. Place the filling onto the lower half of the wrapper and mold it into a cylinder 3 in/8 cm long and 1 in/3 cm wide. Fold the two sides of the wrapper in and roll to enclose as tightly as possible. Complete all the other rolls.

7. Deep-fry in 350°F/177°C oil until golden brown, 3 to 4 minutes. Remove from the oil and place on a wire rack to drain.

8. Serve with the Soy Dipping Sauce on the side.

CHILI DIPPING SAUCE

YIELD: 1½ CUPS/360 ML

2 oz/57 g fresh Fresno or similar chiles

1 oz/28 g shallots

1 oz/28 g garlic

1 oz/28 g ginger

½ cup/120 mL chicken stock

1 fl oz/30 mL lime juice

1 tsp/5 mL rice vinegar

2 tsp/10 g sugar

1 tsp/3 g salt

Purée the chiles, shallots, garlic, ginger, stock, lime juice, vinegar, sugar, and salt together in a blender until they form a smooth sauce.

SOY DIPPING SAUCE

YIELD: 1½ CUPS/360 ML

1½ cups/360 mL light soy sauce, not low-sodium

½ oz/14 g finely minced ginger

2 green onions, finely chopped

1 tbsp/15 mL dark rice vinegar

1 tsp/5 mL sesame oil

Combine the soy sauce, ginger, green onions, vinegar, and sesame oil, and adjust seasoning as needed.

ORANGE-GLAZED CHICKEN WINGS

YIELD: 8 PORTIONS

4 lb/1.81 kg trimmed chicken wings	2 tbsp/15 g sliced ginger
1 fl oz/30 mL vegetable oil	2 tbsp/28 g sugar
1 fl oz/30 mL Shaoxing wine or sherry	Zest and juice of 1 orange
Salt, as needed	1 tbsp/15 mL dark soy sauce
2 garlic cloves, crushed	1 tbsp/15 mL light soy sauce, not low-sodium
1 green onion, minced	1 tbsp/15 mL Vietnamese chili paste
	½ cup/120 mL water

1. Wash the chicken wings and cut any excess skin and tendons away. Dry the chicken wings.

2. In a rondeau over medium-high heat, sauté the chicken wings in the vegetable oil until lightly brown, 2 to 3 minutes.

3. Add the wine and continue to cook for 30 seconds. Season with salt and continue to cook over moderate heat, stirring frequently, until the chicken is almost cooked through, 10 to 15 minutes.

4. Add the garlic, green onion, ginger, sugar, orange zest, orange juice, soy sauces, chili paste, and water, bring to a boil, cover with a lid, and cook over moderate heat until the chicken wings are tender.

5. Once the chicken wings are tender, increase the heat, remove the lid, and let the sauce reduce to a glaze coating the chicken wings. Serve hot.

ROTI PRATA (FLAKY BREAD)

Known as *roti canai* in Malaysia, this flatbread has evolved from Indian and Pakistani cuisines. As a street-food snack, this flatbread is especially popular in Singapore for breakfast. It is often served with curry gravy or a bowl of spiced lentils.

YIELD: 16 ROTI

2 lb/907 g all-purpose flour	3½ fl oz/105 mL vegetable oil, ghee, or shortening, plus as needed
1 oz/28 g sugar	
2 tsp/6 g salt	1 pint/480 mL water
2 eggs, beaten	1 fl oz/30 mL unsweetened condensed milk

1. In a bowl, combine the flour, sugar, and salt. Add the eggs, oil, water, and condensed milk. Combine well and knead into a soft dough. Return the dough to the mixing bowl, cover with plastic, and allow to rest for about 30 minutes.

2. Divide the dough into 16 small balls. Coat each dough ball in oil, cover, and set aside to rest for a minimum of 2 hours.

3. With oiled hands, flatten the dough balls into rounds thicker in the center than on the perimeter. Stretch the dough as far as possible. (Experts fling the dough like a fishing net to achieve ultra-thin rounds.)

4. Once the dough is stretched, fold the edges inward until you have a round shape 6 in/15 cm in diameter.

5. Fry each piece of roti individually on a hot griddle until golden brown and crispy, 1 to 2 minutes per side, adding more oil as necessary.

CHEF'S NOTE — In colder climates or very air-conditioned kitchens, it is advisable to use oil for the dough, as ghee or shortening harden at cooler temperatures and make the dough difficult to work with.

PITA BREAD

YIELD: ABOUT 20 PIECES

22 fl oz/660 mL warm water (70 to 80°F/21 to 27°C)

2½ tsp/10 g active dry yeast

1 lb/454 g bread flour

1 lb/454 g whole wheat flour, not stone ground

¾ oz/21 g salt

1. Combine the warm water and yeast to rehydrate.

2. Add the flours and pour the salt on top.

3. Knead the dough until it is quite elastic, 3 to 4 minutes. Place in a large container, cover with plastic wrap, and allow the dough to double in size, 30 to 90 minutes depending on the humidity and temperature of the room.

4. After the dough has doubled, fold the dough down and allow to double again.

5. Scale the dough into 2-oz/57-g pieces, shape into dinner rolls, and allow to rest for 20 minutes.

6. Roll the dough into thin disks and bake immediately at 450°F/232°C directly on the hearth or on a preheated sheet pan in the oven.

7. Allow the pita to fully puff up and brown just slightly before removing from the oven. Place the pita under a very lightly damp cloth to prevent drying out.

CHEF'S NOTE

Many culinary cultures have comparable flatbreads with different kinds of wheat flours. In order to achieve the pocket in pita bread, the right technique is crucial. It is important that, after portioning the dough, it is shaped into a dinner roll, in order to distribute the gluten proteins evenly. After a brief resting, the dough needs to be baked immediately after it has been rolled. Ideally, pita bread is baked directly on the very hot hearth, a pizza stone or, if neither is available, on a preheated sheet pan.

TZATZIKI, OR CAÇIK

YIELD: 8 PORTIONS

3 English cucumbers, peeled, seeded, shredded on a box grater

Salt, as needed

2 garlic cloves, mashed to a paste

1 tbsp/15 mL white wine vinegar

1 fl oz/30 mL extra-virgin olive oil

3 cups/720 mL strained Greek yogurt

2 tbsp/6 g mint, cut into chiffonade

1. Place the cucumbers in a colander, sprinkle with salt, and allow to sit for about 15 minutes to drain any excess water.

2. Combine the cucumbers with the garlic, vinegar, oil, yogurt, and mint, and adjust the seasoning to taste.

CHEF'S NOTE | This Eastern Mediterranean yogurt and cucumber dip, known as *tzatziki* in Greece and *caçik* in Turkey, is found accompanying many dishes in cuisines all over the region. It is important to use a firm, Greek-style yogurt for this dish; a Bulgarian or similar yogurt has too much liquid and will result in a very thin dip.

PEANUT SAUCE FOR SATAYS

YIELD: 1 PINT/480 ML

¼ cup/60 mL reserved marinade from Malaysian Chicken Satay (page 80)

¼ cup/60 mL vegetable oil

4 garlic cloves, peeled

2 shallots

1 guajillo chile, seeded and soaked

1 tsp/2 g very small dried shrimp, soaked in hot water for 10 minutes

1½ tsp/4 paprika

1 pint/480 mL chicken stock

3 oz/85 g finely ground roasted peanuts

2 oz/57 g sugar

Salt, as needed

1. Combine the reserved marinade and oil in a blender. Add the garlic, shallots, chile, dried shrimp, and paprika, and purée until smooth.

2. Heat a saucepan over medium heat. Add the puréed ingredients and cook until fragrant and the oil separates from the mixture, 5 to 8 minutes.

3. Add the stock and the ground peanuts, bring to a boil, and simmer gently for about 1 hour. Add water as necessary to adjust viscosity.

4. The finished sauce should be at a heavy nappé. As the sauce cooks, oil will rise to the surface. Mix in to re-emulsify. Once the sauce has cooked, adjust seasoning with sugar and salt.

RED ONION RELISH

YIELD: 8 PORTIONS

3½ oz/99 g sugar

4 fl oz/120 mL rice or palm vinegar

Salt, as needed

1 lb 8 oz/680 g English cucumbers, seeded, sliced ¼ in/6 mm thick

1 lb/454 g minced red onions

1. In a saucepan, combine the sugar, vinegar, and salt. Simmer briefly to dissolve all ingredients.

2. Allow to cool, and combine with the cucumbers and red onions. Allow to marinate for about 30 minutes before serving.

TOMATO KETCHUP

YIELD: 2 QT/1.92 L

3½ oz/99 g sugar	2 roasted red peppers (about 10 oz/284 g), peeled, minced
1 fl oz/30 mL water	1 cup/240 mL red wine vinegar
3½ oz/99 g minced onions	½ cup/120 mL balsamic vinegar
1 tbsp/9 g minced garlic	1 tbsp/10 g salt, plus as needed
6 lb/2.72 kg canned tomatoes, seeded	1 tsp/2 g cayenne

1. In a saucepan, combine the sugar and the water and cook slowly, without stirring, until the sugar slightly caramelizes.
2. Add the onions, garlic, tomatoes, and roasted red peppers and allow to simmer slowly for about 15 minutes.
3. Add both vinegars and continue to simmer until the mixture has thickened. Adjust seasoning with salt and cayenne.
4. In a blender, purée the mixture until very smooth, and strain as needed.

WALNUT-HERB SAUCE

YIELD: 8 PORTIONS

2 lemons, cut into segments, pith and membrane removed	3 oz/85 g walnuts, toasted
1 pinch cayenne	1 oz/28 g mint
2 fl oz/60 mL olive oil	1½ tsp/4 g minced garlic
2 fl oz/60 mL water	Salt, as needed
1 oz/28 g chopped flat-leaf parsley	Ground black pepper, as needed

Combine the lemon segments, cayenne, oil, water, parsley, walnuts, mint, and garlic in a food processor and process to a coarse paste. Adjust seasoning as needed.

CHAPATI BREAD

YIELD: 8 PORTIONS

1 lb/454 g atta flour (Indian whole wheat flour)

⅓ oz/10 g salt

1 fl oz/30 mL ghee or vegetable oil (optional)

9 fl oz/270 mL lukewarm water

Ghee or oil, as needed, for cooking

1. Combine the flour, salt, ghee, and water in a mixing bowl and knead into a smooth and pliable dough. Cover the dough with plastic wrap and allow to rest for 1 hour.

2. Shape the dough into sixteen 1½-oz/43-g dough balls. Allow to rest for another 15 minutes, and roll into a thin circle on a very lightly floured surface.

3. Cook the chapatis on a lightly greased griddle or skillet over medium-high heat until lightly browned on both sides, about 1 minute on each side. Alternatively, the bread can also be cooked on a grill, if a lower-fat version is preferred.

4. Serve immediately, or allow to cool on a wire rack before serving.

CHEF'S NOTE

Atta flour is a popular whole wheat flour in India that provides a unique texture and flavor to a wide variety of flatbreads in the region's cuisine. In the milling process of this flour, the bran and endosperm of durum wheat are ground separately and later recombined, resulting in a very fine consistency. If atta flour is not available, equal parts of whole wheat flour and bread flour can be used as a substitute. Avoid stone-ground whole wheat flour, as it is too coarsely textured. Deep-frying the dough at about 375°F/191°C until puffy will result in a very popular bread known as *poori*. In order to achieve a perfectly puffed bread, the dough needs to be fried immediately after it has been rolled and hot oil needs to be constantly poured over the bread as it fries. Once done, allow the bread to drain on a wire rack.

CILANTRO-CASHEW CHUTNEY

YIELD: 3 CUPS/720 ML

1 bunch cilantro, thoroughly dried	½ cup/120 mL plain Bulgarian yogurt
1 jalapeño, stem and seeds removed	4 oz/113 g unsalted cashews
1 fl oz/30 mL lemon juice	Salt, as needed
½ tsp/1 g ground cumin	Ground black pepper, as needed

1. Combine the cilantro, jalapeño, lemon juice, cumin, and yogurt in a blender and purée to a fine paste.

2. Add the cashews and puree until smooth.

3. Add more yogurt or nuts to adjust consistency; the chutney should have the consistency of a strained yogurt or thick sour cream. Adjust seasonings and serve.

CHEF'S NOTE

Chutneys are often mistakenly defined as resembling a jam or preserve. Served as table-side condiments in South Asia, chutneys are much more diverse than that. Commonly, they are based on one or more vegetables and a spice mix. Prepared raw, cooked, or fermented, chutneys vary tremendously. They can be dry or wet, smooth or coarse, spicy or mild. The main purpose of all chutneys is to complement the very aromatic main dish and to provide a well-rounded dining experience.

RUSSIAN DRESSING

YIELD: 1 PINT/480 ML

1½ cups/360 mL mayonnaise

½ cup/120 mL ketchup

1 oz/28 g finely minced sweet onions

1 tsp/5 mL Worcestershire sauce

Tabasco sauce, as needed

Salt, as needed

Ground black pepper, as needed

Combine the mayonnaise, ketchup, onions, Worcestershire, and Tabasco, and adjust seasoning with salt and pepper as needed.

SAUERKRAUT FOR REUBEN SANDWICH

YIELD: 1 LB 8 OZ/680 G

12 oz/340 g minced onions

1 oz/28 g lard, or duck or goose fat

1 lb 8 oz/680 g sauerkraut

1 cup/240 mL chicken stock

1 bay leaf

Salt, as needed

Sugar, as needed

1. Sweat the onions in the fat until translucent, about 3 minutes.

2. Add the sauerkraut and enough chicken stock to submerge by half. Add the bay leaf and adjust seasoning with salt and sugar. Cover tightly with a lid and simmer gently until tender, about 30 minutes, adding more liquid as necessary.

3. Once tender, remove the lid and continue to cook until all excess moisture is evaporated. Adjust seasoning as needed and set aside.

RAW TOMATILLO AND AVOCADO SALSA

YIELD: 1 CUP/240 ML

2 jalapeños, stems removed, halved lengthwise	1 oz/28 g coarsely chopped cilantro leaves and stems
10 tomatillos, husked, rinsed, and quartered	1 small avocado, pitted, peeled, and cut into large dice
1 clove garlic, peeled	Salt, as needed
1 small white onion (2 oz/57 g), peeled	

1. In a blender, purée the jalapeños, tomatillos, garlic, and onion until smooth.
2. Add the cilantro and avocado and briefly blend until slightly coarse. Adjust seasoning with salt.

GREEN PAPAYA SLAW

YIELD: 8 PORTIONS

2 lb/907 g green papaya, peeled, halved, and seeded	1 clove garlic, minced
2 oz/57 g carrots, peeled	1 tbsp/15 mL red wine vinegar
1 fl oz/30 mL lime juice	1 fl oz/30 mL molasses
1 oz/28 g coarsely chopped cilantro	Salt, as needed
1 tsp/3 g finely minced ginger	Ground black pepper, as needed

1. Grate the papaya and carrots on a coarse box grater and combine.
2. Add the lime juice, cilantro, ginger, garlic, vinegar, and molasses, mix well, and adjust seasoning with salt and pepper.

> **CHEF'S NOTE** It is crucial to use green, unripe papaya for this preparation, as the ripe ones are too sweet and soft, which makes the finished salsa lack the crunchy texture and the desired tart flavor.

MEXICAN CREAM

YIELD: 1 PINT/480 ML

1 pint/480 mL heavy cream

1 tbsp/15 mL buttermilk

1 tbsp/15 mL sour cream

1. Combine the cream, buttermilk, and sour cream and heat gently to 80°F/27°C.
2. Allow to ferment at room temperature for 1 day.
3. Cool and refrigerate until ready to use.

CHEF'S NOTE | If there are food-safety concerns because of the fermentation, substitute *crema agria*, which is available in most Mexican specialty stores.

FISH & SEAFOOD

CHAPTER 3

Seafood includes all edible forms of aquatic life, like finfish, mollusks, crustaceans, and sea vegetation. Many sources define a fish as a gill-breathing animal, controlling motion with its fins. In many species, the skin is covered with protective scales. Mollusks are invertebrate marine creatures with a soft, boneless body, including squid, cuttlefish, and octopus. Mussels, oysters, sea snails, and clams, members of the same group, are encased in a hard, calcified shell. Crustaceans, such as crabs, lobsters, crayfish, and shrimp, are characterized by a segmented body and an exoskeleton. Edible sea vegetation includes sea beans, kelp, seaweed, lotus roots, and water lilies. A staple in many coastal cuisines, sea vegetation has received a lot of attention in recent years due to its sustainable cultivation methods, impressive growth rates, and beneficial nutritional profiles.

High levels of complete proteins, healthy fats, vitamins, and minerals make seafood an important part of the human diet. In many studies, regular consumption of seafood has been linked to reduced risk of heart disease as well as to healthy brain development in children. Most nutritionists agree that the risks of seafood, such as accumulation of pollutants like mercury, polychlorinated biphenyl, and pesticide residues, are outweighed by the benefits. In order to limit these risks, seafood should only be purchased from reputable suppliers, sourcing from certified waters and fish farms.

PURCHASE AND STORAGE

Due to its highly perishable nature, fresh fish and seafood has historically been available exclusively in areas close to the source, often with seasonal limitations. Farm raising, technological advances in refrigeration and storage, and an improved infrastructure have created today's relative easy access to fresh seafood. Updated food-safety regulations and their successful implementation have further impacted the mobile food scene. In the past, ceviche, sashimi, and other raw preparations were limited to a small number of restaurants, but they can now be enjoyed in open-air food courts or straight from a food truck.

To satisfy the different needs of food-service operators, fresh fish and seafood are available in a wide range of market forms. Whole fish can be purchased completely intact, drawn, dressed, or headed and gutted. Precut fish is available as steaks or fillets. Bivalves like mussels, clams, or oysters come live, shucked, or cooked on the half-shell. Shrimp can be obtained head-on, peeled, deveined, or butterflied. In addition to all fresh items, a great variety of frozen, precooked, and otherwise preprepared convenience products are widely available.

Significant price increases have made it challenging for many to afford seafood. In addition to the perfect preparation, controlling and maintaining the highest quality of incoming fresh fish is vital in order to justify the price. Upon receiving, fresh fish needs to be inspected for the following signs of freshness:

- Temperature of the fresh fish needs to be 40°F/4°C or less
    - Frozen fish needs to be completely frozen with no signs of frost, as this suggests improper packaging or thawing and refreezing

122 CHAPTER 3 Fish & Seafood

- The fish should have a good overall appearance
  - No cuts or bruising
  - Fins should be pliable and not dried out
  - Scales should be tightly adhering to the body, covered with clear slime
- Flesh responds to gentle pressure
- Clear, bright, bulging eyes
- Maroon, sweet-smelling gills
- Overall sea-like, sweet, inoffensive smell
- No signs of "belly burn," deteriorated flesh along the rib cage, caused by enzymes and bacteria when the guts have been left in the fish too long
- Fish fillets need to be inspected by smell, gentle pressure, and overall appearance

Ideally, fresh seafood is received daily and sold within a short period. If daily deliveries are not an option, proper storage will help to significantly extend shelf life. Whole fish or live bivalves need to be packed in shaved or flaked ice on perforated pans, and changing the ice daily is crucial to avoid accumulation of unwanted fluids. Mussels, clams, and oysters should be stored in their original mesh bags or open-packed in ice; they will suffocate if they are kept in tightly closed plastic bags. Fish fillets, shucked bivalves, or peeled crustaceans should be stored in stainless-steel pans placed on ice. Direct contact with melting ice will compromise flavor and texture.

SUCCESSFUL FISH AND SEAFOOD COOKERY

The vast diversity and unique characteristics of species can make seafood cookery quite confusing. Classifications help us to understand and appreciate similarities and differences. A common way to categorize fish is by skeletal structure. Roundfish, including salmon, cod, and bass, have a center spinal cord with one fillet on each side. Flounder, sole, and halibut, categorized as flatfish, have both eyes on the same side of the head and a center backbone surrounded by two upper and two lower fillets. Last, non-bony fish like monkfish, skate, swordfish, and shark have soft cartilage instead of hard bones.

Fish can also be sorted by activity level. Included in the group of high-activity fish are salmon, mackerel, swordfish, and trout. Fast and powerful swimmers, they have fatty and dark flesh that is known for its distinct flavor. The flesh of medium-activity fish, like bass, grouper, and snapper, has a moderately high oil content with a somewhat milder flavor. The low-oil, bright white flesh of low-activity fish, such as cod, sole, and flounder, is very delicate with a mild and clean taste profile. These distinct characteristics, a result of the fish's lifestyle, can provide guidance for choosing an appropriate cooking method. Medium-activity-level fish are quite versatile and can be cooked in many different ways. The strong flavor of high-activity fishes entails certain cooking methods and side dishes.

The bones of low-activity fishes, with their low fat content and clean flavor, are perfect for fish stocks. Their delicate flesh, however, can easily be overpowered by strong accompaniments and might be too tender for some cooking methods. Some freshwater fishes, especially bottom-dwelling species like catfish, eel, and carp, are infamous for their earthy flavor. In response, it is common practice to purge the live fish in clean water, or complement them with flavorful cooking methods, aromatics, and accompaniments.

Fish and seafood, with its inherent tenderness, is preferably cooked quickly by grilling, sautéing, frying, or gentle poaching and steaming. In most cases, excessive cooking or heating causes fish to become dry and fall apart, while crustaceans and mollusks actually toughen and become rubbery. Exceptions include octopus and conch; to tenderize, they are often simmered for extended periods, occasionally even in a pressure cooker.

Preserved fish and seafood, found in almost every cuisine, have their origins in seasonal abundances during spawning or migration. Preserved by pickling, fermenting, curing, or smoking, the recurring excess is used to provide a stable year-round supply. See Tables 3.1, 3.2, and 3.3 for the appropriate cooking methods of various seafood.

TABLE 3.1 Finfish: Distinct Characteristics and Appropriate Cooking Methods

SPECIES	CHARACTERISTICS	COOKING METHOD
Flounder	Low-activity flatfish White, very tender flesh Delicate, mild flavor	Sauté Shallow poach Deep-fry Broil
Dover sole	Low-activity flatfish Relatively firm flesh compared to other flatfish Superior flavor	Sauté Shallow poach Deep-fry Broil, grill
Halibut	Large low-activity flatfish Sold whole, as fillets, or head off Snow white, delicate flesh Mild taste	Grill, broil Smoke Poach, shallow poach Sauté Serve raw
Turbot	Large low-activity flatfish with bony protrusions on the dark skin White, firm flesh Superior flavor	Poach, shallow poach, steam Grill, broil Sauté, fry Bake Serve raw

TABLE 3.1 *(continued)*

SPECIES	CHARACTERISTICS	COOKING METHOD
Cod	Low-activity roundfish Delicate, flaky white flesh Mild flavor	Poach, shallow poach Broil Sauté skin-on Fry Broil Salt cure and steam for cod cakes
Haddock	Low-activity roundfish Very similar to cod Very tender, flaky white flesh Mild flavor	Poach, shallow poach Broil Sauté skin-on Fry Broil Salt cure and steam for fish cakes
Pollock	Low-activity roundfish Very similar to cod and haddock Very tender, flaky white flesh Mild flavor	Poach, shallow poach Broil Sauté skin-on Fry Broil Salt cure and steam for fish cakes
Hybrid bass	Farm-raised, medium-activity fish Off-white flesh Slight earthy flavor; complement with strong flavors	Shallow poach Grill, broil Sauté skin-on Fry Sauté and pickle
Red snapper	Medium-activity roundfish White, firm flesh Sweet flavor Should be bought at 5 lb or less	Shallow poach Grill, broil Sauté skin-on Fry Sashimi Ceviche
Grouper	Medium-activity roundfish Sweet, off-white flesh Stays moist when cooked	Shallow poach Grill, broil Sauté, fry Sashimi Ceviche Sauté and pickle

(continued)

Successful Fish and Seafood Cookery **125**

TABLE 3.1 (*continued*)

SPECIES	CHARACTERISTICS	COOKING METHOD
Porgy	Medium-activity roundfish Also known as sea bream or dorade Portion-size fish, preferably cooked whole Relatively bony Mild flavor, medium-firm texture	Grill whole Bake Broil Sauté
Tilefish	Medium-activity roundfish Pink flesh, turns white when cooked Tender flesh	Grill Bake Sauté Fry Poach Sashimi
Salmon, Atlantic	High-activity roundfish Exclusively farm raised White tongue Shiny and moist orange flesh High fat	Smoke, hot and cold Poach, shallow and deep Grill Broil Sauté skin-on Sashimi Fry
Salmon, Pacific	High-activity roundfish Larger than Atlantic salmon Black tongue Medium to dark red flesh Lower oil content than Atlantic salmon	Smoke, hot and cold Poach, shallow and deep Bake Grill Broil Sauté skin-on Fry
Trout, rainbow	High-activity roundfish Freshwater species Portion-size fish Delicate, buttery, ivory-colored flesh	Hot smoke Grill Broil Sauté Fry Poach
Arctic char	High-activity roundfish Relative of trout and salmon Dark red flesh High oil content	Grill Broil Poach Sauté skin-on Sashimi

TABLE 3.1 (*continued*)

SPECIES	CHARACTERISTICS	COOKING METHOD
Tuna, bluefin	High-activity roundfish Fat content varies depending on variety Dark flesh	Confit in olive oil Grill Pan sear Sashimi
Mackerel	High-activity roundfish Dark, oily flesh Strong flavor	Grill Salt cure Sauté Smoke
Swordfish	Large non-bony fish Pinkish white flesh with high oil content	Broil Grill Sauté
Monkfish	Non-bony flatfish Commonly sold head off, as loins Firm, mild white flesh	Bake Fry Grill Sauté
Skate	Non-bony flatfish Related to sharks Firm flesh, becomes softer as it cooks	Fry Sauté Shallow poach
Catfish	Bottom-dwelling freshwater fish Mild flavor after purging White flesh	Fry Grill Sauté Smoke
Sardine	Small herring species Delicate, fatty flesh Ideally 7 in/18 cm or less	Broil Fry Grill Sauté Sauté and pickle Smoke
Tilapia	Farmed around the world Economical fish Off-white to pink flesh, turns white when cooked Very mild flavor	Broil Grill Poach Sashimi Sauté Fry

(*continued*)

TABLE 3.1 (*continued*)

SPECIES	CHARACTERISTICS	COOKING METHOD
Eel	Shape resembles a snake Best quality when received alive and allowed to purge in freshwater Very fatty, firm flesh Able to survive outside water for several days	Broil Grill Sauté Smoke Stew

TABLE 3.2 Miscellaneous Seafood: Distinct Characteristics and Appropriate Cooking Methods

SPECIES	CHARACTERISTICS	COOKING METHOD
Clams	Hard, calcified shell Size varies depending on variety Bottom-dwelling, needs to be purged of sand Available live, canned, shucked, individually quick frozen (IQF) half-shells, frozen	Chowder Fry for larger clams Grill in shell Serve raw on half-shell Steam
Mussels	Dark blue shell or New Zealand green shell mussels Slightly sweet flavor	Steam Stews
Oysters	Many varieties Cold-water oysters have a deeper flavor Available live, shucked, or frozen	Bake on half-shell Serve raw on half-shell
Squid	Invertebrate Very high yield Available fresh, cleaned, or IQF rings Slightly sweet, firm texture when cooked properly Overcooking makes squid rubbery Bright white flesh	Braise Fry Stews Squid ink often used as a coloring agent for rice and pasta
Octopus	Invertebrate White flesh Firm flesh when cooked properly Skin comes off easily after cooking	Bake Grill Sashimi Soups Stews

TABLE 3.3 Aquatic Vegetation: Distinct Characteristics and Appropriate Cooking Methods

NAME	CHARACTERISTICS	COOKING METHOD
Hijiki seaweed	Available dried Expands upon soaking, about five times Brown strands Nutty flavor	Part of stews Salads Simmer
Wakame	Available dried Rich green color Slippery texture, becomes slimy upon long cooking Tough ribs and stems should be removed	Miso soup Salads Stews
Giant kelp/kombu	Available dried or fresh Grows in huge "underwater forests" Dark green to brown color Chewy texture Very rich in naturally occurring glutamates	Base for Japanese dashi Cut into ribbons, cooked like noodles Salads
Passe-pierre/sea beans	Crisp, naturally salty sprigs Grows on salt marches and beaches Bright green	Due to their naturally occurring salt content, they do not need to be seasoned Quick sauté Raw in salads
Lotus root	Freshwater plant Long aquatic root Dark skin, needs to be peeled Unique lacey pattern Stays crunchy upon cooking	Batter fry Salads Sliced thin and served raw Stir-fry Stuffed fried

Seafood has always been and will continue to be an important part of the human diet. In regions close to water, restaurateurs and home cooks take advantage of the abundance of fresh fish and will often buy the catch of the day straight off the boat. Street-food stands nearby offer the fish cooked on a grill or makeshift stove for immediate consumption. Sustainable farming and harvesting techniques, as well as responsible utilization, will help to ensure a steady supply of wholesome food for future generations.

BOUILLABAISSE

YIELD: 8 PORTIONS

1 lb/454 g sea bass fillet, or monkfish, branzino, or similar fish, cut into large dice

8 oz/227 g peeled deveined shrimp, cut into large dice

Salt, as needed

Ground black pepper, as needed

2 fl oz/60 mL extra-virgin olive oil

1 fl oz/30 mL Pernod

1 tsp/0.5 g saffron threads

8 oz/227 g medium-dice onions

2 garlic cloves, minced

8 oz/227 g paysanne-cut leek

1 bulb fennel, cut into medium dice

2 qt/1.92 L Fish Stock (page 174)

8 oz/227 g peeled medium-dice potatoes

8 oz/227 g mussels

Cayenne, as needed

Garlic and Saffron Mayonnaise (page 175)

Crusty bread, as needed

1. Season the fish and shrimp with salt and pepper and combine with 1 oz/30 mL olive oil, Pernod, and saffron in bowl. Allow to marinate under refrigeration for 1 hour.

2. In a rondeau or similar pan, sweat the onions in 1 oz/30 mL olive oil until translucent, about 5 minutes. Add the garlic, leeks, and fennel and continue to sweat for 1 minute.

3. Add the stock and potatoes and bring to a boil over high heat. Lower the heat to establish a gentle simmer, and continue simmering until all vegetables are tender and almost cooked through, 5 to 10 minutes.

4. Add the mussels and continue to simmer until they begin to open, about 2 minutes.

5. Add the marinated fish and cook at a gentle simmer until it is cooked through and flakes when light pressure is applied, 1 to 2 minutes. Adjust the seasoning with salt, pepper, and cayenne.

6. To serve, arrange the cooked seafood and vegetables in a soup bowl and ladle the broth over it. Serve Garlic and Saffron Mayonnaise and crusty bread on the side.

CHEF'S NOTE

There are many variations of this traditional fish stew/soup from the Provence region of France. Most commonly it contains at least three different kinds of fish and shellfish, often mussels, sea urchin, octopus, or squid. Classic aromatics include, among others, Pernod, saffron, orange, garlic, and a generous amount of olive oil. In a restaurant-type setting, all fish and vegetables are cooked together but served separately from the resulting flavorful broth. From this perspective, bouillabaisse bears resemblance to "boiled dinners" as they are found in many cultures.

CIOPPINO

Cioppino, originating in San Francisco, bears strong resemblance to an Italian seafood stew known as cacciucco. Both are typically made from the catch of the day cooked gently in a white wine–flavored tomato sauce and served with olive oil and crusty bread on the side.

YIELD: 8 PORTIONS

8 oz/227 g small-dice onions

2 garlic cloves, peeled

5 green onions, thinly sliced

1 green pepper, cut into small dice (about 5 oz/142 g)

1 bulb fennel, cored, tops removed, cut into small dice (about 9 oz/255 g)

1 fl oz/30 mL extra-virgin olive oil

4 fl oz/120 mL white wine

2 lb/907 g canned tomatoes, chopped

1 qt/960 mL chicken stock

1 pint/480 mL tomato purée

2 tsp/2 g minced oregano

1 tsp/1 g minced thyme

1 bay leaf

Salt, as needed

Ground black pepper, as needed

1 lb/454 g Manila clams, scrubbed

1 lb/454 g mussels, beards removed, scrubbed

8 oz/227 g sea bass or similar fish fillet, skin removed, cut into large dice

12 oz/340 g shrimp, 21/25 count, peeled and deveined (16)

8 oz/227 g sea scallops, cartilage removed

Garnish

1 cup/35 g whole basil leaves

Extra-virgin olive oil, as needed

Crusty bread, sliced, as needed

1. In a rondeau or similar pan, sweat the onions, garlic, green onions, green pepper, and fennel in the oil over low to medium heat until the vegetables begin to soften, about 5 minutes.

2. Add the white wine and cook over medium heat until the wine has fully evaporated and developed a slightly caramelized flavor, 5 to 7 minutes.

3. Add the tomatoes, stock, tomato purée, oregano, thyme, and bay leaf, cover with a lid, and simmer gently for about 30 minutes, adding more stock as needed to achieve a light to medium nappé consistency.

4. Remove the bay leaf and adjust seasoning with salt and pepper.

5. At service, bring the tomato mixture to a boil over high heat. Add the clams and mussels, cover with a lid, and simmer gently until the mussels and clams begin to open, 3 to 5 minutes.

6. Add the fish, shrimp, and scallops and continue simmering, covered with a lid, until the clams and mussels are completely open, the shrimp and scallops are firm, and the fish flakes under gentle pressure, 3 to 5 minutes. Discard any clams or mussels that do not open.

7. Add the basil leaves, and adjust seasoning as needed. Serve in a bowl with a drizzle of olive oil on top and crusty bread on the side.

COCONUT SEAFOOD CHOWDER

This soup combines classical Western cooking methods with common Thai ingredients and flavors, a culinary approach often found along the Pacific coast in areas with a large Southeast Asian population.

YIELD: 8 PORTIONS

1 stalk lemongrass (about ¾ oz/21 g)	1 cup/240 mL white wine
2 garlic cloves, thinly sliced	Salt, as needed
2 tbsp/30 mL very finely minced galangal	Ground white pepper, as needed
4 kaffir lime leaves	1 qt/960 mL coconut milk
2 fl oz/60 mL vegetable oil	½ cup/120 mL heavy cream
8 oz/227 g peeled small-dice red potatoes	8 oz/227 g red snapper or similar fish fillet, skinned and diced
8 oz/227 g quartered white mushrooms	
1 oz/28 g Thai red curry paste	8 oz/227 g lump crabmeat
1 pint/480 mL clam juice	Juice of 1 lime
1 pint/480 mL chicken stock	1 cup/35 g whole basil leaves

1. In a rondeau or similar pan, sweat the lemongrass, garlic, galangal, and lime leaves in the vegetable oil over low to medium heat until aromatic, about 1 minute.

2. Add the potatoes and continue to cook over low heat for 2 minutes more. Take care that the potatoes do not brown.

3. Add the mushrooms and continue to cook gently until they stop releasing moisture, about 5 minutes.

4. Add the red curry paste and continue cooking until aromatic, about 1 minute.

5. Add the clam juice, chicken stock, and wine. Adjust seasoning as needed with salt and white pepper, and gently simmer gently until the potatoes are tender, about 10 minutes.

6. Add the coconut milk and heavy cream. If necessary, adjust seasoning once more.

7. At service, add the fish and crabmeat, and simmer until the fish flakes under gentle pressure, about 1 minute. Adjust seasoning with lime juice, salt, and white pepper, and add the basil leaves.

8. To serve, arrange the cooked seafood and vegetables in a soup bowl and ladle the soup on top.

THAI HOT AND SOUR SOUP

YIELD: 8 PORTIONS

1 lb 8 oz/680 g shrimp, 21/25 count, peel and heads on	6 kaffir lime leaves, bruised
2 lemongrass stalks	4 plum tomatoes, cut lengthwise into eighths
1 oz/28 g Thai red curry paste	8 oz/227 g straw mushrooms, cut in half
1 fl oz/30 mL vegetable oil	3 fl oz/90 mL Thai fish sauce, or as needed
1 tbsp/8 g sliced galangal	1 tbsp/12 g palm sugar
2 qt/1.92 L chicken or seafood stock	1 cup/240 mL lime juice
6 Thai bird chiles, coarsely minced	1 cup/48 g coarsely cut cilantro

1. Peel and devein the shrimp. Rinse and reserve the shells and heads. Slice the shrimp in half and reserve.

2. Trim the lemongrass of any dried and/or discolored parts. Slice each stalk in half lengthwise and cut into 1-in/3-cm pieces. Reserve.

3. In a saucepan over low to medium heat, sweat the curry paste in the vegetable oil until aromatic, about 1 minute.

4. Add the shrimp shells and heads, lemongrass, and galangal to the pan, sweat briefly, and then add the stock. Simmer gently for about 15 minutes.

5. Strain into a clean pot. Add the chiles, lime leaves, tomatoes, mushrooms, fish sauce, and sugar to the seafood broth and simmer gently for 1 minute.

6. Add the shrimp, bring the broth to a simmer, and add the lime juice and cilantro.

7. Serve immediately in bowls.

CHEF'S NOTE In order to enjoy this iconic Thai soup, it needs to be aggressively sour and spicy. Just like many other dishes from that region, it is supposed to tickle the taste buds in all directions: distinctly salty, sour, and very spicy, with a very subtle note of sweetness.

STEAMED MUSSELS WITH SPANISH CHORIZO

YIELD: 8 PORTIONS

8 oz/227 g small-dice Spanish chorizo	1 lb 8 oz/680 g diced tomatoes
1 cup/240 mL extra-virgin olive oil	8 oz/227 g diced piquillo peppers
1 cup/128 g minced onions	Salt, as needed
2 tbsp/18 g minced garlic	Ground black pepper, as needed
4 lb/1.81 kg mussels, scrubbed, debearded	1 cup/48 g chopped parsley
	½ cup/24 g coarsely cut cilantro
2 cups/480 mL dry white wine	Crusty bread, such as baguette or ciabatta, as needed

1. In a rondeau or similar pot, render the chorizo in the olive oil over medium heat until slightly caramelized, about 2 minutes.

2. Add the onions and sweat gently over medium heat until tender, about 2 minutes. Add the garlic and continue to sweat until fragrant, about 30 seconds.

3. Add the mussels, white wine, tomatoes, and peppers, cover with a lid, and cook over high heat until the mussels have opened, about 2 minutes. Discard any mussels that have not opened.

4. Adjust seasoning with salt and pepper, as needed. Add the parsley and cilantro to the mussels, and toss well to combine.

5. Serve in a soup bowl with crusty bread.

FRIED FISH CAKES WITH CUCUMBER SALAD

YIELD: 8 PORTIONS

Spice Paste

1½ tbsp/10 g coarsely chopped Thai bird chiles

1½ oz/43 g coarsely cut shallots

4 garlic cloves, peeled

¼ cup/12 g coarsely cut cilantro, preferably with roots

2 tbsp/16 g coarsely cut galangal

6 kaffir lime leaves

2 lb 8 oz/1.13 kg saltwater white-fleshed fish fillet, skinned

1 lb/454 g Chinese long beans or green beans, sliced into paper-thin rounds

2 fl oz/60 mL fish sauce

2 fl oz/60 mL vegetable oil, or as needed

Spicy Thai Cucumber Salad (page 175)

1. With a mortar and pestle, finely grind the chiles, shallots, garlic, cilantro, galangal, and lime leaves.

2. Coarsely dice the fish and add to a food processor, processing until it forms a slightly coarse paste. Scrape the inside of the food processor as needed to ensure an even texture.

3. In a mixing bowl, thoroughly combine the spice paste, sliced beans, and fish sauce with the chopped fish. Mix well, until sticky to the touch. In gently simmering water, cook a small sample of the ground fish, taste it, and adjust seasoning as needed with fish sauce.

4. With oiled hands, shape the ground fish into 2- to 2½-oz/57- to 71-g cakes. Sauté in a generous amount of oil over medium heat until the cakes reach an internal temperature of 155°F/68°C and are golden brown on both sides, about 2 minutes on each side.

5. Remove from the skillet, drain on a wire rack for about 2 minutes, and serve with some of the cucumber salad.

GRILLED FISH WITH TAPENADE

YIELD: 8 PORTIONS

8 red mullet, porgy, sea bream, branzino, or similar portion-size fish (14 to 16 oz/397 to 454 g each)

Salt, as needed

Ground black pepper, as needed

1 cup/240 mL extra-virgin olive oil

Lemon juice, as needed

Tapenade (page 176)

1 loaf crusty French bread, such as a baguette

1. With a sturdy pair of scissors, cut away all fins from the fish and remove all scales. Score the flesh with a knife, parallel to the rib bones, down to the bone, 2 or 3 times on each side of the fish.

2. Season the fish with salt and pepper and rub with the olive oil.

3. On a very hot, freshly cleaned and oiled grill, cook the fish until cooked through, about 3 minutes on each side, until the flesh begins to flake upon gentle pressure. Finish in an oven if needed.

    Larger fish might char too much on the grill before they cook through. They can be seared on a grill to achieve the flavor and the attractive grill marks and can then be finished in an oven at 400°F/204°C until the fish is cooked to an internal temperature of 145°F/63°C. The amount of time will vary depending on the size of the fish.

    For smaller or very delicate fish, a grilling basket is a useful tool. It allows to cook and turn multiple fish at the same time without the risk of breaking the fish.

4. After it is done, sprinkle the fish with lemon juice and serve with the Tapenade and crusty bread on the side.

CHILI CRAB

YIELD: 8 PORTIONS

8 soft-shell crabs (3 to 4 oz/85 to 113 g)	¼ cup/60 mL mild chili sauce
2 tbsp/16 g minced ginger	1 tbsp/8 g sugar
2 tbsp/18 g minced garlic	½ tsp/1 g ground white pepper
1 tsp/2 g Thai bird chiles, minced	Salt, as needed
2 fl oz/60 mL vegetable oil	½ cup/120 mL water
1 tbsp/6 g mashed fermented black beans	1 tbsp/8 g cornstarch
	2 eggs, beaten
1 tbsp/15 mL Chinese cooking wine or sherry	2 tbsp/24 g coarsely cut cilantro
½ cup/120 mL tomato sauce	French bread, or sliced or steamed Chinese buns, deep fried

1. Cut about ½ in/1 cm behind the eyes and mouth of the crab and squeeze out the content of the sac behind the eyes. Remove the gills from under the pointed end of the crab. Remove the apron from under the crab and rinse and pat the crab dry.

2. In a wok over moderate heat, stir-fry the ginger, garlic, and chiles in the vegetable oil until fragrant, about 30 seconds. Add the black beans, stir-fry for a few seconds, then add the crab and continue to stir-fry for 1 minute, until the crab turns pink. Remove the crab from the wok and reserve.

3. Add the wine and cook for about 5 seconds. Add the tomato sauce and chili sauce and bring to a quick boil. Add the sugar and white pepper, and adjust seasoning with salt as needed. Return the crabs to the sauce and simmer gently for 1 minute, until the crab is cooked through.

4. Combine the water and cornstarch to make a slurry. Thicken the sauce with the slurry as needed for a light to medium nappé.

5. Add the eggs and continue to stir until the eggs are fully cooked. Add the cilantro, and serve 1 crab per plate, with a generous amount of sauce and deep-fried Chinese buns or crusty French bread.

CHEF'S NOTE Inspired by the national dish of Singapore, this recipe uses soft-shell crab, which makes it more convenient to eat.

STUFFED BAKED SQUID

YIELD: 8 PORTIONS

8 whole medium-size squid (5 to 6 oz/142 to 170 g each)

Filling

2 oz/57 g pancetta, minced

2 fl oz/60 mL extra-virgin olive oil

5 oz/142 g minced onions

8 garlic cloves, minced

½ cup/120 mL white wine

12 oz/340 g canned tomatoes, crushed

3 oz/85 g minced green olives

1 tbsp/9 g minced fresh thyme

1 bunch green onions, minced

1 cup/100 g fresh white bread crumbs

Salt, as needed

Ground black pepper, as needed

½ cup/120 mL white wine

1 fl oz/30 mL extra-virgin olive oil

Juice of 1 lemon

Dried bread crumbs, as needed

1. Separate the tentacles from the heads of the squid and finely dice them; set aside. Remove the clear cartilage from the head as well as the beak at the base of the tentacles of the squid. Discard the clear cartilage and the beak.

2. For the filling, in a skillet over medium heat, render the pancetta in the olive oil until crispy, about 5 minutes. Add the onions and sweat gently until they begin to soften, about 2 minutes. Add the garlic and continue to sweat gently until fragrant, about 30 seconds.

3. Add the white wine and reduce over medium heat until the wine is completely evaporated and begins to have a slightly caramelized aroma, about 5 minutes.

4. Add the tomatoes, olives, and thyme and continue to cook over moderate heat until the tomatoes are very soft and begin to turn into a soft pulp, about 5 minutes. Add the diced squid tentacles and continue to cook for about 30 seconds. Add the green onions and bread crumbs and adjust seasoning with salt and pepper as needed.

5. Stuff the squid tubes (heads) about three-quarters full and secure the opening with a toothpick. Place the stuffed squid tubes into an oiled ovenproof dish large enough to hold the squid in a single layer, season with salt, and add white wine until about ½ inch/6 mm up the squid. Drizzle the squid with the olive oil and lemon juice, and sprinkle with bread crumbs. Bake at 400°F/204°C for about 15 minutes. Serve hot.

FISH AND CHIPS

YIELD: 8 PORTIONS

3 lb/1.36 kg haddock fillets	Beer Batter (page 176)
Salt, as needed	Vegetable oil or lard, as needed, for deep-frying
Ground black pepper, as needed	
1 tbsp/15 mL lemon juice	French Fries (page 177)
1 tsp/5 mL Worcestershire sauce	Malt vinegar, as needed
All-purpose flour, as needed	

1. Cut the haddock fillets into 2- to 3-oz/57- to 85-g pieces and season with salt, pepper, the lemon juice, and the Worcestershire.

2. Dredge the fillets in flour and shake off any excess.

3. Dip in the prepared Beer Batter and fry immediately.

4. In a deep-fryer, fry in 350°F/177°C oil or lard until lightly browned, 3 to 5 minutes. Drain on a wire rack. Serve on a bed of well-salted French Fries drizzled with malt vinegar as per guest's request.

CHEF'S NOTE — Probably one of the most iconic street foods of the British Isles, fish and chips comes in many different varieties. Traditionally, cod has been used for this dish, but overfishing and the resulting high prices of cod have made haddock a favorite ingredient for fish and chips. Another popular fish for this dish is plaice, a relatively abundant flatfish in the North Sea. The fried fish is commonly served on a bed of chunky diced or sliced fried potatoes and sprinkled with vinegar, often malt vinegar.

FISH IN MILD COCONUT MILK

YIELD: 8 PORTIONS

Spice Paste

1 guajillo chile or similar chile, seeded

8 oz/227 g coarsely cut shallots

2 garlic cloves, peeled

2 tbsp/10 g coarsely cut lemongrass

1 tsp/3 g ground turmeric

1 tbsp/15 mL tamarind pulp

2 fl oz/60 mL hot water

1 oz/28 g vegetable oil

1 pint/480 mL coconut milk

Salt, as needed

8 sea bass, snapper, or similar fish fillets, skin on, scaled (6 oz/170 g each)

Steamed rice, as needed

1. Soak the chile in water for about 15 minutes to soften.

2. Combine the chile with the shallots, garlic, lemongrass, and turmeric in a blender and process to a fine paste, adding water as needed to facilitate the blending.

3. Combine the tamarind pulp with the hot water until fully dispersed and strain through a fine-mesh sieve. Discard the solids and reserve the strained liquid.

4. In a wok or similar pan, sweat the spice paste in the oil over medium heat until all moisture is evaporated and the solids begin to separate from the oil.

5. Add the coconut milk and the strained, softened tamarind paste. Bring to a boil and adjust seasoning with salt.

6. Cut the fish into 3-oz/85-g pieces, season with salt, and poach very gently in the spiced coconut milk until the fish is cooked and begins to flake upon gentle pressure, about 5 minutes. Serve in a bowl, on a bed of steamed rice.

CHILEAN TUNA CEVICHE

YIELD: 8 PORTIONS

2 lb/907 g ahi tuna, cut into ½-in/1-cm dice

Salt, as needed

1 cup/240 mL lime juice, or as needed

1 tbsp/15 mL light sesame oil

1 fl oz/30 mL light soy sauce, not low-sodium

1½ tsp/4 g finely minced ginger

½ cup/78 g minced pitted green olives

½ cup/78 g minced pitted black olives

2 green onions, minced

Black pepper, as needed

Garnish

1 lb/454 g roasted fingerling potatoes, sliced on the bias

8 oz/227 g red cabbage leaves, cut into ultra-fine chiffonade

Salt, as needed

¼ cup/10 g chives cut into ½-in/1-cm pieces

1. Generously season the tuna with salt and allow to sit for 10 minutes. Gently rinse and dry the tuna.

2. Combine the tuna with the lime juice, sesame oil, soy sauce, ginger, olives, and green onions and allow to marinate for 10 minutes. Adjust seasoning with lime juice, salt, and pepper, as needed.

3. Combine the roasted sliced potatoes with the red cabbage, and season with salt. Arrange 3 oz/85 g of tuna ceviche on 2 oz/57 g of cabbage and potato mix in bowls. Garnish with the chives.

GREEN MEXICAN CEVICHE

YIELD: 8 PORTIONS

3 lb/1.36 kg mahimahi, cut into ¾-in/2-cm dice

½ cup/120 mL lime juice

1 lb/454 g tomatillos, husks removed, rinsed, diced

24 manzanilla olives, pitted, finely diced

4 oz/113 g small-dice white onions

2 jalapeños, cut into small dice (¼ oz/7 g)

2 firm Hass avocados, cut into small dice (4 oz/113 g each)

1 cup/43 g cilantro stems and leaves, finely cut

½ cup/120 mL extra-virgin olive oil

Salt, as needed

Garnish

Saltine crackers, as needed

1. Combine the fish with the lime juice, cover, and refrigerate for 1 hour.

2. Remove the fish from the refrigerator and combine with the tomatillos, olives, onions, jalapeños, avocados, cilantro, and oil. Adjust seasoning with salt to taste.

3. Serve a well-chilled 6-oz/170-g portion in a bowl with saltine crackers on the side.

COLOMBIAN CEVICHE WITH COCONUT MILK

YIELD: 8 PORTIONS

1 brown coconut	3 oz/85 g thinly sliced red onion
Ceviche	¾ cup/180 mL lime juice
2 garlic cloves, peeled	**Garnish**
1 habanero chile, seeded and deveined (¼ oz/7 g)	2 tbsp/6 g finely cut cilantro
3 lb/1.36 kg red snapper fillets	¼ cup/24 g shaved coconut, lightly toasted
Salt, as needed	

1. To produce the coconut milk, toast the whole coconut in an oven at 400°F/204°C for 5 to 10 minutes to help break the hard exterior. Holding the coconut in one hand over a bowl, crack it gently with a meat cleaver until the hard shell breaks. Catch the draining coconut juice in the bowl, strain it, and set aside.

2. With the cleaver, pry the shell apart. Scrape out the dense coconut flesh and purée it in a blender with as much hot water as is necessary to create a smooth purée. Strain the puréed coconut solids through a cheesecloth-lined strainer, and squeeze the solids to extract as much liquid as possible.

3. In a mortar and pestle, process the garlic and habanero chile into a paste and set aside.

4. Cut the red snapper fillets into thin slices and season generously with salt. Allow the fish to sit for about 10 minutes.

5. Toss the sliced fish with the habanero and garlic paste, and marinate for 10 minutes.

6. At service, place the red snapper in a bowl, add the lime juice, sliced red onion, coconut milk, cilantro, and shaved coconut, and adjust seasoning with salt as needed.

OCTOPUS "FAIRGROUND-STYLE"

YIELD: 8 PORTIONS

3 lb/1.36 kg whole octopus

1 bay leaf

1 tbsp/6 g black peppercorns

Salt, as needed

1 lb/454 g peeled yellow potatoes, cut into large dice

1 cup/128 g minced onions

½ cup/120 mL extra-virgin olive oil, plus more as needed

1 tbsp/7 g smoked Spanish paprika

1. Blanch the octopus in 2 gal/7.68 L of boiling water three times, changing the water after each time.

2. In an appropriate-size pot, submerge the octopus in cold water, covering by 1 in/3 cm. Add the bay leaf and peppercorns and bring to a gentle simmer. Add salt as needed and simmer very gently until the octopus is very tender, 1 to 3 hours depending on the size of the octopus.

3. Once the octopus is very tender, remove it from the water, allow to cool, and cut into ¼-in/6-mm slices.

4. Strain the cooking liquid and return it to the pot. Add the potatoes and cook until fork-tender, 10 to 15 minutes. Drain and reserve.

5. In a rondeau or similar pan over medium heat, sweat the onions in the olive oil, about 5 minutes. Remove from the heat, add the potatoes and octopus, and toss gently to combine.

6. Serve on a plate and sprinkle with the smoked paprika. Drizzle with additional olive oil as needed. Serve with small cocktail skewers.

BRAISED SWORDFISH KEBOB IN SWEET AND SAVORY SAUCE

YIELD: 8 PORTIONS

Sweet and Savory Sauce

1 cup/128 g minced onions

1 fl oz/30 mL extra-virgin olive oil

3 garlic cloves, minced

5 oz/142 g small-dice celery

3 oz/85 g chopped green olives

1 oz/28 g raisins

4 plum tomatoes, fresh or canned, chopped

8 fl oz/240 mL fish or chicken stock

1½ oz/43 g capers

Salt, as needed

Ground black pepper, as needed

3 lb/1.36 kg swordfish fillets, cut into 1½-in/4-cm dice

Salt, as needed

Ground black pepper, as needed

2 fl oz/60 mL extra-virgin olive oil

8 bamboo skewers, 8 in/20 cm

1½ oz/43 g pine nuts

2 tbsp/6 g basil, cut into chiffonade

1. For the sauce, sweat the onions in the olive oil over moderate heat until tender, about 5 minutes. Add the garlic and continue to sweat until aromatic, about 30 seconds. Add the celery, olives, and raisins, and continue to sweat gently until they begin to soften, about 2 minutes.

2. Add the tomatoes, stock, and capers, and continue to cook over moderate heat until the tomatoes are very soft and begin to disintegrate and turn into a soft pulp. Adjust seasoning with salt and pepper and set aside.

3. Season the diced swordfish with salt and pepper and toss in the olive oil. Skewer 6 oz/170 g of swordfish per skewer, and sear in a skillet until well browned on all sides, about 1 minute per side.

4. Add the Sweet and Savory Sauce. Simmer the skewers very gently to an internal temperature of 145°F/63°C, about 5 minutes. Serve 1 skewer per portion, topped with the sauce. Sprinkle with the pine nuts and basil.

VIETNAMESE GRILLED SHRIMP CAKE ON SUGARCANE

YIELD: 8 PORTIONS

Shrimp Cake

4 oz/113 g minced shallots

1 tbsp/9 g minced garlic

2 oz/57 g lard

1 fl oz/30 mL fish sauce

1 egg

1 tbsp/12 g palm sugar

½ tsp/1 g ground white pepper

2 tbsp/16 g cornstarch

1 lb/454 g shrimp, peeled and deveined

4 green onions, minced

8 oz/227 g canned sugarcane

Condiments

16 sheets rice paper, 6-in/15-cm diameter rounds

1 head red lettuce, leaves separated (14 to 16 oz/397 to 454 g)

1 cup/92 g bean sprouts

1 cup/43 g whole mint leaves

Hoisin-Peanut Sauce (page 177)

Vietnamese Dipping Sauce (page 178)

1. In a skillet, sweat the shallots and garlic in the lard over moderate heat until tender, about 2 minutes. Allow the mixture to cool and then combine with the fish sauce, egg, palm sugar, white pepper, and cornstarch in a food processor and purée into a fine paste.

2. Add the shrimp and process to a slightly coarse paste. Add the green onions and adjust seasoning with fish sauce, as needed.

3. Cut the sugarcanes lengthwise into 16 sticks about ¼ in/6 mm in thickness and about 3 to 4 in/8 to 10 cm in length.

4. With wet hands, shape about 1½ oz/43 g shrimp paste around each sugarcane stick about ½ in/1 cm thick and leaving 1 in/3 cm sugarcane exposed on each end. With oiled hands, smooth the surface.

5. In a steamer lined with cabbage leaves or cheesecloth, steam the shrimp paste sticks for 5 minutes, until firm to the touch and 155°F/68°C.

6. At service, grill the steamed shrimp sticks on each side until well browned, 1 to 2 minutes on each side.

7. Remove the shrimp paste from the sugarcane and place on a softened rice paper layered with a piece of lettuce, bean sprouts, and mint leaves. Wrap tightly and dip into the dipping sauce of your choice.

Form the forcemeat around the sugarcane.

Steam the skewers in a cabbage-lined steamer.

Recipes 153

SEAFOOD SAUSAGE HOT DOG

YIELD: 8 PORTIONS

12 to 14 ft/3.7 to 4.3 m lamb casings, ¾ in/2 cm diameter	2 egg whites
1 lb/454 g diced lean white fish fillet	6 oz/170 g shrimp, peeled and deveined
1 lb/454 g shrimp, peeled, deveined, and diced	6 oz/170 g skinless salmon fillet
Salt, as needed	1 tbsp/3 g minced chives
2 tsp/4 g Old Bay Seasoning	8 hot dog buns
1 oz/28 g panko bread crumbs	Pommery mustard or similar mustard, as needed
1 cup/240 mL heavy cream, chilled	Creamed Savoy Cabbage (page 180)
	Crispy Fried Shallots (page 181)

1. Soak the lamb casings in 2 qt/1.92 L water at 100°F/38°C for about 30 minutes.

2. For the forcemeat, combine the diced fish, shrimp, salt, and Old Bay Seasoning on a sheet pan. Place in the freezer until halfway frozen.

3. Soak the panko bread crumbs in the heavy cream and reserve.

4. Grind the semi-frozen fish–shrimp mix through the fine plate (⅛ in/3 mm) of a meat grinder.

5. Process the ground fish in a food processor to a very smooth paste. Add the egg whites and the cream–bread crumb mix and continue to process until homogenous.

6. Grind the shrimp, salmon, and chives through the medium plate (¼ in/6 mm) of a meat grinder and thoroughly combine with the forcemeat.

7. Cook a small sample to make a taste test, and adjust seasoning with salt and pepper as needed.

8. With a sausage stuffer, fill the forcemeat into the well-soaked lamb casings; twist links of 4 to 5 in/10 to 13 cm.

9. Poach in well-salted water at 165°F/74°C to an internal temperature of 155°F/68°C. Once done, shock the cooked sausages in ice water until well chilled throughout, 10 to 15 minutes. Dry gently and store for later use.

10. At service, gently sauté the sausages over medium heat until well browned on all sides, about 3 minutes. Spread the hot dog bun with the mustard and fill the bun halfway up with the Creamed Savoy Cabbage. Place the hot dog on top and sprinkle with Crispy Fried Shallots.

Recipes   155

TUNA AND GOAT CHEESE EMPANADAS

YIELD: 8 PORTIONS

4 oz/113 g minced onions	1 lb/454 g cooked tuna
1 fl oz/30 mL extra-virgin olive oil	8 oz/227 g fresh goat cheese
4 garlic cloves, minced	Salt, as needed
4 oz/113 g chopped pitted green olives	Ground black pepper, as needed
2 oz/57 g chopped capers	2 lb/907 g puff pastry dough
2 oz/57 g toasted pine nuts	Egg wash, as needed
2 tsp/2 g sweet paprika	Salsa, as needed

1. In a skillet over low heat, sweat the onions in the olive oil until very soft, about 10 minutes. Add the garlic and continue to cook until fragrant, about 10 minutes. Add the olives, capers, pine nuts, and paprika and continue to cook gently over low heat for 1 minute.

2. In a mixing bowl, combine the onions, olives, and pine nuts with the tuna and goat cheese and toss gently to combine. Adjust seasoning with salt and pepper as needed.

3. On a floured surface, roll out the puff pastry dough to a ⅛-in/3-mm thickness, dock with a fork to prevent excess puffing of the dough, and cut out 16 circles of 3 in/8 cm diameter. Gently re-roll the leftover dough to achieve a better yield.

4. Place about 2 oz/57 g of the tuna filling onto each dough circle, brush the edges with egg wash, and fold in half into a crescent. Using a fork, pinch the edges of each crescent to seal the empanadas.

5. Brush the empanadas with egg wash and bake at 425°F/218°C until golden brown, about 10 minutes.

6. Serve on a plate with a salsa of your choice.

GRILLED FISH TACOS

YIELD: 8 TACOS

3 lb/1.36 kg mahimahi fillets
Salt, as needed

Marinade

½ cup/120 mL vegetable oil
1½ fl oz/45 mL lime juice
1½ tbsp/9 g chili powder
1½ tsp/3 g ground cumin
1½ tsp/3 g ground coriander
2 garlic cloves, minced

Southwestern Slaw (page 182)
8 flour or corn tortillas, 8 in/20 cm diameter
Lime-Flavored Sour Cream (page 181)

1. Cut the mahimahi into 16 equal slices, 2 to 3 oz/57 to 85 g each, and season with salt as needed.

2. Gently combine the vegetable oil, lime juice, chili powder, cumin, coriander, and garlic with the fish. Allow the fish to marinate for about 30 minutes.

3. Grill the fish over high heat until well marked and cooked through, about 1 minute on each side.

4. Place about 2 tbsp/30 mL of Southwestern Slaw into a corn tortilla and top with two pieces of fish. Drizzle with the Lime-Flavored Sour Cream and serve.

SALT COD FISH FRITTERS

YIELD: 8 PORTIONS

1 lb 8 oz/680 g boneless salt cod (bacalao)

Sofrito

4 garlic cloves, minced

2 oz/57 g small-dice onions

1 red pepper

1 green pepper

1 fl oz/30 mL extra-virgin olive oil

8 oz/227 g all-purpose flour

2 tsp/9 g baking powder

1 cup/240 mL water

½ cup/120 mL minced chives

2 green onions, minced

2 tsp/4 g ground black pepper

Vegetable oil, as needed

Aioli (page 182)

Picada (page 183)

1. To reduce the salt content of the fish, place the salt cod in a saucepan and add enough water to submerge it by 2 in/5 cm. Bring to a simmer, turn off the heat, and drain the water. Repeat the process 3 or 4 times, tasting the fish after each draining to check for saltiness. Repeat as often as necessary until the fish tastes pleasantly salty, comparable to well-seasoned fish. With your hands, flake the cooked cod into hazelnut-size chunks and reserve.

2. For the sofrito, sweat the garlic, onions, and peppers in the olive oil over low to medium heat until very tender, 5 to 7 minutes, and reserve.

3. In a mixing bowl, combine the flour and baking powder. Add the water and mix thoroughly to break down any lumps. Add the chives, green onions, and pepper and combine thoroughly. Add the flaked cod and the sofrito.

4. Shape the fritters with tablespoons and deep-fry at 350°F/177°C until golden brown and crispy through, 2 to 4 minutes. After the fitters are done, allow to drain on a wire rack. Serve hot fritters on a plate with either Aioli or Picada.

BRANDADE OF SALT COD

YIELD: ABOUT 8 PORTIONS

1 lb/454 g salt cod fillets (bacalao)	Grated nutmeg, as needed
1 clove garlic, minced	Cayenne, as needed
3 fl oz/90 mL olive oil	Ground black pepper, as needed
1 cup/240 mL heavy cream, or as needed	1 tbsp/15 mL lemon juice
8 oz/227 g russet potatoes, cooked and mashed	Salt, as needed
	1 baguette

1. To reduce the salt content of the fish, place the salt cod in a saucepan and add enough water to submerge it by 2 in/5 cm. Bring to a simmer, turn off the heat, and drain the water. Repeat the process 3 or 4 times, tasting the fish after each draining to check for saltiness. Repeat as often as necessary until the fish tastes pleasantly salty, comparable to well-seasoned fish. With your hands, flake the cooked cod into hazelnut-size chunks and reserve.

2. In a saucepan over low to medium heat, sweat the garlic in the olive oil for 2 to 3 minutes.

3. Add the cream and bring to a boil. Combine the cream and the flaked cod in a food processor and process until smooth. Add the mashed potatoes and mix into a smooth paste. Adjust the flavor with nutmeg, cayenne, black pepper, and lemon juice, and add salt as needed. Add more cream as needed to adjust consistency.

4. Serve brandade in a small cup accompanied by a thinly sliced, crispy toasted baguette.

SHRIMP PANCAKES

YIELD: 8 PORTIONS

3 oz/85 g minced onions	1 tsp/4 g baking powder
2 fl oz/60 mL extra-virgin olive oil	1 cup/240 mL water
¼ tsp/0.5 g Spanish paprika	12 oz/340 g shrimp, deveined and minced
2 tbsp/6 g coarsely chopped flat-leaf parsley	Olive oil, as needed, for frying
6 oz/170 g all-purpose flour	Aioli (page 182)
Salt, as needed	Picada (page 183)

1. In a skillet over low heat, sweat the onions in the oil until very tender, about 10 minutes. Add the paprika and continue to cook until fragrant, about 30 seconds. Add the parsley.

2. In a bowl, combine the flour, salt, and baking powder; add the water and mix to combine. Add the shrimp and the onion mixture.

3. To fry the pancakes, heat a ½-in/1-cm level of olive oil in a skillet to about 350°F/177°C.

4. Drop batter by the tablespoon into the oil, flattening the pancakes into 2- to 3-in/5- to 8-cm rounds using the back of a spoon that has been dipped in hot oil. Fry until golden, 2 to 3 minutes, turning once.

5. Serve pancakes accompanied by Aioli or Picada.

MUSSELS WITH OLIVES

YIELD: 8 TAPAS-SIZE PORTIONS

24 mussels, scrubbed, debearded

3 oz/90 mL dry white wine

1 bay leaf

3 oz/85 g minced onions

2 garlic cloves, minced

1 oz/28 g extra-virgin olive oil

12 oz/340 g canned tomatoes, chopped

2 oz/57 g minced black olives

2 salted anchovy fillets

2 tbsp/6 g finely cut chives

Salt, as needed

Ground black pepper, as needed

¼ cup/21 g finely grated manchego cheese

1. In a rondeau or similar pot, combine the mussels, wine, and bay leaf and bring to a boil. Cover tightly and cook over high heat until the mussels open, 3 to 5 minutes. Discard any mussels that do not open.

2. Remove the mussels from the shells and reserve. Strain the cooking liquid and set aside. Separate the mussel shells and keep one half of the shells, discarding the rest.

3. In a separate pan, sauté the onions and garlic in the olive oil until translucent, 1 to 2 minutes. Add the tomatoes, olives, and anchovies and continue to sauté gently until tender, 2 to 3 minutes.

4. Add the mussel cooking liquid and reduce over medium-high heat until almost fully evaporated, 5 to 10 minutes.

5. Once the liquid has almost fully evaporated, take the skillet off the heat, add the mussels and chives, and adjust seasoning with salt and pepper.

6. Place the mussels back into the reserved half-shells and sprinkle with the cheese. Serve immediately.

SPICY FRIED FISH

YIELD: 8 PORTIONS

2 tbsp/30 mL tamarind paste

½ cup/480 mL hot water

3 lb/1.36 kg whole smelts or similar small fish

Salt, as needed

1 tbsp/6 g ground turmeric

Cornstarch, as needed, for dredging

Vegetable oil, as needed, for deep-frying

Malaysian Shrimp Paste Sambal (page 183)

1. Combine the tamarind paste with the hot water, mix well to fully disperse, and strain through a fine-mesh sieve. Reserve.

2. Clean and gut the fish and season with salt as needed.

3. In a bowl, combine the seasoned fish with the strained tamarind paste and allow to marinate for about 10 minutes.

4. Drain the fish, sprinkle with the turmeric, and mix thoroughly.

5. Dredge the fish in cornstarch, shake off the excess, and deep-fry at 375°F/191°C until golden brown and cooked through, 3 to 4 minutes. Serve with Malaysian Shrimp Paste Sambal.

CHEF'S NOTES

The key to success in this dish is to make sure that the fish gets crispy and well browned as it fries. Too often, many chefs are preoccupied with a fear of overcooking, which often results in food with an unsatisfying lack of flavor and texture. It is safe to say that doneness is secondary to the value of texture and flavor.

Should a small fish not be available, any mildly flavored fish fillet can be cut into goujons or strips of 2 to 3 in/5 to 8 cm in length and about ½ in/1 cm in width. These strips can be cooked the same way.

GRILLED SPICED FISH PASTE

YIELD: 8 PORTIONS

Spice Paste

3 guajillo chiles or similar chiles, seeded

6 oz/170 g coarsely cut shallots

6 garlic cloves, peeled

1 tbsp/7 g ground turmeric

12 macadamia nuts

2 stalks (1½ oz/43 g) lemongrass, trimmed and coarsely cut

1 tsp/2 g ground coriander

3 lb/1.36 kg skinless sea bass fillets or similar fish

1 oz/28 g sugar

1 tsp/2 g ground white pepper

Salt, as needed

1 cup/240 mL coconut milk

Banana leaves, as needed

Malaysian Shrimp Paste Sambal (page 183)

1. Submerge the chiles in enough water to cover by 2 in/5 cm, and soak for 15 minutes to soften. Drain well.

2. Combine the chiles with the shallots, garlic, turmeric, macadamia nuts, lemongrass, and coriander in a blender and purée to a smooth paste. Add small amounts of water if necessary to facilitate the blending.

3. Dice the fish and mix with the sugar, white pepper, and salt. Process the fish in a food processor to a coarse paste.

4. Add the spice paste and the coconut milk to the fish and process to a fine paste.

5. Cut the banana leaves into 6-in by 9-in/15-cm by 23-cm pieces, and hold them briefly over an open flame or under a broiler until they soften and become more pliable.

6. Place 2 tbsp/30 mL of fish paste onto the center of each banana leaf. Parallel the natural lines of the banana leaf and fold one edge of the banana leaf to cover the fish paste. Fold the other edge in and press down gently; the resulting package should be 9 in/23 cm long, 1 in/3 cm wide, and ½ in/1 cm thick. Use toothpicks to secure both ends.

7. Grill over high direct heat until cooked through and the banana leaf is well charred, about 5 minutes. Serve as a sandwich filling or on steamed rice, accompanied by the Malaysian Shrimp Paste Sambal.

SQUID IN BLACK INK SAUCE

YIELD: 8 TAPAS-SIZE PORTIONS

1 lb 8 oz/680 g whole squid with tentacles

Stuffing

2 fl oz/60 mL olive oil, plus more as needed

2 oz/57 g minced onions

2 oz/57 g minced piquillo peppers

2 garlic cloves, minced

2 oz/57 g minced Serrano ham

1 oz/28 g bread crumbs

Salt, as needed

Sauce

4 oz/113 g minced onions

4 fl oz/120 mL dry white wine

4 fl oz/120 mL tomato purée

4 oz/113 g minced piquillo peppers

1 tbsp/15 mL squid ink

Salt, as needed

Ground black pepper, as needed

1. Clean the squid. Remove the cartilage, eyes, and beak if present and discard. Cut the tentacles into small pieces and sauté very briefly over high heat in a skillet in the olive oil, about 30 seconds. Remove from the pan and reserve.

2. Add the onions, piquillo peppers, and garlic to the pan and cook slowly over low heat until slightly caramelized, about 10 minutes. Add the Serrano ham and cook briefly. Return the reserved tentacles to the skillet, add the bread crumbs, and season with salt as needed.

3. Stuff the squid tubes (the cleaned heads) with this mixture and secure them with a toothpick.

4. Sear the stuffed squid in olive oil on all sides, remove from the pan, and set aside.

5. Add the onions to the squid's pan drippings and sweat gently over low heat for about 10 minutes. Add the wine and reduce until fully evaporated. Add the tomato purée, piquillo peppers, and squid ink and heat through.

6. Purée in a blender until very smooth, adding water as needed to facilitate the blending. Adjust seasoning with salt and pepper, as needed.

7. Place the seared stuffed squid in a pan large enough to hold them tightly in one layer. Add the puréed sauce, cover tightly with a lid, and cook gently over very low heat until the squid is heated through, about 15 minutes. Serve 2 or 3 per portion on a plate with the sauce.

GRILLED SWORDFISH SKEWER WITH ROASTED POTATO SALAD

YIELD: 8 PORTIONS

4 oz/113 g coarsely cut onions	1 cup/240 mL extra-virgin olive oil
2 fl oz/60 mL lemon juice	Flat metal skewers, ½ in/1 cm
3 lb/1.36 kg swordfish fillet	40 small fresh bay leaves
Salt, as needed	Roasted Potato Salad (page 179)
Ground black pepper, as needed	

1. In a blender, combine the onions and lemon juice and purée until very smooth.

2. Cut the swordfish into 1-oz/28-g pieces, season with salt and pepper, and combine with the lemon juice–onion mix. Add the olive oil and allow to marinate for up to 1 hour.

3. Skewer 6 oz/170 g swordfish onto each flat metal skewer with a bay leaf between each piece.

4. Grill over high heat, preferably charcoal, for 1 to 2 minutes on each side, until the swordfish is cooked to an internal temperature of 145°F/63°C and well charred on all sides.

5. At service, remove the metal skewer and serve on top of Roasted Potato Salad.

SHRIMP IN GARLIC

YIELD: 8 TAPAS-SIZE PORTIONS

1 lb 8 oz/680 g shrimp, 16/20 count, head and peel on, deveined

Salt, as needed

12 garlic cloves, very thinly sliced

1 tsp/2 g crushed black pepper

¼ tsp/0.5 g red pepper flakes (optional)

1 cup/240 mL extra-virgin olive oil

½ cup/120 mL dry white wine

2 cups/100 g coarsely chopped flat-leaf parsley

Baguette or similar bread, as needed

1. Season the shrimp with salt.

2. In a sauté pan over low heat, gently sweat the garlic, black pepper, and red pepper flakes in the olive oil about 30 seconds.

3. Add the wine and bring to a boil briefly. Add the shrimp and poach at about 165°F/74°C until the shrimp are cooked through, about 5 minutes.

4. Once cooked, remove the shrimp from the olive oil and simmer the oil-wine mix over medium heat until the wine has evaporated and the oil looks clear; take great care not to brown the garlic.

5. Return the shrimp to the oil and add the chopped parsley. Serve shrimp in a bowl with the oil, accompanied by the bread to dip in the oil.

AROMATIC FISH ESCABECHE

YIELD: 8 PORTIONS

3 lb/1.36 kg fresh sardines, smelts, or similar fish, cleaned and gutted	1 tbsp/6 g ground cumin
Salt, as needed	1½ tsp/3 g red pepper flakes
Ground black pepper, as needed	1 tsp/2 g ground ginger
All-purpose flour, as needed	1 pinch saffron threads
Extra-virgin olive oil, as needed, for frying	1 cup/240 mL red wine vinegar
	1 oz/28 g sugar
6 garlic cloves, sliced	4 bay leaves
	½ cup/120 mL water

1. Season the fish with salt and pepper, dredge in flour, and shake off the excess. Deep-fry the fish in olive oil at 375°F/191°C until golden brown, crispy, and cooked through, 3 to 4 minutes. Remove the fish from the skillet and allow to drain on a wire rack.

2. In a skillet, sweat the garlic in about 4 oz/113g of olive oil over low heat for about 1 minute. Add the cumin, red pepper flakes, ginger, and saffron, and continue to cook over low heat until fragrant, about 30 seconds.

3. Add the vinegar, sugar, bay leaves, and water. Bring to a boil and adjust seasoning with salt, and add vinegar as needed to adjust acidity. It should be a pleasant balance of aromatic and tart with a gentle sweetness.

4. Arrange the fish in a dish, pour the vinegar mixture over it, and allow to sit for at least 1 hour, but preferably overnight. Serve at room temperature.

FISH STOCK FOR BOUILLABAISSE

YIELD: 2 QT/1.92 L

4 oz/113 g large-dice onions

2 oz/57 g leeks, white part only, cut into large dice

2 oz/57 g large-dice celery

1 fl oz/30 mL extra-virgin olive oil

4 garlic cloves, sliced

4 lb/1.81 kg fish bones and heads, gills removed

8 plum tomatoes, fresh or canned, crushed

2 tbsp/18 g orange zest, no pith

1 fl oz/30 mL Pernod or similar anise liqueur

3 bay leaves

2 sprigs thyme

¼ tsp/0.5 g cayenne

2½ qt/2.4 L cold water

Salt, as needed

Ground black pepper, as needed

1. In a stockpot or similar pot, sweat the onions, leeks, and celery in the olive oil over moderate heat until they begin to get tender, 3 to 5 minutes. Add the garlic and sweat until aromatic, about 1 minute. Add the fish heads and bones and continue to sweat gently over low to medium heat for 2 minutes.

2. Add the tomatoes, orange zest, Pernod, bay leaves, thyme, cayenne, cold water, salt, and pepper and bring to a boil. Simmer gently over medium heat for about 30 minutes, skimming frequently.

3. Adjust seasoning, strain gently through a fine-mesh strainer, and keep refrigerated until needed.

GARLIC AND SAFFRON MAYONNAISE

YIELD: 1 PINT/480 ML

1 pint/480 mL pure olive oil	1 tsp/5 g salt
6 garlic cloves, peeled	1 tbsp/6 g fresh bread crumbs
2 tsp/1 g saffron threads	Juice of 1 lemon
2 egg yolks, at room temperature	2 tsp/4 g cayenne

1. In a blender, combine the olive oil, garlic, and saffron, and purée until smooth.

2. In a mixing bowl, combine the egg yolks with the salt, bread crumbs, lemon juice, and cayenne until fully incorporated.

3. Gradually, in a slow stream, add the olive oil, garlic, and saffron purée to the egg mixture, whisking constantly.

4. If needed, add small amounts of water to adjust viscosity; the sauce should be slightly spreadable. Adjust seasoning with salt, as needed.

SPICY THAI CUCUMBER SALAD

YIELD: 8 PORTIONS

3 European cucumbers (2 lb/907 g), peeled	12 oz/340 g finely minced red onions
½ cup/120 mL lime juice	½ cup/24 g whole mint leaves
¼ cup/50 g sugar	½ cup/24 g coarsely cut cilantro
Salt, as needed	¼ cup/35 g coarsely chopped roasted peanuts
3 Thai bird chiles, finely sliced	

1. Cut the cucumbers in half lengthwise, remove all the seeds, and cut into thin slices.

2. In a mixing bowl, combine the sliced cucumbers with the lime juice, sugar, salt, chiles, and onions, and marinate for 15 minutes.

3. Add the mint, cilantro, and peanuts, toss, and adjust seasoning as necessary. Serve well chilled.

TAPENADE

YIELD: 1½ CUPS/360 ML

12 oz/340 g salt-cured black olives

4 oz/113 g capers in brine, drained

2 oz/57 g salted anchovy fillets

2 fl oz/60 mL lemon juice

½ oz/14 g Dijon mustard

4 fl oz/120 mL extra-virgin olive oil

Ground black pepper, as needed

1. Taste the olives, capers, and anchovies. If they are too salty, submerge them for 10 minutes in cold water, then drain, rinse and pat dry, and check again.

2. In a food processor, combine the olives, capers, anchovies, lemon juice, mustard, oil, and pepper and process into a coarsely textured, slightly cohesive paste.

3. Reserve to allow flavors to develop for at least 1 hour before serving.

BEER BATTER

YIELD: 1 QT/960 ML

10 oz/284 g all-purpose flour

1 oz/28 g sugar

1 oz/28 g salt

1 tbsp/12 g baking powder

1 tsp/2 g ground black pepper

1 pint/480 mL dark beer or bock

1. In a mixing bowl, combine the flour, sugar, salt, baking powder, and pepper.

2. Add the beer and mix until smooth. Allow the batter to rest for 30 minutes before use.

FRENCH FRIES

YIELD: 8 PORTIONS

3 lb/1.36 kg russet potatoes, 100 count

Oil, as needed, for deep-frying

Salt, as needed

1. Peel the potatoes, cut into sticks of ¼-in/6-mm thickness, and submerge in cold water to rinse away exterior starch. Wash the potatoes in several changes of cold water.
2. Dry the potatoes and fry in a deep fryer at 275°F/135°C until the exterior of the fries has a sandpaper-like texture but has not browned yet.
3. On a wire rack, drain the potatoes, and allow to cool and air-dry in a refrigerator for about 3 hours.
4. Fry the potatoes at 325°F/163°C until golden brown and crispy. Remove from the hot oil, shake off excess, and toss in salt.

HOISIN-PEANUT SAUCE

YIELD: 3 CUPS/720 ML

1 pint/480 mL hoisin sauce

1 cup/240 mL water

3 oz/85 g minced yellow onions

½ cup/120 mL white rice vinegar

1 fl oz/30 mL sriracha or similar ground chili paste

3 oz/85 g finely chopped roasted peanuts

1. In a saucepan, combine the hoisin sauce, water, onions, and vinegar and simmer gently over low heat for 5 minutes. Add water as needed to maintain a medium to heavy nappé. Set aside to cool.
2. Add the sriracha and peanuts and serve at room temperature.

Recipes 177

VIETNAMESE DIPPING SAUCE

YIELD: 1 PINT/480 ML

4 garlic cloves, thinly sliced

2 tsp/10 mL sriracha or similar chili paste

2 Thai bird chiles

½ cup/120 mL fish sauce

1¼ cups/300 mL hot water

2 fl oz/60 mL lime juice with pulp

4 oz/113 g sugar

1 oz/28 g very finely grated carrots

1. With a mortar and pestle, pound the garlic, sriracha, and chiles until a slightly coarse paste is achieved.

2. In a mixing bowl, combine the fish sauce, hot water, lime juice, sugar, carrots, and chili-garlic paste. Mix until the sugar has dissolved. Serve at room temperature.

> **CHEF'S NOTE** Dipping sauces are a crucial component of Vietnamese culinary culture. This one, known as *nuoc cham*, is probably the most common. Every chef and household uses a different version. The ingredients are pretty much the same; just the proportions vary.

ROASTED POTATO SALAD

YIELD: 8 PORTIONS

1 lb 8 oz/680 g fingerling potatoes

Salt, as needed

Ground black pepper, as needed

Extra-virgin olive oil, as needed

8 oz/227 g shredded green beans

8 oz/227 g halved cherry tomatoes

Dressing

5 fl oz/150 mL extra-virgin olive oil

2 fl oz/60 mL sherry vinegar

1 tbsp/15 mL balsamic vinegar

½ cup/24 g coarsely chopped flat-leaf parsley

½ cup/78 g pitted Kalamata olives, cut in half lengthwise

¼ cup/33 g chopped capers

1 tbsp/8 g chopped anchovies

1 tsp/3 g minced garlic

1. Cut the potatoes into large obliques, season with salt and pepper, and toss in olive oil.
2. Roast the potatoes at 425°F/218°C until golden brown and fully cooked; set aside.
3. In a generous amount of rapidly boiling, well-salted water, cook the beans until tender. Shock in ice water; set aside.
4. In a bowl, toss the roasted potatoes with the green beans, tomatoes, and all other ingredients until well combined, and allow to stand at room temperature for 30 minutes.
5. Adjust seasoning with salt and pepper, as needed. Serve slightly warm.

CHEF'S NOTE

An oblique cut is used primarily with long, cylindrical vegetables such as parsnips or carrots. Place the peeled vegetable on a cutting board. Make a diagonal cut to remove the stem end. Hold the knife in the same position and roll the vegetable a quarter turn (approximately 90 degrees). Slice through it on the same diagonal, forming a piece with two angled edges. Be sure to decrease the angle of the diagonal as the vegetable gets larger in diameter. This will ensure uniform cuts that will cook evenly. Repeat until the entire vegetable has been cut.

Recipes 179

CREAMED SAVOY CABBAGE FOR SEAFOOD HOT DOG

YIELD: 8 PORTIONS

1 head savoy cabbage	Ground black pepper, as needed
1½ cups/360 mL heavy cream	Pinch of grated nutmeg
Salt, as needed	3 oz/85 g dried cranberries, soaked

1. Cut two-thirds of the cabbage into a fine chiffonade (⅛ in/3 mm), and cut the remaining one-third of the cabbage into coarse chunks.

2. Cook the coarse chunks in 1 gal/3.84 L of well-salted water for 5 to 8 minutes, until tender, and purée in a blender until very smooth.

3. Add the heavy cream, adjust seasoning with salt, pepper, and nutmeg, and chill down rapidly. Reserve.

4. Cook the cabbage chiffonade in 1 gal/3.84 L of well-salted water until tender, 3 to 5 minutes. Drain well, gently squeeze out excess moisture, and combine with the puréed cabbage mix.

5. Add the cranberries, adjust seasoning with salt and pepper, and reserve for later use. Serve hot.

CRISPY FRIED SHALLOTS

YIELD: 8 PORTIONS

1 lb/454 g shallots, sliced ⅛ in/ 3 mm thick

1 tbsp/8 g cornstarch, or as needed

1 qt/960 mL vegetable oil

1. In a mixing bowl, toss the shallots with the cornstarch to evenly coat them with a thin layer.

2. In a 2-qt/1.92-L saucepan, heat the oil to about 200°F/93°C. Place the shallots into the warm oil and increase the heat to high until the oil is at 325°F/163°C. Maintain 325°F/163°C until the shallots are golden brown and crispy throughout.

3. With a spider or similar tool, remove the shallots from the oil and allow to drain on a wire rack until cool. Gently blot with an absorbing towel and keep in a dry spot for later use.

CHEF'S NOTE | The temperature of the oil for the crispy fried shallots is initially very low. This is done to drive out any moisture so that the shallots will stay crispy once they turn golden brown.

LIME-FLAVORED SOUR CREAM

YIELD: 1 CUP/240 ML

1 cup/240 mL Mexican Cream (page 119)

½ cup/120 mL buttermilk

2 tsp/6 g finely grated lime zest

1 tbsp/15 mL lime juice

Salt, as needed

Combine the Mexican Cream, buttermilk, lime zest, lime juice, and salt, and mix well.

Recipes 181

SOUTHWESTERN SLAW

YIELD: 8 PORTIONS

1 lb/454 g green cabbage

Salt, as needed

1 fl oz/30 mL lime juice

1 fl oz/30 mL honey

2 oz/57 g finely minced red onions

½ oz/14 g jalapeños, seeded and finely minced

¼ cup/12 g coarsely cut cilantro

Ground black pepper, as needed

1. Cut the cabbage into coarse chunks and chop in a food processor until coarsely chopped.

2. In a mixing bowl, mix the chopped cabbage with salt, work well, and allow to sit for about 15 minutes.

3. Squeeze excess moisture out of the cabbage and combine with the lime juice, honey, onions, jalapeños, and cilantro. Adjust seasoning with salt and pepper, as needed.

AIOLI

YIELD: 1 PINT/480 ML

8 garlic cloves, peeled and chopped

Salt, as needed

2 egg yolks

1 pint/480 mL pure olive oil

1. Combine the garlic and salt and crush into a coarse paste in a mortar or with the side of a knife.

2. Combine with the egg yolks in a bowl, and gradually pour in the oil in a slow, steady stream until emulsified. Adjust seasoning as needed.

> **CHEF'S NOTE**
> To prepare this recipe in a food processor, combine the garlic, salt, and egg yolks in the bowl. With the processor running on low speed, slowly add the oil in a fine stream.

PICADA

YIELD: 3 CUPS/720 ML

6 oz/170 g baguette, cut into ½-in/1-cm slices

1 pint/480 mL extra-virgin olive oil

8 oz/227 g blanched roasted almonds

8 oz/227 g blanched roasted hazelnuts

8 garlic cloves, minced

Salt, as needed

½ cup/24 g chopped flat-leaf parsley

Ground black pepper, as needed

1. Fry the bread in the olive oil until golden brown and crispy throughout. Keep the oil for later use.

2. In a food processor, grind the almonds, hazelnuts, garlic, bread, and salt to a coarse paste. Add the parsley and continue to process.

3. In a mixing bowl, combine the bread-nut mixture with the olive oil left over from frying the bread to form a slightly coarse, spreadable paste. Adjust seasoning with salt and pepper as needed. Serve at room temperature.

MALAYSIAN SHRIMP PASTE SAMBAL

YIELD: 8 PORTIONS

10 red Fresno chiles (8 oz/227g) or similar chiles, seeded and deveined

1 tbsp/15 mL Malaysian shrimp paste, toasted

Salt, as needed

Juice of 1 lime

With a mortar and pestle, pound the chiles to a fine paste with the shrimp paste and salt. Add the lime juice and adjust seasoning as needed.

CHEF'S NOTE

Malaysian shrimp paste, also known as *belacan*, is a very fragrant condiment common in Malaysian cooking. It is made by grinding and salting small shrimp and allowing them to ferment, then pressing it into sliceable blocks. In order to enhance the flavor, Malaysian shrimp paste is usually toasted before use.

CHAPTER 4

VEGETABLES

Plant food has always been vital to our diet, and early humans ate a primarily vegetarian diet. Their principal foods were wild fruits, seeds, leaves, stalks, tubers, and roots, supplemented by the meat of hunted or scavenged animals. Many anthropologists agree that the gradual change from a nomadic to a domestic lifestyle with the inception of agriculture about 10,000 years ago considerably reduced the diversity of our plant food, but facilitated the creation of a reliable supply. To achieve the greatest nutritional benefit and best taste from this new resource, our ancestors developed methods to make produce more palatable and digestible, the foundation of today's diverse vegetable cookery with its cultural and regional variations.

Today, produce is viewed differently from region to region. For most cultures, it is an appreciated, integral part of the daily meals. Meat comes to the table in relatively small doses, with perhaps an occasional meat dish for sharing, accompanied by several vegetable and grain preparations. To accentuate the flavor, small amounts of meat might sometimes be incorporated into vegetable dishes. In South and Southeast Asia, vegetarian or vegan cultures are widespread. These cuisines have created exciting vegetarian and vegan dishes, popular and coveted far beyond their regional boundaries.

Some industrialized Western cultures serve vegetables as an accompaniment to meat, poultry, or fish. Regrettably, the vegetables are often outshone by the featured item and prepared with a lack of passion. As a result, many see the vegetable side dish as a mere nutritional necessity with little appeal. However, a look at older or traditional cookbooks reveals that these cuisines actually offer a great variety of attractive vegetable preparations. Inspired by a harvest surplus, or by a limited availability of meat or fish, these time-honored dishes place the vegetable in the center of the plate, perhaps, if desired, with some meat on the side. Examples include the famous French cassoulet, braised greens with ham hocks from the southern United States, and Rutabaga Stew (page 207) from Germany.

STORAGE

Harvesting produce does not end its life. Vital processes, causing desirable and undesirable changes, continue. Climacteric fruits, like pears, avocado, or bananas, begin to ripen after harvest and become delectably sweet and enjoyable. Stored too long, they will begin to decay. Others, like cherries, apples, and berries, will not continue to ripen off the plant. Since they have to be harvested at peak ripeness, the quality of delicate berries and others deteriorates rapidly during transport and storage. Many vegetables, once disconnected from their original food and energy source, switch into survival mode and begin to convert accumulated nutrients for their own nourishment. True new potatoes, sweet and creamy when they come out of the ground, will turn starchy within a few days. Mature potatoes, on the other hand, will turn their starches into sugar and actually become sweet if they are stored too cold. And crisp leafy vegetables can become limp very quickly if moisture loss is not controlled. All of these changes can be manipulated and slowed down by proper storage. Temperature control is one of the most effective ways to prevent loss of quality. However, prolonged exposure to the average refrigerator temperature of 40°F/4°C can actually damage some produce. Bananas turn black, tomatoes lose flavor, and avocados darken. For these and many other items, a storage temperature of about 50°F/10°C is advisable.

PREPARATION

Popular belief suggests that it is better to eat vegetables raw or undercooked, as heating supposedly strips the produce of its nutritional benefits. In rare cases, or if the vegetable is poorly prepared, this might be true. Properly executed, cooking actually improves palatability and digestibility as well as nutritional accessibility.

Based on the characteristics of different vegetable categories, appropriate cooking methods vary. For color retention, young and crisp green vegetables are often rapidly boiled in well-salted water before they are finished with butter and aromatics. Immature squashes, on the other hand, are much better grilled, sautéed, or stewed. An aggressive dry heat supports their inherent delicate flavor, while boiling in liquid would turn them mushy and tasteless. Mature squashes, as well as roots and tubers, benefit from roasting. Their starches and sugars, caramelized from the high heat of the oven, create a well-browned and flavorful exterior. Root vegetables, to draw attention to their firm texture and their natural sweetness, are often cooked in a small amount of liquid with butter and a natural sweetener like sugar or honey. In this process, known as glazing, the liquid is allowed to evaporate, leaving a shiny, sweet coating around the cooked vegetable. Young leafy vegetables can be sautéed or stir-fried, whereas mature greens such as collards, kale, or mustard greens are most enjoyable after a long and slow braise.

Culinary fruits, in contrast, are mostly enjoyed raw or minimally prepared. The classical menu sequence of most cuisines places them at the end, as a finale or climax of the menu. Traditional European Christmas gifts often include fruits as a treat or reward for good behavior. English proverbs, as in "the fruits of our labor," also express our general mind-set. All this love and affection might in part be due to the fact that plants actually design their fruits to be appealing; their irresistibility is the reward for dispersing the seeds.

Street-food vendors prefer easy, executable methods like grilling or frying. Braised dishes are popular too. Their hot-holding capability makes them perfect candidates for a service with limited means. See Table 4.1 for vegetables and their appropriate cooking methods.

TABLE 4.1 Cooking Methods and Suitable Vegetables

METHOD	SUITABLE VEGETABLE CATEGORIES	SAMPLES
Sautéing/Stir-frying	Naturally tender young vegetables	Broccoli Carrots Mushrooms Napa cabbage Spinach Sugar snap peas Yellow squash Zucchini
Glazing	Root vegetables Some tubers	Beets Carrots Celeriac Rutabagas Sweet potatoes Turnips
Grilling	Young, high-moisture vegetables Tubers	Bell peppers Eggplant Green asparagus Potatoes Green onions Sweet potatoes Yellow squash Zucchini
Rapid boiling before finishing	Tender young vegetables	Baby carrots Brussels sprouts Green beans Snow peas Sugar snap peas
Simmering in liquid	Legumes Tubers Root vegetables	Mature beans Potatoes Sweet potatoes Whole beets

TABLE 4.1 (*continued*)

METHOD	SUITABLE VEGETABLE CATEGORIES	SAMPLES
Roasting	Tubers Roots Mature squashes Sturdy vegetables	Brussels sprouts Carrots Cauliflower Garlic cloves Peppers Plantains Potatoes Turnips Whole shallots
Frying (commonly batter or breading coated)	Tubers All other naturally tender vegetables	Potatoes Sweet potatoes
Braising/stewing	Sturdy leafy vegetables Root vegetables Cabbages Stalks	Carrots Cauliflower Celery Collard greens Fennel Kale Mustard greens Peppers Red, green, or savoy cabbage Rutabagas Squashes

The culinary scene around produce is changing. Traditionally limited to only a few fried items, like French Fries (page 177), onion rings, and fried green tomatoes, today's street food presents many exciting vegetable dishes.

Expanding produce departments and revitalized farmers' markets stand witness to the growing demand for a wholesome diet. The direct cooperation between individual food-service operators and nearby farmers, once often greeted with a lofty smile, has become a viable business option, as more and more patrons are willing to pay a premium for sustainably produced food.

Prepared skillfully, with enthusiasm and respect for the ingredients, produce certainly can be the star on the plate. Once the potential is recognized, nobody will feel the need to hide the vegetable or eat it only out of a sense of obligation; patrons will actually ask for it.

EGGPLANT PARMESAN

YIELD: 8 PORTIONS

3 lb/1.36 kg eggplant

Salt, as needed

Ground black pepper, as needed

Breading

All-purpose flour, as needed

1 pint/480 mL egg wash

8 oz/227 g bread crumbs

Oil, as needed, for pan frying

Tomato Sauce (page 191)

8 oz/227 g grated mozzarella cheese

8 oz/227 g grated Parmesan cheese

Grilled Garlic Bread (page 248)

1. Peel the eggplant and cut into ½-in/1-cm slices. Toss the eggplant slices in a small amount of salt and allow to sit in a colander until eggplant appears moist, about 15 minutes.

2. Pat the eggplant dry and season with black pepper. Dredge the sliced eggplant in flour and shake off the excess. Dip in the egg wash and shake off the excess. Dredge in the bread crumbs, making sure the eggplant is evenly coated.

3. Pan-fry the eggplant slices over medium heat in a relatively generous amount of oil until golden brown on both sides, 1 to 2 minutes per side. Once done, allow to drain on a wire rack.

4. Ladle a thin layer of Tomato Sauce onto the bottom of an ovenproof casserole dish or hotel pan and top with one layer of the fried eggplant. Top the eggplant with one-third of the grated cheeses. Repeat with more tomato sauce, fried eggplant, and another one-third of the cheese. Add tomato sauce on top and cover with the last one-third of the cheese.

5. Bake the Eggplant Parmesan in a 350°/177°C oven until well browned and bubbly, 20 to 30 minutes. Serve on a deep plate with a piece of Grilled Garlic Bread.

TOMATO SAUCE

YIELD: 2 QT/1.92 L

1 lb/454 g minced onions

3 fl oz/90 mL extra-virgin olive oil

4 garlic cloves, minced

4 lb/1.81 kg tomatoes, canned with juice

2 cups/480 mL tomato purée

1 tbsp/3 g chopped oregano

Salt, as needed

Ground black pepper, as needed

¼ cup/12 g basil, cut into fine chiffonade

1. In a stockpot or similar pot, sweat the onions in the olive oil over very moderate heat until very tender, about 15 minutes.

2. Add the garlic and continue to sweat gently until fragrant, about 30 seconds.

3. Add the tomatoes, tomato purée, and oregano. Bring to a boil and simmer very gently over low heat for about 45 minutes, adding water as needed to maintain a medium nappé. Adjust seasoning with salt and pepper, as needed.

4. Purée the sauce in a food mill or food processor until slightly coarse. Adjust seasoning and add the basil.

RADISH SALAD WITH PORK CRACKLINGS

In Mexican cooking, chicharrones, also known as *pork rinds*, are made by deep-frying cooked and dehydrated pork skin until it is crispy and puffy. Commonly obtained commercially, they are used for stews and stuffing for tortas and tacos. In other Latin American and Caribbean countries, chicharrones are made from pork skins and the underlying meat. One of the most popular cuts for this is pork belly.

YIELD: 8 PORTIONS

1 lb 8 oz/680 g radishes, thinly sliced	6 fl oz/180 mL pure olive oil
2 oz/57 g red onions, sliced paper-thin against the grain	Salt, as needed
	Coarsely cracked black pepper, as needed
2 cups/142 g radish sprouts	½ oz/14 g mint, cut into chiffonade
2 fl oz/60 mL lime juice	½ oz/14 g coarsely chopped cilantro
2 fl oz/60 mL orange juice	4 oz/113 g pork cracklings

1. In a bowl, combine the radishes, onions, and radish sprouts.
2. Add the lime juice, orange juice, and olive oil. Adjust seasoning with salt and pepper.
3. Add the mint and cilantro.
4. Combine everything with the pork cracklings and serve immediately.

TOMATO-BRAISED CAULIFLOWER

YIELD: 8 PORTIONS

8 oz/227 g diced onions	2 cauliflower heads (3 to 3½ lb/1.36 to 1.59 kg), trimmed, cut into bite-size florets
3 fl oz/90 mL extra-virgin olive oil	
8 garlic cloves, minced	2 lb/907 g canned tomatoes with juice
4 bay leaves	Salt, as needed
1 tsp/2 g red pepper flakes	½ oz/14 g basil leaves

1. In a rondeau or similar pot, sweat the onions in the olive oil over moderate heat until very tender, about 5 minutes. Add the garlic, bay leaves, and red pepper flakes and continue to cook until fragrant, about 30 seconds. Add the cauliflower and sweat gently, stirring occasionally, for 5 minutes.

2. Crush the tomatoes and add, with their juice, to the cauliflower.

3. Bring to a boil over low to medium heat, adjust seasoning, and cook, covered with a tight-fitting lid, until the cauliflower is tender and most of the liquid has been absorbed, about 30 minutes.

4. Verify doneness after about 20 minutes. The cauliflower should be fork-tender. If necessary, remove the lid to evaporate excess liquid. At the moment of service, adjust seasoning, add the basil leaves, and serve in a bowl.

SAMFAINA

YIELD: 1½ QT/1.44 L

1 lb 8 oz/680 g large-dice onions	1 lb 8 oz/680 g zucchini, seeded, cut into ¾-in/2-cm dice
4 fl oz/120 mL extra-virgin olive oil	1 lb 8 oz/680 g red peppers, roasted, peeled, cut into ¾-in/2-cm dice
4 garlic cloves, thinly sliced	1 lb/454 g canned whole tomatoes with juice
1 lb/454 g Japanese eggplant, skin on, cut into ¾-in/2-cm dice	Salt, as needed
	Ground black pepper, as needed

1. In a rondeau or similar pot over low heat, sweat the onions in the olive oil until very tender, about 10 minutes. Add the garlic and cook until fragrant, about 30 seconds.

2. Add the eggplant and zucchini and continue to sweat gently until they begin to get tender and until the liquid has evaporated, 5 to 8 minutes, stirring occasionally.

3. Add the peppers and tomatoes, reduce the heat, and simmer uncovered until the liquid has again evaporated and the vegetables are very soft. Adjust seasoning as needed with salt and pepper. Serve in a bowl or on a plate.

CHEF'S NOTES	Samfaina is often referred to as the Catalonian ratatouille. It can be served as a one-pot meal accompanied by some crusty bread or as an adjunct to grilled meat, poultry, or seafood.
	On occasion, the vegetables will be allowed to cook for long enough for the samfaina to reach an almost jam-like texture, and it is served as an accompanying sauce.

ROMESCO SAUCE WITH GRILLED VEGETABLES

YIELD: 8 PORTIONS

2 red peppers	Salt, as needed
2 zucchini	Ground black pepper, as needed
2 Japanese eggplant	8 fl oz/240 mL extra-virgin olive oil
2 russet potatoes	2 fl oz/60 mL sherry vinegar
2 sweet potatoes	Romesco Sauce (page 198)

1. Grill or broil the red peppers until the skin is blistered away from all sides. Place the peppers into a container with a tight-fitting lid or a paper bag and allow them to sweat for 5 minutes. Remove the skin and seeds and cut into quarters.

2. Cut the remaining vegetables into ¼-in/6-mm-thick slices, adjusting the angle as needed to achieve similar-size slices.

3. Season all of the vegetables with a generous amount of salt and pepper and toss with 2 fl oz/60 mL of olive oil.

4. Grill the vegetables over high heat until well-marked and browned on both sides and cooked through, 1 to 2 minutes per side.

5. Arrange the vegetables attractively on a platter, drizzle with the remaining olive oil and the sherry vinegar, and serve with the Romesco Sauce.

ROMESCO SAUCE

Romesco sauce, an iconic component of Spanish cookery, has its origins in Catalonian cuisine. This sauce reflects a traditional Spanish sauce-making technique in which the main item is puréed and body and viscosity is achieved by incorporating ground nuts or bread. The Picada sauce on page 183 follows a similar principle. On many tables in Spain, this sauce is the focus and the fish, seafood, meat, or vegetable is considered of secondary importance.

YIELD: 1 QT/946 ML

2 oz/57 g skinned hazelnuts	1 lb/454 g plum tomatoes
3 oz/85 g skinned almonds, blanched	3 fl oz/90 mL extra-virgin olive oil
4 garlic cloves, peeled	2 fl oz/60 mL sherry vinegar
2 oz/57 g baguette or similar bread, sliced ¼ in/6 mm thick	2 tbsp/6 g chopped flat-leaf parsley
	Salt, as needed
2 lb/907 g red peppers	Ground black pepper, as needed

1. Roast the hazelnuts, almonds, garlic, and bread at 350°F/177°C until lightly browned.

2. Grill the peppers and tomatoes until charred on all sides. Place in a container with a tight-fitting lid. Allow to sweat for 5 minutes, and remove the skins.

3. Combine the hazelnuts, almonds, garlic, bread, peppers, tomatoes, olive oil, vinegar, parsley, salt, and pepper in a food processor and purée into a slightly coarse paste. If needed, adjust viscosity with water. Adjust seasoning as needed with salt and pepper.

VEGETABLE KHORMA

Khorma, occasionally spelled korma, curma, qorma, or kurmais, is an Indian meat or vegetable stew. Made with ground nuts, seeds, and dairy and/or coconut milk, a khorma is commonly creamy and mild. Bold and hot spices are generally avoided or used only in small amounts.

YIELD: 8 PORTIONS

Spice Paste

12 oz/340 g sliced onions

2 oz/57 g ghee

1 tbsp/9 g sliced garlic

1 oz/28 g Fresno chiles, seeded

1 tbsp/9 g blue poppy seeds

1 tbsp/6 g sweet paprika

1 cup/240 mL Bulgarian or similar yogurt

3 tbsp/25 g chickpea flour

¼ cup/18 g desiccated coconut

2 oz/57 g cashews

1 cup/48 g coarsely cut cilantro, with stems

1 lb 8 oz/680 g large-dice red potatoes

1 cauliflower head (1½ to 2 lb/680 to 907 g), cut into bite-size florets

8 oz/227 g large-dice red peppers

8 oz/227 g carrots, peeled, cut into obliques

8 oz/227 g green beans, halved

1 oz/28 g ghee

8 oz/227 g cherry tomatoes, halved

Salt, as needed

1. For the spice paste, sweat the onions in the ghee over moderate heat until very tender and slightly caramelized, about 10 minutes.

2. Add the garlic, chiles, poppy seeds, and paprika and continue to sweat gently until aromatic. Combine with the yogurt, chickpea flour, coconut, cashews, and cilantro in a blender and purée to a fine paste, adding water as needed to facilitate the blending. Set aside.

3. In a rondeau, sweat the potatoes, cauliflower, peppers, carrots, and beans in the ghee over moderate heat until they begin to get tender, 5 to 10 minutes.

4. Add water until barely covered, bring to a boil, adjust seasoning with salt, and simmer gently over moderate heat until all the vegetables are fork-tender, 10 to 15 minutes.

5. Add the spice paste to the vegetables, and simmer for about 2 more minutes. Add the cherry tomatoes, and adjust the seasoning and viscosity until the sauce is a medium nappé.

SPICY STIR-FRIED EGGPLANT

YIELD: 8 PORTIONS

2 lb/907 g Japanese eggplant	1 medium-dice red pepper
Salt, as needed	2 tbsp/25 g sugar
1 tbsp/9 g minced ginger	1½ fl oz/45 mL light soy sauce, not low-sodium
3 garlic cloves, minced	
2 fl oz/60 mL vegetable oil	1 fl oz/30 mL dark rice vinegar
1 fl oz/30 mL chili bean paste	1 green onion, minced
1 medium-dice green pepper	

1. Cut the eggplant into obliques, sprinkle with salt, and set aside for 10 minutes.

2. In a wok over medium-high heat, sweat the ginger and garlic in the vegetable oil until fragrant, about 10 seconds. Add the chili bean paste and continue sweating.

3. Add the eggplant and peppers and stir-fry over moderate heat until fork-tender, 3 to 5 minutes.

4. Add the sugar and continue to stir-fry until the ingredients begin to caramelize. Deglaze with the soy sauce and vinegar. Adjust seasoning as needed. Add the green onions, toss gently, and serve in a bowl.

CHEF'S NOTES

Chili bean paste is a salty paste made from fermented soybeans and chiles. Its main flavor profile is fermented soy with a strong, spicy aftertaste. It can be substituted with a soy paste with the addition of dried hot chiles.

Dark rice vinegar, also known as black rice vinegar, is a very popular condiment in Chinese cooking. It has a strong, almost smoky flavor and is commonly found in many stir-fried and braised dishes. It is not commonly found in dressings or used for cold dishes, because its strong flavor will overpower many other flavors.

ROASTED EGGPLANT PURÉE WITH YOGURT AND WALNUTS

YIELD: 8 PORTIONS

2 large eggplant (1½ to 2 lb/680 to 907 g), cut in half lengthwise

Salt, as needed

3 fl oz/90 mL extra-virgin olive oil

2 oz/57 g toasted walnuts

3 garlic cloves, sliced

3 tbsp/45 mL lemon juice

1 cup/240 mL Greek yogurt, strained

3 tbsp/9 g mint, cut into chiffonade

3 tbsp/9 g chopped flat-leaf parsley

¼ tsp/0.5 g cayenne

Ground black pepper, as needed

Garnish

2 fl oz/60 mL olive oil

1 tbsp/3 g mint, cut into chiffonade

1 cup/120 g toasted walnuts, chopped

Pita Bread (page 111)

1. Rub the flesh side of the eggplant with salt and brush with 1 to 2 tbsp/15 to 30 mL of olive oil per half. With a paring knife, score the flesh about 1 in/3 cm deep.

2. In an oven at 400°F/204°C, roast the eggplant, flesh side up, until lightly charred and cooked through, 10 to 15 minutes. Remove the skin, coarsely chop the eggplant flesh, and set aside.

3. In a food processor, combine the walnuts, garlic, lemon juice, yogurt, mint, and parsley and process into a fine paste.

4. Add the eggplant flesh and cayenne and process into a slightly coarse paste. Adjust seasoning with salt, pepper, and cayenne.

5. At service, sprinkle with olive oil, mint, and walnuts and serve in a cup accompanied by Pita Bread.

SPICY TOFU WITH MUSHROOMS

YIELD: 8 PORTIONS

1 oz/28 g dried shiitake mushrooms

8 oz/227 g oyster mushrooms

8 oz/227 g button-size white mushrooms

1½ tsp/4 g Sichuan pepper

1 tsp/2 g red pepper flakes

2 fl oz/60 mL vegetable oil

2 tbsp/30 mL chili bean paste

2 green onions, minced

2 tsp/6 g ginger, minced

4 garlic cloves, minced

1 tbsp/15 mL Shaoxing wine or sherry

2 fl oz/60 mL light soy sauce, not low-sodium

2 lb/907 g silken tofu, cut into ½-in/1-cm dice

Salt, as needed

Cornstarch slurry, as needed

Garnish

1 green onion, sliced

2 garlic cloves, thinly sliced

1. Soak the shiitakes in water for 12 hours. Remove the stems and cut into small dice.

2. Remove all tough parts of the oyster mushrooms and tear them parallel to the gills into bite-size pieces; set aside. Cut the white mushrooms into quarters.

3. In a skillet over low heat, fry the Sichuan pepper and red pepper flakes in the oil until lightly browned, 30 seconds to 1 minute. Strain the oil into a wok and discard the solids.

4. In the flavored oil over medium heat, sweat the chili bean paste, green onions, ginger, and garlic until fragrant, about 20 seconds. Add the soaked shiitake mushrooms and stir-fry slowly for 1 minute. Add the fresh mushrooms and stir-fry until they have shrunk in size by about half and stop exuding moisture as they cook.

5. Add the wine and soy sauce. Carefully place the diced tofu over the cooked mushrooms in the wok, sprinkle with salt, cover with a lid, and simmer gently for 3 minutes.

6. Very gently mix the tofu with the mushrooms, and thicken lightly with cornstarch slurry to medium nappé, so the juices lightly coat the tofu and mushrooms. Adjust seasonings as needed. Serve in a bowl and garnish with the sliced green onion and garlic.

CHEF'S NOTES

This dish exemplifies a common flavor profile of Sichuan. Known as *Má Là* in Chinese, this "numb and spicy" flavor combines the burn of the dried chiles with the numbing sensation of the Sichuan peppers. These are not a true pepper, but the dried flower bud of a prickly ash tree.

Silken tofu is a very soft tofu with the mouthfeel of fine custard. It has a high water content and needs to be handled gently to prevent breaking it during cooking.

GRILLED SWEET POTATOES

YIELD: 8 PORTIONS

3 lb/1.36 kg sweet potatoes, peeled, sliced lengthwise ¼ in/6 mm thick

Salt, as needed

Ground black pepper, as needed

3 fl oz/90 mL extra-virgin olive oil

2 oz/57 g pomegranate molasses

1. Season the sweet potato slices with salt and pepper and toss in the olive oil.

2. Grill on both sides over moderate to high heat until cooked through and well caramelized, 1 to 2 minutes per side.

3. Once the sweet potato is done, brush with the pomegranate molasses and flip over to brush the other side. Allow the pomegranate molasses to caramelize on both sides. Remove from the grill quickly, to prevent the pomegranate molasses from burning.

4. Arrange on a platter and drizzle generously with olive oil. Serve on a plate.

CHEF'S NOTE Pomegranate molasses, a common ingredient in Middle Eastern cooking, adds a tart and acidic dimension to many dishes. It is made by reducing the juice of tart pomegranate varieties.

VEGETABLES IN SPICY COCONUT MILK

YIELD: 8 PORTIONS

2 garlic cloves, minced	8 oz/227 g white mushrooms, cut into quarters
2 red Thai bird chiles, minced	
1 tbsp/6 g minced galangal	8 oz/227 g bok choy, stems cut into large dice, leaves cut into chiffonade
1 stalk lemongrass (½ to ¾ oz/14 g to 21 g), minced	
	4 oz/113 g cherry tomatoes
2 fl oz/60 mL vegetable oil	1 pint/480 mL coconut milk
3 tbsp/45 mL Thai red curry paste	4 lime leaves, bruised
1 red pepper (5 to 6 oz/142 g to 170 g), cut into large dice	2 tbsp/30 mL Thai fish sauce
	2 tbsp/25 g palm sugar
8 oz/227 g sugar snap peas, strings removed	1 cup/35 g basil leaves
	½ cup/24 g coarsely cut cilantro
8 oz/227 g carrots, cut into obliques	

1. In a wok or similar pan over moderate heat, sweat the garlic, chiles, galangal, and lemongrass in the vegetable oil until aromatic, about 1 minute. Add the curry paste and continue to sweat over moderate heat for about 30 seconds.

2. Add the red pepper, peas, carrots, mushrooms, bok choy, and tomatoes. Continue to stir-fry until everything is well coated and begins to get tender, 2 to 3 minutes.

3. Add the coconut milk and lime leaves, and adjust seasoning with fish sauce and palm sugar as needed. Bring to a boil and simmer gently over low heat until everything is fork-tender, about 10 minutes. Taste and adjust seasoning and viscosity as needed to reach medium nappé.

4. At service, add the basil and cilantro and mix gently. Serve in a deep bowl.

RUTABAGA STEW

YIELD: 8 PORTIONS

One 1-lb/454-g smoked ham hock

3 qt/2.84 L chicken stock

1 lb/454 g large-dice onions

2 oz/57 g lard

1 lb 8 oz/680 g cured and smoked pork butt, cut into large dice

3 lb/1.36 kg large-dice rutabagas

1 lb/454 g yellow potatoes, peeled, cut into large dice

Salt, as needed

Ground black pepper, as needed

¼ cup/12 g parsley, chopped not too finely

Coarsely cracked black pepper (optional)

1. Simmer the ham hock in the stock over low to medium heat until fork-tender, 1½ to 3 hours. Once tender, remove the hock from the stock and take off all meat from the bone and skin, dice it, and set aside. Reserve the resulting ham hock and stock.

2. In a stockpot over medium heat, sweat the onions in the lard until translucent, 5 to 8 minutes. Add the pork butt and continue to sweat for 2 to 3 minutes.

3. Add the rutabagas, potatoes, cooked ham hock meat, and stock, bring to a boil, and simmer gently over low to medium heat until everything is tender, 30 to 45 minutes. Adjust seasoning as needed.

4. At service, add the parsley and optionally add a generous amount of coarsely cracked black pepper. Serve in a soup bowl.

CHEF'S NOTE | This dish is a good representative of the one-pot dishes in German cuisine. Hearty and easy to prepare with simple means, these types of stews provide a substantial meal, especially during cold winter seasons.

EGGS IN CURRY

YIELD: 8 PORTIONS

2 fl oz/60 mL vegetable oil	1 tbsp/6 g ground turmeric
1½ tsp/3 g cumin seeds	1½ tsp/3 g ground chile
1½ tsp/3 g black mustard seeds	1½ qt/1.44 L crushed tomatoes
1 sprig curry leaves	Salt, as needed
8 oz/227 g medium-dice yellow onions	Ground black pepper, as needed
	16 hard-cooked eggs, peeled
4 garlic cloves, sliced	Vegetable oil, as needed
1 tbsp/9 g minced ginger	1 tbsp/6 g garam masala
1 tbsp/6 g ground coriander	1 cup/48 g coarsely cut cilantro

1. Heat the vegetable oil in a wok over medium heat, and add the cumin seeds and mustard seeds and fry until they crackle, 10 to 20 seconds.

2. Add the curry leaves and cook until wilted, 10 to 20 seconds.

3. Add the onions and cook over moderate heat until golden brown, 5 to 10 minutes.

4. Add the garlic and ginger and continue to cook until fragrant, about 30 seconds. Add the coriander, turmeric, and ground chile and continue to cook gently until fragrant, 10 to 20 seconds.

5. Add the tomatoes and simmer slowly until the sauce thickens, 15 to 20 minutes. Adjust seasoning with salt and pepper.

6. Fry the eggs in the vegetable oil over medium heat until golden brown on all sides, 2 to 3 minutes. Add the eggs to the tomato curry sauce and continue to cook until the eggs are heated through. Add the garam masala and cilantro; mix gently and serve immediately. Serve eggs with sauce in a bowl.

CHEF'S NOTE

Garam masala, literally meaning "warming spices," is a combination of spices originating in Indian cuisine. The exact mixture varies, but common components are black pepper, cardamom, cinnamon, clove, and cumin seeds.

GRILLED ZUCCHINI KEBOB

YIELD: 8 PORTIONS

Charmoula

2 garlic cloves, minced

1½ tsp/3 g ground coriander

¼ preserved lemon, finely diced

½ oz/14 g minced parsley

½ oz/14 g minced cilantro

½ tsp/0.5 g ground saffron

½ tsp/1 g sweet paprika

¼ tsp/0.5 g cayenne

3 fl oz/90 mL extra-virgin olive oil

1 fl oz/30 mL lemon juice

3 lb/1.36 kg zucchini, quartered lengthwise, seeded, cut into large dice

Salt, as needed

1 fl oz/30 mL olive oil

8 flat metal skewers

Garnish

2 tbsp/6 g chopped flat-leaf parsley

2 tbsp/6 g coarsely cut cilantro

1. To make the charmoula, combine the garlic, coriander, preserved lemon, parsley, cilantro, saffron, paprika, cayenne, olive oil, lemon juice, and 1 fl oz/30 mL water and mix well.

2. Season the zucchini with salt and toss in the olive oil; thread on the skewers.

3. Grill over very high heat until slightly charred and cooked through, 1 to 2 minutes per side. Brush with the charmoula and allow it to caramelize slightly. The zucchini should be slightly charred and fork-tender.

4. Serve skewer garnished with parsley and cilantro.

CHEF'S NOTES

Charmoula is a popular marinade used in northwestern African cuisines. It is commonly used for fish and seafood, vegetables, and meat. Recipes for charmoula vary greatly from region to region and from family to family, but garlic, coriander, cumin, and preserved lemon are found in almost every version.

Preserved lemons are a significant component in North African, especially Moroccan, cuisine, as well as in southern Indian cuisine. Preserved lemons are made by fermenting fresh lemons in a brine made from lemon juice, salt, and spices for weeks or months at room temperature. After fermentation, the most valuable part is the rind, with its gentle tartness and very intense lemon flavor.

GRILLED CORN ON THE COB

YIELD: 8 PORTIONS

8 cobs sweet corn, husked	4 limes
Vegetable oil, as needed	¾ cup/180 mL mayonnaise
Salt, as needed	4 oz/113 g grated queso cotija
8 heavy-duty bamboo skewers	Dried pequin chile, finely ground, as needed

1. Rub the corn with oil and season with salt.

2. Grill on a medium-hot grill until slightly charred on all sides and heated through, 5 to 10 minutes.

3. Remove the ears from the heat, and spear each with a bamboo skewer.

4. Squeeze the lime juice over the corn, spread with the mayonnaise, and sprinkle with the cheese and ground chile. Serve hot.

CHEF'S NOTES

Queso cotija is a hard cow's milk cheese from Mexico with a delicate, slightly salty flavor. If not available, queso fresco or a similar cheese may be substituted.

Pequin chiles are very small, very hot peppers that are used frequently in northeastern Mexican and other Latin cuisines.

CARIBBEAN VEGETABLE KEBOB

YIELD: 8 PORTIONS

Kebob

24 cipollini onions, peeled

24 large garlic cloves, peeled

2 ripe plantains

2 red peppers

2 green peppers

1 pineapple

24 cherry tomatoes

8 flat metal skewers

Grilling Sauce

8 oz/227 g diced pineapple

2 fl oz/60 mL lime juice

2 fl oz/60 mL molasses

2 garlic cloves, peeled

¼ Scotch Bonnet chile, seeded, minced

Salt, as needed

Ground black pepper, as needed

1. Briefly parboil the onions and garlic in salted water over high heat until semi-tender, 30 seconds to 1 minute. Shock in ice water and set aside.

2. Roast the plantains at 350°F/177°C until cooked halfway and partially fork-tender, 5 to 10 minutes. Allow to cool, and peel.

3. Cut the red and green peppers, plantains, and pineapple into about 1-in/3-cm dice. Thread the onions, garlic, peppers, pineapple, and tomatoes alternately onto the skewers.

4. For the Grilling Sauce, combine the diced pineapple, lime juice, molasses, garlic, and chile in a blender and purée until smooth.

5. Simmer the sauce in a saucepan over low heat and reduce until it reaches a light to medium nappé.

6. Season all kebobs with salt and pepper and grill over direct high heat until tender and slightly charred, 2 to 3 minutes per side. Brush with the Grilling Sauce and continue to grill until caramelized, about 1 minute.

PAKORA FRIED VEGETABLE SKEWER

YIELD: 8 PORTIONS

½ head cauliflower	1½ tsp/3 g garam masala
8 large white mushrooms	½ tsp/1 g garlic powder
Vegetable oil, as needed	¼ tsp/0.5 g cayenne
1 carrot	1 tbsp/10 g salt
1 zucchini	
1 green pepper	Salt, as needed
Batter	Ground black pepper, as needed
3½ oz/99 g chickpea flour	8 bamboo skewers
3½ oz/99 g all-purpose flour	All-purpose flour, as needed, for dredging
1½ tsp/6 g baking powder	Cilantro-Cashew Chutney (page 116)

1. Cut the cauliflower into bite-size florets and briefly parboil over high heat until semi-tender, about 30 seconds.

2. In a skillet over very high heat, sauté the mushrooms in vegetable oil until slightly caramelized.

3. Cut the carrot into obliques and parboil over high heat until semi-tender, about 30 seconds.

4. Cut the zucchini lengthwise into quarters, remove the seeds, and cut into dice. Add to a skillet and sauté over very high heat until slightly caramelized.

5. Cut the pepper into large dice.

6. For the batter, combine the flours, baking powder, garam masala, garlic powder, cayenne, and salt in a mixing bowl. Add 1 pint/480 mL water and mix until smooth.

7. Season all the vegetables with salt and pepper after they are cooked. Place one piece of each vegetable onto each skewer. Dredge the skewers in flour and shake off excess. Dip in the batter to coat completely.

8. Deep-fry at 350°F/177°C until golden brown and crispy, 3 to 5 minutes. Drain on a wire rack. Serve skewer on a plate accompanied by Cilantro-Cashew Chutney.

CHEF'S NOTE

Many culinary cultures include batter-fried dishes in their repertoire. Pakora, served in Indian cuisine, uses a batter based on chickpea flour in which vegetables, or sometimes bread, are dipped and deep-fried until crispy. This version is made with half chickpea flour and half all-purpose flour to allow some leavening and to make the crust more tender and airy.

PAN-FRIED QUESADILLAS

Quesadillas, originating in Mexico, can be defined as a flour or corn tortilla with a filling containing cheese and other ingredients. Quesadillas vary tremendously from region to region, and it is a challenge to find two Mexican chefs who agree on quesadillas.

YIELD: 8 PORTIONS

Dough

14 oz/397 g masa harina

2 cups/480 mL warm water

Filling

Huitlacoche Filling (page 219)

Nopales Filling (page 220)

Vegetable oil, as needed, for frying

Salsa Verde (page 248)

1. To make the dough, combine the masa harina and warm water in a stand mixer.
2. Knead the resulting dough for 5 to 8 minutes; it should feel like soft clay and be slightly above body temperature. Allow the dough to rest for 15 minutes.
3. Divide the dough into 16 Ping-Pong–size balls. Using a tortilla press lined with plastic on both sides, press a dough ball into a thin tortilla. Press once and rotate 180 degrees before pressing again to achieve an even thickness of about ⅛ in/3 mm.
4. Remove the top sheet of plastic and place about 1 oz/28 g of one of the fillings onto the dough.
5. Use the lower sheet of plastic to fold the dough in half and seal the edges by pinching.
6. Gently slide the quesadilla into preheated vegetable oil in a cast-iron skillet and cook over medium heat until well browned on both sides, 1 to 2 minutes per side. Allow to drain on a wire rack, and serve quesadillas with Salsa Verde.

CHEF'S NOTES

Made with a raw dough based on masa, this dish resembles what is known in many regions as an empanada. Yet one of the CIA's Latin American cuisine experts, Chef Iliana de la Vega, assured me that this is a true quesadilla.

Masa harina is the commercially available dried form of masa, the dough traditionally used in Mexico for corn tortillas and tamales, among other things. Masa is made by briefly boiling and then soaking field corn overnight in a solution made from water and limestone, also known as slaked lime or cal. The soaked corn is ground on a metate, a traditional grinding stone dating back to Mesoamerican times, into varying degrees of coarseness depending on its desired use.

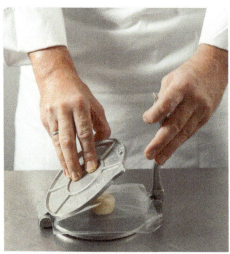
Press the corn tortilla dough between two pieces of heavy-duty plastic wrap in a tortilla press.

Remove the top piece of heavy-duty plastic wrap from the pressed tortilla.

Spoon the filling into the tortilla and use the plastic to fold the tortilla over, encasing the filling.

Pan fry the quesadillas until golden on both sides.

HUITLACOCHE FILLING

YIELD: 8 PORTIONS

3 oz/85 g minced onions

2 garlic cloves, minced

1 fl oz/30 mL pure olive oil

1 serrano, seeded, minced (about
1 tbsp/7 g)

8 oz/227 g huitlacoche

Juice of 1 lime

¼ tsp/0.5 g dried epazote

¼ tsp/0.5 g Mexican oregano

Salt, as needed

Ground black pepper, as needed

8 oz/227 g grated queso Chihuahua or similar
cheese

1. Sweat the onions and garlic in the olive oil in a skillet over moderate heat until translucent, about 2 minutes.

2. Add the serrano and continue to cook. Add the huitlacoche and simmer gently over low to medium heat for 4 to 5 minutes.

3. Add the lime juice, epazote, and oregano and adjust seasoning with salt, pepper, and more lime juice as needed. Add the cheese.

CHEF'S NOTE

Huitlacoche, also known as *corn smut* or *corn truffle,* is a specialty in Mexican cuisine. It is corn that has been infected by a parasitic fungus, causing the kernels to swell and turn black. While it does not look particularly appetizing to the untrained eye, huitlacoche has a very pleasant, smoky aroma and the property of enhancing other flavors due to the natural occurrence of glutamic acid in the fungus.

NOPALES FILLING

YIELD: 8 PORTIONS

1 lb/454 g nopales	Ground black pepper, as needed
1 fl oz/30 mL pure olive oil	½ oz/14 g coarsely cut cilantro
3 oz/85 g minced onion	8 oz/227 g grated queso Chihuahua
Juice of 1 lime	or similar cheese
Salt, as needed	

1. Clean the nopales of all spikes and cut into medium dice.

2. In a very hot skillet, sear the nopales in the olive oil until slightly browned on all sides, 2 to 3 minutes.

3. Add the minced onion and continue to cook until translucent, about 2 minutes.

4. Adjust seasoning as needed with lime juice, salt, and pepper. Add the cilantro and the cheese.

CHEF'S NOTES

Nopales are the hand-size fleshy pad segments of the prickly pear. Although preferred fresh in Mexico, southern Texas, and New Mexico, canned versions are available. Be careful not to overcook nopales; just like okra, they have the tendency to thicken surrounding liquids to a mucus-like consistency. This effect can be limited by sautéing nopales at a high temperature in a small amount of fat.

Queso Chihuahua is a semisoft cow's milk cheese named after its place of origin, the Mexican state of Chihuahua. This cheese has a mild flavor and is suitable for melting applications. If needed, Jack or a similar cheese can be substituted for queso Chihuahua.

TACOS WITH POBLANO PEPPERS IN CREAM

This taco filling, known as *rajas con crema*, is very popular in central and southern Mexico. Literally translated, it means "strips with cream."

YIELD: 8 PORTIONS

8 poblano peppers

8 oz/227 g sliced onions

2 fl oz/60 mL vegetable oil

1 cup/240 mL Mexican Cream (page 119) or crème fraîche

Salt, as needed

Corn Tortillas (page 279)

3 oz/85 g panela cheese or similar cheese

1. Roast the poblano peppers over an open flame until the skin is charred on all sides. Place the roasted peppers in a paper bag or a container with a tight-fitting lid and allow the peppers to sweat for 10 to 15 minutes.

2. Peel the peppers and remove all seeds and membrane skins. Cut the flesh into ½-in/1-cm-wide strips.

3. In a skillet over low heat, sweat the onions in the vegetable oil until translucent and very tender, 5 to 8 minutes. Add the sliced pepper and the Mexican Cream. Continue to cook until heated through and the cream has reduced to a thick viscosity, 3 to 5 minutes.

4. Adjust seasoning with salt and serve in preheated tortillas topped with the cheese.

CHEF'S NOTE | Panela cheese, or queso panela, is a semisoft Mexican cow's milk cheese with characteristics comparable to mozzarella. Panela is particularly well suited for frying and grilling because it does not melt easily when heated.

VEGETABLE SANDWICH WITH MANCHEGO CHEESE

YIELD: 8 PORTIONS

Dressing

½ tsp/0.5 g chopped thyme

2 garlic cloves, minced

2 fl oz/60 mL Dijon mustard

2 tbsp/30 mL sherry vinegar

2 tbsp/30 mL honey

2 fl oz/60 mL extra-virgin olive oil

Grilled Vegetables

2 medium zucchini

2 Japanese eggplant

2 red peppers

2 poblano peppers

8 medium portobello mushrooms

Salt, as needed

Ground black pepper, as needed

4 fl oz/120 mL extra-virgin olive oil

8 ciabatta rolls or similar rolls

Herbed Tapenade (page 249)

1 cup/240 mL toasted pine nuts

8 oz/227 g manchego cheese, sliced

8 oz/227 g baby arugula

Olive oil, as needed

Sherry vinegar, as needed

1. Combine the thyme, garlic, mustard, vinegar, honey, and olive oil for the dressing.

2. Cut the zucchini and eggplant into ¼- to ½-in/½- to 1-cm-thick slices on a bias. Adjust the angle as necessary to achieve similar-size slices.

3. Roast the red peppers and poblanos under a broiler, turning frequently, until the skin is completely blistered. Allow to sweat for 10 minutes in a closed container. Peel, remove the seeds, and cut into slices.

4. Remove the stems and gills of the mushrooms.

5. Season all the vegetables with a generous amount of salt and pepper and toss with the olive oil. Grill the vegetables over high heat until well browned on both sides and almost cooked through, 1 to 2 minutes per side.

6. Brush the vegetables on both sides with the dressing and allow to caramelize on both sides over high heat, 30 seconds to 1 minute per side. Once done, remove the vegetables from the grill and set aside.

7. Split the ciabatta rolls, toast under a broiler, and spread tapenade on both sides.

8. Distribute the grilled vegetables evenly onto the lower halves of the rolls. Sprinkle the pine nuts onto the vegetables, top with the sliced cheese, and allow to melt under a broiler.

9. Top with the baby arugula, drizzle with some olive oil and sherry vinegar, and top with the other half of the roll. Serve on a plate.

LEEK QUICHE

Quiches, originally open-faced pies with a savory custard, bacon, and cheese from the Alsace and Lorraine regions of France, have evolved into a very popular quick lunch or even breakfast. Nowadays, an endless choice of ingredients can be found featured in quiche.

YIELD: 8 PORTIONS (2 PIECES)

Dough

1 lb/454 g all-purpose flour, chilled

1 tbsp/10 g salt

9½ oz/269 g medium-dice butter, ice cold

5 fl oz/150 mL water, ice cold

Leek Filling

2 lb/907 g leeks, light green and white parts, sliced

2 garlic cloves, minced

2 oz/57 g unsalted butter

Salt, as needed

Ground black pepper, as needed

2 eggs

½ cup/120 mL half-and-half

Pinch of grated nutmeg

4 oz/113 g grated Gruyère cheese

1. For the quiche dough, combine the flour and salt. Add the butter to the flour and break the butter into hazelnut-size pieces. Add the cold water and mix to barely incorporate. Chunks of butter should be visible in the dough. Wrap in plastic and allow to rest under refrigeration for at least 30 minutes.

2. Roll the dough out to a ⅛-in/3-mm thickness, and line 2 pie tins with the dough. Blind-bake the dough in a 400°F/204°C oven until lightly browned, about 10 minutes.

3. For the leek filling, sweat the leeks and garlic in the butter over medium heat until tender, 5 to 10 minutes, and season with salt and pepper as needed. Set aside and allow to cool.

4. Thoroughly combine the eggs with the half-and-half. Combine the egg mixture with the cooked leeks, add the nutmeg, and adjust seasoning as needed.

5. Pour the leek mixture into the blind-baked quiche crusts and top with the grated cheese. Bake the quiches at 375°F/191°C in a convection oven until golden and thoroughly cooked, 10 to 15 minutes. Allow to rest for at least 10 to 15 minutes in a warm area.

6. At service, cut each quiche into 8 wedges.

SAMOSAS

YIELD: 8 PORTIONS (24 SMALL SAMOSAS)

Filling

2 lb/907 g Yukon gold or similar potatoes

1 tsp/2 g coriander seeds

1 tsp/2 g cumin seeds

2 fl oz/60 mL vegetable oil

12 oz/340 g minced yellow onions

1 tbsp/9 g minced ginger

1 jalapeño, minced

½ tsp/0.5 g cayenne

½ cup/32 g green peas

¼ cup/12 g coarsely cut cilantro

Salt, as needed

2 oz/57 g all-purpose flour

3 fl oz/90 mL water

12 Chinese spring roll wrappers

Vegetable oil, as needed, for frying

Cilantro-Cashew Chutney (page 116), as needed

1. For the filling, bake the potatoes at 400°F/204°C until thoroughly cooked. Cut the potatoes in half lengthwise and force the potatoes, flesh side down, through a medium-size wire rack into a hotel pan; the skins will stay behind on the wire rack. Mash with your hands into a chunky and slightly cohesive mass. Set aside.

2. In a wok or similar pan over medium to high heat, fry the coriander and cumin seeds in the oil until they begin to pop, 10 to 30 seconds. Add the onions and sweat gently until they are well caramelized, 5 to 8 minutes. Add the ginger and jalapeño and cook until fragrant, about 30 seconds. Add the cayenne and sweat briefly, about 10 seconds.

3. Add the potatoes, peas, and cilantro. Mix gently and adjust seasoning with salt as needed. Make sure to maintain a chunky yet cohesive texture.

4. Combine the flour and water into a paste and set aside.

5. Cut the spring roll wrappers in half into long rectangles and place one vertically in front of you. To assemble, place 1 to 2 tbsp of the filling in a thin layer on the spring roll wrapper about 1 in/3 cm away from the lower end and fold the end over the filling to form a triangle. Continue to fold in triangles, resembling a flag fold. At the last fold, seal the edges with the flour and water paste.

6. Deep-fry in 360°F/182°C vegetable oil until golden brown; remove and drain on a wire rack. Serve samosas on a plate with Cilantro-Cashew Chutney or a chutney of your choice.

| CHEF'S NOTE | Samosas, well-liked snacks in India for many centuries, have now gained popularity with regional interpretations all over the world. A samosa can be defined as a fried, triangular pastry with a savory filling. This recipe, which uses Chinese spring roll wrappers, is very popular in Myanmar. |

Pressing the halved cooked potato through a cooling wire rack removes the flesh in an evenly chunky mixture, leaving the skin behind.

Place a spoonful of filling on the lower right side of the wrapper before proceeding with the flag fold.

Fold the wrapper over, encasing the filling and forming a triangle shape.

Deep-fry the samosas until golden and crisp.

228　CHAPTER 4　Vegetables

PORTOBELLO SANDWICH WITH MADEIRA-GLAZED ONIONS AND BRIE

YIELD: 8 PORTIONS

2 fl oz/60 mL extra-virgin olive oil	Salt, as needed
12 oz/340 g sliced onions	Ground black pepper, as needed
2 garlic cloves, minced	1 romaine heart (8 oz/227 g)
2 fl oz/60 mL Madeira wine	16 slices artisan sourdough bread
½ tsp/1 g dried oregano	1 lb/454 g Brie or similar cheese, cut into ¼-in/6-mm slices
8 large portobello mushrooms	

1. In a saucepan or similar pan, sweat the onions in 1 fl oz/30 mL of the olive oil over moderate heat until very tender and slightly caramelized, 8 to 10 minutes. Add the garlic and cook until aromatic, about 30 seconds. Add the Madeira wine and oregano and reduce until the wine is completely evaporated. Set aside.

2. De-stem the mushrooms and remove the gills, then toss the mushrooms in the remaining olive oil, and season with salt and pepper. Grill or broil until fully cooked, pliable, and slightly browned, 2 to 3 minutes. When cool enough to handle, slice the mushrooms.

3. To assemble the sandwiches, place some romaine lettuce onto 8 slices of bread and top with the sliced mushrooms. Top with the cooked onions, the sliced cheese, and a second slice of bread.

4. Press gently and serve immediately. Alternatively, the sandwich can be toasted in a panini press.

TOMATO AND LAMB BREADS

YIELD: 8 PORTIONS

Dough

10 fl oz/300 mL lukewarm water

1 tbsp/15 mL honey

½ tsp/2 g active dry yeast

8 oz/227 g whole wheat flour

8 oz/227 g bread flour

1 fl oz/30 mL extra-virgin olive oil

2 tsp/6 g salt

Topping

3 oz/85 g minced onions

1 fl oz/30 mL extra-virgin olive oil

3 garlic cloves, minced

6 oz/170 g lamb, ground very finely

12 oz/340 g canned tomatoes, drained, chopped

1 tsp/3 g sweet paprika

⅛ tsp/0.25 g cayenne

⅛ tsp/0.25 g ground cinnamon

⅛ tsp/0.25 g ground allspice

1 tsp/1 g chopped oregano

Salt, as needed

Ground black pepper, as needed

1 tbsp/15 mL lemon juice

1. In a mixer with a dough hook, combine the water, honey, and yeast and mix gently to rehydrate the yeast, about 1 minute. Add the flours, olive oil, and salt and mix on low speed to achieve a smooth and pliable dough, about 1 minute. Keep the dough in a bowl, covered with plastic wrap, in a warm spot and allow the dough to double in size, 30 to 90 minutes.

2. In a skillet over medium heat, cook the onions in the olive oil until soft and slightly caramelized, 5 to 8 minutes. Add the garlic, lamb, tomatoes, paprika, cayenne, cinnamon, allspice, and oregano and continue cooking until soft and all the liquid has evaporated, 5 to 10 minutes. Adjust seasoning with salt, pepper, and lemon juice.

3. Cut the dough into eight 3-oz/85-g pieces, roll them into buns, and allow to rest, covered with plastic wrap, for 15 minutes.

4. Roll the dough into very thin circles measuring about 8 in/20 cm, dock the dough with a fork or stipple with your fingers, spread thinly with the topping, and immediately bake directly on the hearth or on a pizza stone at 450°F/232°C until lightly browned but still pliable, 2 to 4 minutes.

CHEF'S NOTES

Also known as *lahmacun,* this flatbread is very popular at Turkish street-food stands in Germany and is oftentimes served as a wrapper around vegetables, kebobs, or meatballs.

To prevent the bread from blistering during baking, it is crucial to dock or stipple the dough after rolling and to bake the flatbread immediately after it is rolled and topped.

230 CHAPTER 4 Vegetables

ONION CAKE

YIELD: 8 PORTIONS

Dough

11 fl oz/330 mL lukewarm water

2 tsp/8 g active dry yeast

1 lb/454 g all-purpose flour

1 oz/28 g butter, softened

1 tbsp/10 g salt

Filling

4 oz/113 g bacon, cut into small dice

2 oz/57 g vegetable oil

3 lb/1.36 kg sliced onions

Salt, as needed

Ground black pepper, as needed

¾ cup/180 mL whole milk

¾ cup/180 mL sour cream

3 eggs, beaten

Pinch of grated nutmeg

4 oz/113 g grated Gruyère cheese

1. To make the dough, combine the water and yeast in the bowl of an electric mixer. Add the flour, softened butter, and salt. Mix thoroughly and knead to achieve a smooth and pliable dough, 1 to 2 minutes. Place the dough into a mixing bowl, cover with plastic wrap, store in a warm space, and allow the dough to double in size.

2. Fold the dough over on itself a few times, cover with plastic again, and allow it to double in size again, 30 to 90 minutes.

3. To make the filling, render the bacon in the vegetable oil in a large skillet over medium heat until crispy, 1 to 2 minutes. Remove the bacon and set aside.

4. In the bacon's pan drippings and fat, sweat the onions over medium heat, stirring frequently, until very tender and slightly caramelized, about 20 minutes. Season with salt and pepper as needed and set aside to cool.

5. Thoroughly combine the milk, sour cream, and eggs in a large mixing bowl. Add the cooked onions and the crispy bacon, mix well, and adjust seasoning with salt, pepper, and nutmeg.

6. Butter and flour a 12- by 18-in/30- by 46-cm sheet pan and roll the dough to fit that pan. Lay the dough in the pan, cover with plastic, and let rest for 20 to 30 minutes. Spread the onion, egg, and sour cream mix over the dough and top with the cheese.

7. Bake the onion cake at 400°F/204°C until fully cooked and well browned on top. After baking, allow the onion cake to rest for about 15 minutes and then cut into 16 pieces.

CHEF'S NOTE

Known as *Zwiebeluchen*, this specialty from southwestern Germany is commonly served during late summer and early fall, accompanied by the first new wines of the season. Known as *Federweisser* in Germany, these young, still actively fermenting wines provide a perfect flavor match for the onion cake. These wines are not available outside Germany. Vinho Verde from Portugal or Grüner Veltiner from Austria are good substitutes.

Recipes   233

MANIOC FRIES

YIELD: 8 PORTIONS

3 lb/1.36 kg whole manioc	Ground black pepper, as needed
1 gal/3.84 L cold water	Cayenne, as needed
Vegetable oil, as needed for frying	Tomato Ketchup (page 114)
Salt, as needed	

1. Peel the manioc and cut into sticks measuring ¼ by ¼ by 2 in/6 mm by 6 mm by 5 cm. Submerge in the cold water and wash thoroughly to remove excess surface starch. Allow to drain in a colander and pat dry with a clean kitchen towel.

2. Deep-fry the manioc at 275°F/135°C until fork-tender but not browned, 3 to 5 minutes. Drain well, set aside, and allow to cool completely.

3. At service, deep-fry at 325°F/163°C until golden brown and crispy, 5 to 7 minutes. Toss with salt, pepper, and cayenne and serve immediately, accompanied by the ketchup.

ONION FRITTERS

This dish is a southern Indian variation of the well-known pakora, which consists of vegetables deep-fried in a chickpea batter. Pakora is particularly popular in quick-service restaurants and street-food stands in London.

YIELD: 8 PORTIONS

Batter

6 oz/170 g chickpea flour (besan)

1 tbsp/15 mL vegetable oil

1 tsp/2 g ground coriander

2 tsp/4 g ground cumin

Salt, as needed

1 jalapeño, minced

1 cup/240 mL warm water

1 lb/454 g thinly sliced onions

1 cup/240 mL coarsely cut cilantro

Chickpea flour (besan), as needed

Vegetable oil, as needed, for frying

Honey-Tomato-Almond Chutney (page 250)

1. Combine the flour, oil, coriander, cumin, salt, jalapeño, and water and mix thoroughly. Add more water as needed to achieve a consistency comparable to a pancake batter. Allow the batter to rest for 30 minutes.

2. Combine the onions and cilantro and dust with chickpea flour until evenly coated with a thin layer. Combine the onions with the batter until evenly coated.

3. Fry 1- to 2-oz/28- to 57-g fritters at 375°F/191°C until crispy and golden brown on all sides, 2 to 4 minutes. Remove and drain on a wire rack.

4. Serve fritters on a plate, with the Honey-Tomato-Almond Chutney served separately.

PLANTAIN FRITTERS

YIELD: 8 PORTIONS

2 lb/907 g green plantains

Vegetable oil, as needed, for frying

Dipping Water

6 garlic cloves, peeled

4 green onions

1 Scotch Bonnet chile, stem and seeds removed

1 oz/28 g salt

Salt, as needed

Ground black pepper, as needed

Aioli (page 182)

Poblano Coulis (page 250)

1. Peel the plantains and cut them into 2-in/5-cm rounds. Deep-fry in vegetable oil at 350°F/177°C until well browned, 2 to 4 minutes. Drain on a wire rack and press, using a wooden board or a skillet, to a thickness of ¼ in/6 mm.

2. For the dipping water, purée the garlic, green onions, chile, and salt with 1 qt/960 mL water in a blender until very smooth.

3. At service, dip the precooked and pressed plantains in the dipping water, shake off excess liquid, and fry at 375°F/191°C until well browned and very crispy, 3 to 5 minutes.

4. Allow to drain on a wire rack and season with salt and pepper as needed. Serve on a plate with Aioli or Poblano Coulis.

CHEF'S NOTE | Known as *tostones*, these plantain fritters are a well-liked snack in many Latin American and Caribbean cuisines. Their popularity is comparable to that of French fries in central Europe. They can be served plain, with dipping sauces, or as an accompaniment to meat or vegetables. It is vital to the success of this dish to use very firm, green plantains. Ripe plantains are too soft and brown too quickly.

Deep-fry the plantain pieces until they are golden.

Use the bottom of a skillet to press the plantain into a disk.

Pour the dipping water over the disks, and then shake off the excess.

Deep-fry the plantain disks a second time until golden and crisp.

DEEP-FRIED POTATO BALLS

YIELD: 8 PORTIONS

3 lb/1.36 kg Yukon gold or similar potatoes

1 fl oz/30 mL vegetable oil

1½ tsp/3 g red pepper flakes

1 tsp/4 g brown mustard seeds

2 tbsp/10 g husked black lentils (urad dal)

1 sprig curry leaves

12 oz/340 g minced onions

2 tbsp/16 g minced ginger

¾ oz/21 g minced serranos

1 tsp/3 g ground turmeric

½ cup/24 g coarsely cut cilantro

Salt, as needed

Batter

8 oz/227 g chickpea flour (besan)

½ tsp/1 g cayenne

Salt, as needed

11 fl oz/330 mL water

Vegetable oil, as needed, for frying

Cilantro-Cashew Chutney (page 116)

1. Bake the potatoes at 400°F/204°C until tender or easily pierced with a paring knife, 30 to 45 minutes. Cut the potatoes in half lengthwise and force the potatoes, flesh side down, through a medium-size wire rack into a hotel pan; the skins will stay behind on the wire rack.

2. Once the potatoes are cool enough to touch, mash with your hands into a chunky and slightly cohesive mass. Set aside.

3. In a skillet or wok over medium heat, heat the oil, add the red pepper flakes, mustard seeds, and black lentils, and fry until the mustard seeds begin to pop, about 30 seconds.

4. Add the curry leaves and cook over medium heat until wilted, 5 to 10 seconds. Add the onions and cook over low to medium heat until well caramelized, 8 to 10 minutes.

5. Add the ginger, serranos, and turmeric and sweat until aromatic, about 30 seconds.

6. Add the potatoes and cilantro, combine gently, and adjust seasoning with salt.

7. Combine the flour, cayenne, salt, and water into a smooth batter. Add water as needed.

8. Shape the potato filling into 1-in/3-cm balls.

9. Dip the potato balls in the batter and fry in 350°F/177°C vegetable oil until golden brown, 3 to 5 minutes. Remove and drain on a wire rack.

10. Serve on a plate, accompanied by the Cilantro-Cashew Chutney.

SPANISH POTATO OMELET

YIELD: 8 PORTIONS

3 lb/1.36 kg Yukon gold or similar potatoes, peeled, sliced ⅛ in/3 mm thick	Salt, as needed
	Ground black pepper, as needed
8 oz/227 g sliced onions	16 eggs
4 fl oz/120 mL extra-virgin olive oil	Aioli (page 182)

1. In a large skillet over medium heat, covered with a lid, cook the potatoes and onions gently in 2 fl oz/60 mL of the olive oil until fork-tender, 5 to 10 minutes. Stir occasionally without breaking the potatoes. Adjust seasoning with salt and pepper as needed. With a slotted spoon, remove the cooked potatoes and onions to a mixing bowl.

2. In a large bowl, thoroughly beat the eggs and add salt as needed. Gently yet thoroughly combine the eggs with the cooked potato and onion mix without breaking the potato slices.

3. Return the potato-egg mix to the skillet with the remaining olive oil and cook over moderate heat until the egg begins to solidify along the perimeter of the skillet, 2 to 3 minutes.

4. Place the pan into an oven at 375°F/191°C and cook gently until omelet is cooked through and slightly browned. If a large enough pan is not available, work in smaller batches.

5. Slide the omelet out of the skillet and allow to rest for 5 minutes before cutting into wedges and serving with Aioli.

CHEF'S NOTE

Known as *tortilla de patatas*, this popular Spanish dish resembles what is known as a *frittata* or Italian omelet, but there are some distinct differences. A frittata is made with well-browned diced potatoes, among other ingredients, and contains more eggs in relation to the other ingredients. It is important to understand that the Spanish potato omelet is all about the potatoes, while the eggs serve a background role. The key to success is to very gently sauté sliced potatoes in olive oil until they are cooked, and then combine them with just enough eggs to evenly coat the potatoes before cooking the omelet over very moderate heat until cooked through.

GRILLED EAST MEDITERRANEAN CHEESE WITH TOMATOES

YIELD: 8 PORTIONS

3 lb/1.36 kg haloumi, kefalotyri, or panela cheese	4 tomatoes (about 1 lb/454 g), peeled, cut into small dice
Salt, as needed	2 fl oz/60 mL brandy or cognac
Ground black pepper, as needed	1 fl oz/30 mL lemon juice
4 fl oz/120 mL extra-virgin olive oil	2 tbsp/6 g chopped flat-leaf parsley
2 tbsp/16 g capers	

1. Cut the cheese into wedges about 3 in/8 cm long and ½ to ¾ in/1 to 2 cm thick. Season the cheese with salt and pepper, toss in 2 fl oz/60 mL of the olive oil, and cook on a very hot grill until slightly charred on both sides, 30 seconds to 1 minute per side. Arrange on a plate.

2. In a skillet over medium heat, sweat the capers and tomatoes in the remaining olive oil until the tomato begins to get pulpy, about 5 minutes.

3. Add brandy and lemon juice and cook until the moisture is evaporated. Add the chopped parsley and adjust seasoning with salt and pepper.

4. Pour the tomato mix over the grilled cheese and serve immediately.

CHEF'S NOTES

Inspired by the classical cheese saganaki from Greece, this recipe features grilled haloumi cheese. For the traditional saganaki, which literally translates into "little skillet," the cheese is commonly sautéed or pan seared.

Haloumi cheese, a firm, relatively salty cheese originally from Cyprus, is popular in many Middle Eastern cuisines. One of its unique features is that it can be grilled or cooked without melting. If needed, Mexican panela cheese or Greek kefalotyri cheese can be substituted.

BAKED PHYLLO POCKET WITH SPINACH AND FETA

YIELD: 8 PORTIONS

3 oz/85 g minced onions	1 egg, beaten
2 tbsp/24 mL butter	4 oz/113 g feta cheese, crumbled
2 garlic cloves, minced	3 oz/85 g grated mozzarella cheese
1 lb/454 g spinach, lower part of stems removed	Salt, as needed
1 pinch grated nutmeg	Ground black pepper, as needed
1½ tsp/2 g chopped oregano	12 sheets phyllo dough
	12 oz/340 g butter, melted

1. In a skillet over low to medium heat, sweat the onions in the butter until translucent, about 5 minutes. Add the garlic and continue to sweat until fragrant, about 30 seconds.

2. Add the spinach, nutmeg, and oregano and sauté over high heat until the spinach is wilted and all moisture is evaporated, 3 to 5 minutes.

3. Transfer the spinach mixture to a stainless-steel bowl, add the egg and cheeses, and season with salt and pepper as needed. Set aside.

4. Lay 1 sheet of phyllo dough on a cutting board. Brush lightly with melted butter and top with a second sheet of dough. Brush with butter again and top with another sheet. Cut the stack of the phyllo dough in half lengthwise.

5. Cut the stacked phyllo sheets in half vertically to achieve 2 rectangles. On the lower right corner of a phyllo rectangle, place about 2 tbsp of the spinach filling. Fold the filling into the dough in a flag fold to achieve a triangle dough pocket with all sides sealed. Repeat with the other phyllo dough rectangle and the remaining phyllo sheets.

6. Brush the triangles with the melted butter. Bake on a parchment-lined sheet pan at 350°F/177°C until golden brown, about 10 minutes.

CHEF'S NOTE

Known as *spanakopita* in Greece or *börekin* in Turkey, variations of this savory stuffed pastry pocket can be found all over the Middle East, the Balkans, and North Africa. See page 284 for a related preparation from Turkey known as *water börek*.

MARINATED TOMATOES

YIELD: 8 PORTIONS

3 lb/1.36 kg roma tomatoes	2 bunches green onions, thinly sliced
1½ tbsp/18 g black or yellow mustard seeds	2 jalapeños, seeded, minced
Olive oil, as needed	4 garlic cloves, sliced
1½ tbsp/9 g coarsely ground black pepper	2 tbsp/16 g very finely grated ginger
1½ tbsp/9 g ground cumin	1½ cups/360 mL white vinegar
2 tsp/4 g cayenne	5 oz/142 g brown sugar
2 tsp/4 g ground turmeric	Salt, as needed

1. Score the skins of the tomatoes crosswise and remove the green core. In a generous amount of rapidly boiling water, blanch the tomatoes until the skin begins to loosen. Immediately shock the tomatoes in ice water. Peel the tomatoes, cut in half lengthwise, and cut the halves lengthwise again into quarters; set aside.

2. In a saucepan or similar pan over medium-high heat, fry the mustard seeds in the olive oil until they begin to pop, 10 to 15 seconds. Add the pepper, cumin, cayenne, and turmeric and fry for 5 to 10 seconds before adding the green onions, jalapeños, garlic, and ginger and cooking them gently over low to medium heat for 10 seconds.

3. Add the vinegar, sugar, and salt, bring to a rapid boil, and remove from the heat. Adjust seasoning as needed.

4. Gently combine with the blanched and peeled tomatoes and allow to marinate under refrigeration for at least 24 hours. Serve well chilled.

SOUTHEAST ASIAN VEGETABLE PICKLES

YIELD: 8 PORTIONS

1 lb/454 g pickling cucumbers, peeled, seeded, cut into 2- to 3-in/5- to 8-cm sticks

8 oz/227 g carrots, cut into 2- to 3-in/5- to 8-cm sticks

8 oz/227 g jícama, cut into 2- to 3-in/5- to 8-cm sticks

8 oz/227 g napa cabbage, cut into ½-in/1-cm chiffonade

8 oz/227 g daikon radish, cut into 1- to 3-in/3- to 8-cm sticks

8 oz/227 g Chinese long beans, cut into 1- to 3-in/3- to 8-cm pieces

½ cup/80 g salt

Spice Paste

4 fl oz/120 mL peanut oil

1 oz/28 g lemongrass, trimmed, chopped

3 oz/85 g sliced shallots

4 garlic cloves, sliced

1 tbsp/8 g grated ginger

2 oz/57 g desiccated coconut, lightly toasted

2 tsp/4 g ground turmeric

2 fl oz/60 mL peanut oil

6 fl oz/180 mL white vinegar

6 fl oz/180 mL water

2 tbsp/25 g sugar

Salt, as needed

1. Toss all of the vegetables with the salt, and allow to sit for 30 minutes. Wash in a generous amount of water, and allow to drain. Briefly blanch the radish, jícama, and carrots separately for about 30 seconds and the napa cabbage for about 10 seconds in a generous amount of unsalted water; drain and set aside.

2. In a blender, combine the peanut oil, lemongrass, shallots, garlic, ginger, coconut, and turmeric, and purée the spice paste until smooth.

3. In a skillet, cook the puréed spice paste in the oil over moderate heat for about 5 minutes without browning.

4. Add the vinegar, water, sugar, and salt, bring to a boil, and thoroughly combine with the blanched vegetables. Adjust flavor and seasoning as necessary and allow the vegetables to marinate under refrigeration for at least 48 hours. Serve at room temperature.

GRILLED GARLIC BREAD

YIELD: 8 PORTIONS

2 fl oz/60 mL extra-virgin olive oil

4 garlic cloves, sliced

1 loaf French bread

Salt, as needed

Ground black pepper, as needed

1. Combine the olive oil and garlic in a small saucepan, heat gently, and cook over low heat for 1 minute.

2. Slice the bread on a drastic bias into ¼-in/6-mm-thick slices, brush with the garlic oil, and season with salt and pepper.

3. Grill until lightly charred on both sides and crispy throughout, 30 to 60 seconds per side. Serve immediately.

SALSA VERDE

YIELD: 8 PORTIONS

1 lb/454 g tomatillos, husked, washed

1 serrano, stem removed

8 oz/227 g onions, cut into ¼-in/6-mm slices

1 clove garlic, peeled

1 oz/28 g roughly cut cilantro, with stems

1 oz/28 g lard

1 cup/240 mL chicken stock

Salt, as needed

Ground black pepper, as needed

1. On a grill or in a comal, mark the tomatillos, serrano, onions, and garlic until slightly charred. Set aside to cool.

2. In a blender, purée the tomatillos, serrano, onions, garlic, and cilantro, adding water to facilitate the blending.

3. In a saucepan over high heat, heat the lard until it smokes. Add the puréed vegetables, bring to a boil, and simmer over medium heat, stirring constantly, for 2 to 3 minutes.

4. Add the chicken stock, and simmer until thick enough to coat a spoon, 10 to 15 minutes. Adjust seasoning with salt and pepper and serve.

HERBED TAPENADE

YIELD: 1 PINT/480 ML

10 oz/284 g green olives, pitted	½ cup/120 mL extra-virgin olive oil
10 oz/284 g black olives, pitted	Ground black pepper, as needed
3 oz/85 g minced capers	1½ tsp/5 g minced oregano
4 garlic cloves, minced	2 tbsp/6 g basil, cut into chiffonade
Juice of 1 lemon	

1. If necessary, soak the olives and capers to reduce saltiness.

2. In a food processor, combine the olives, capers, garlic, lemon juice, and olive oil, incorporating the lemon juice and oil slowly. Blend until rather smooth.

3. Adjust seasoning and finish with oregano and basil.

CHEF'S NOTE | Tapenade is a dish that is omnipresent on tables in southern France. Eaten mainly as an hors d'oeuvre, a spread on crusty bread, or an accompaniment to grilled fish, tapenade adds a distinct salty kick to a meal.

POBLANO COULIS

YIELD: 1 PINT/480 ML

2 to 2½ lb/907 to 1.13 kg poblano peppers

2 garlic cloves, sliced

2 fl oz/60 mL extra-virgin olive oil

1 fl oz/30 mL lime juice

1 tbsp/12 g sugar

Salt, as needed

Ground black pepper, as needed

1. Over an open fire or under a broiler, roast the poblanos until the skin is blistered on all sides, 2 to 3 minutes. Place in a bowl, cover tightly with plastic wrap or with a lid, and allow to sweat for 5 minutes. Remove the skins, seeds, and stems and cut coarsely.

2. In a saucepan over medium heat, sweat the garlic gently in the olive oil until fragrant, about 30 seconds. Add the poblanos and cook gently for 1 minute.

3. Combine with the lime juice, sugar, salt, and pepper in a blender and purée until smooth, adding water as needed to facilitate blending. Adjust seasoning as needed and chill rapidly to retain the bright color. Serve cold or at room temperature.

HONEY-TOMATO-ALMOND CHUTNEY

YIELD: 1 PINT/480 ML

3 garlic cloves, minced

1 oz/28 g minced ginger

1 fl oz/30 mL vegetable oil

1 cup/240 mL rice vinegar

2 lb/907 g tomatoes, peeled, chopped

6 oz/170 g honey

3 oz/85 g raisins

4 oz/113 g almonds, toasted, finely chopped

1 tsp/2 g cayenne

Salt, as needed

1. In a saucepan or similar pan over medium heat, sweat the garlic and ginger in the vegetable oil until aromatic, about 30 seconds.

2. Add the vinegar, tomatoes, honey, raisins, almonds, cayenne, and salt and simmer until the chutney reaches medium nappé.

3. Adjust seasoning with salt, vinegar, and honey to achieve a balanced sweet and sour flavor.

POTATO, GARLIC, AND OLIVE SPREAD

YIELD: 8 PORTIONS

3 lb/1.36 kg russet potatoes	1½ cups/120 mL extra-virgin olive oil
3 oz/85 g whole almonds, blanched, peeled	Salt, as needed
	Ground black pepper, as needed
2 oz/57 g garlic cloves, peeled	2 to 3 fl oz/60 to 90 mL lemon juice
3 oz/85 g Kalamata olives, pitted	Pita Bread (page 111)
3 oz/85 g green olives, not bitter, pitted	

1. Bake the potatoes at 400°F/204°C until they can easily be pierced with a paring knife, 30 to 45 minutes.

2. In the meantime, toast the almonds at 400°F/204°C until slightly golden brown, 3 to 5 minutes; set aside.

3. In a food processor, chop the garlic very fine, add the toasted almonds and the olives, and continue to process until chunky.

4. Once the potatoes are fully cooked, cut them in half lengthwise and force them, flesh side down, through a medium-size wire rack into a hotel pan; the skins will stay behind on the wire rack.

5. Mash the potatoes with a masher and add the garlic mixture and olive oil. Combine thoroughly. Adjust seasoning with salt, pepper, and lemon juice and add more olive oil if needed to achieve a spreadable consistency. Serve at room temperature with Pita Bread.

CHEF'S NOTE — This spread, known as *skordalia* or *skorthalia* in Greece, is a great addition to any meal. It is most commonly found on Eastern Mediterranean mezze platters as a spread for pita bread, and it also serves very well as a spread for Mediterranean-inspired sandwiches.

GRAINS, LEGUMES, NOODLES, & BREAD

CHAPTER 5

GRAINS

Prized for their nutritional value and long shelf life, grains, edible seeds of cereal plants, are our most important food crop. Grains, as part of the human diet, had their humble beginnings with the onset of agriculture about 10,000 years ago. Growing human settlements put greater stress on natural resources, causing people to look for alternative food sources. In an effort to overcome the limited appeal of these hard and mostly indigestible raw seeds, our ancestors had to come up with ways to make them more attractive. After learning to remove the inedible husk, distinct preparation methods were devised, including milling, sprouting, parching, fermenting, baking, and simply cooking in liquid. Over time, the several thousand different species of edible grains available to us have dwindled down to only a few varieties of international importance. Today's most common grains are corn, rice, wheat, barley, sorghum, millet, oat, and rye. Others, of mostly regional or nutritional significance, include buckwheat, quinoa, teff, and amaranth.

The unique characteristics of each variety lead to distinct applications and preparations. Wheat, famous for its ability to create a plastic and elastic protein matrix, is a perfect ingredient for noodles or raised breads. Bulgur wheat, a staple in Middle Eastern cooking, has been created to expedite the very long cooking time of whole wheat berries. Used for salads, soups, and pilafs, bulgur is made by commercially precooking, dehydrating, and cracking the whole seeds.

Barley, rye, and oats are hardy grains, able to thrive in cold climates. Besides being used for porridge, dense sourdough, or flatbread, they are often sprouted and fermented into alcoholic beverages, assuring them a safe spot in many culinary cultures.

Rice, today the chief food source for more than half the world's population, is able to grow in the tropical and semitropical regions. After polishing, the grains are commonly steamed or simmered for risottos or pilafs. In Southeast Asia, rice is often processed into noodles or rice sheets and paper. See Table 5.1 for a list of common grains and grain preparations, their characteristics, and potential applications.

TABLE 5.1 Characteristics and Applications of Grains and Grain Preparations

NAME	CHARACTERISTICS	APPLICATIONS
Corn	Native to the Americas One of the most important grains in human nutrition Very versatile	Corn syrup Desserts Fresh sweet corn Popped corn Pozole Polenta Baking

TABLE 5.1 (*continued*)

NAME	CHARACTERISTICS	APPLICATIONS
Wheat	Native to the Middle and Near East One of the first grains to be cultivated Essential for baking Capability to develop gluten matrix to trap gases for leavening Gives strength and chew to doughs	Bread Cakes Pasta Pilaf Salads
Rice	Cultivated since at least 5000 B.C.E. Chief food source for almost half the world's population Requires vast amounts of water to grow, makes it most suitable for tropical regions	Steamed rice Risotto Pilaf Rice noodles Rice flour Rice sheets
Barley	Hardy grain Nutty flavor, slight chewiness Malted barley flour is often added to all-purpose flour as food for yeast	Sprouting for malt Pilaf Soups Hot cereals
Oats	Relatively high fat content Rolled oats are used uncooked for some applications	Hot cereals Granola Müsli Baking Cookies Soups Salads
Rye	Hardy grain, thrives in cold climates Important grain in Northern and Eastern European cuisines Hearty dark breads and some local specialties Rye produces a very weak gluten network, resulting in very dense dough	Pumpernickel Rye bread Sprouting
Farro/emmer	Ancient grain in the wheat family from North Africa and the Middle East Common in Italy Complex, nutty taste Cooks creamy like risotto	Pilaf Risotto Salads Whole grains as addition to bread doughs

(*continued*)

TABLE 5.1 (*continued*)

NAME	CHARACTERISTICS	APPLICATIONS
Spelt	An ancient wheat variety introduced to the United States by the Amish Light, nutty flavor Easier to digest than other wheat varieties	Pilaf Risotto Salads Whole grains as addition to bread doughs
Kamut	Ancient Egyptian wheat Rich, buttery flavor and chewy texture	Pilaf Risotto Salads Whole grains as addition to bread doughs
Triticale	Developed in the late 1800s Hybrid of rye and wheat Nutty flavor	Whole-grain baking Pilaf Soups Stews
Millet	Grown throughout the world U.S.-grown is primarily used as birdseed Tiny seeds easy to digest Chewy	Pilaf Soups Stews Salads Bird food
Amaranth	Ancient Aztec grain Nutty flavor Slightly spicy and sticky gelatinous texture High in fiber and protein	Gluten-free baking Pilaf Salads Hot cereals Soups
Buckwheat/kasha	Not related to wheat Actually a fruit seed related to rhubarb Common in Central and Eastern European cuisines Very distinct nutty flavor	Baking Hot cereals Noodles
Quinoa	Tiny, disk-shaped seed, originating in the Andes Mountains of South America Complete set of essential amino acids To minimize bitterness, quinoa should be thoroughly washed or briefly blanched before use	Pilaf Soups Stews Salads

TABLE 5.1 (*continued*)

NAME	CHARACTERISTICS	APPLICATIONS
Sorghum	Comparable to corn One of the top cereal crops in the world Originating in Africa, it is now grown in the United States and Asia	Pilaf Soups Stews Salads Hot cereals Starch production
Teff	Tiny grains, native to East Africa Mild nutty flavor, rich in iron	Injera (Ethiopian flatbread) Hot cereals Pilaf
Wild rice	Native to the Great Lakes region of the United States Not actually a rice Used to be staple food for northern Native American tribes Distinct nutty flavor	Pilaf Soups Stews Salads

COMMERCIAL GRAIN PREPARATIONS

Bulgur wheat	Fully cooked, dehydrated, and cracked whole wheat berries Reconstitutes quickly by rehydrating in boiling water	Pilaf Soup Stews Salads
Couscous	A traditional pasta-like food of North Africa Small dough pebbles made from ground semolina mixed with water Traditionally cooked in a couscousière, a perforated pan above a simmering pot of stew	Traditional Moroccan couscous Salad
Hominy	Dried field corn is soaked in slaked lime or lye Known as pozole in Mexico	Soups Stews Ground for tamales or corn tortillas Hominy grits

MARKET FORMS OF GRAINS AND APPROPRIATE COOKING METHODS

Grains are commercially milled into a variety of market forms. The different degrees of processing help to conveniently prepare a range of interesting grain dishes. For some market forms, the grains are partially or fully cooked, mainly to extend the shelf life, before further processing. See Table 5.2 for an explanation of commercial grains and their potential applications.

Grains **257**

TABLE 5.2 Market Forms of Grains and Their Applications

NAME	PROCESSING	SAMPLES	APPLICATIONS
Whole grains/ groats/ berries	Least processed market form; only the husk has been removed Contains bran, germ, and endosperm Refrigeration will prevent premature rancidity of the oil-rich germ	Brown rice Wheat berries Oat groats	Pilaf Soaked as addition to whole-grain doughs Salads Stews Soups
Pearled or polished	Bran is partially or fully removed Barley is referred to as pearled Rice is called polished	White rice Pearl barley	Pilaf Salads Stews Soups Risotto
Steel cut, cracked	Whole or polished grains Cracked into smaller pieces for faster cooking In some cases precooked and dehydrated	Steel-cut or Irish oats Bulgur wheat Cracked rye	Hot cereals Soaked as addition to whole-grain doughs Salads Tabbouleh Pilaf
Flakes or rolled	Mechanically flaked or flattened For shelf-life extension, whole grains are briefly steamed before flattening Faster cooking	Old-fashioned/ rolled oats Wheat flakes	Hot or cold cereals Salads Granola, müsli Bread doughs Crusts
Meal/grits	Grain is ground to a sandy consistency Stone grinding results in uneven particle size, creating a desired gritty consistency	Cornmeal Polenta Semolina Grits	Polenta Dumplings Puddings Hot cereals
Bran	The thin layer just under the outer husk of the grain Rich in dietary fiber and antioxidants	Wheat bran Oat bran	Enriching doughs and hot cereals
Germ	The embryo of the grain Rich in fat, B vitamins, and vitamin E Processed into a coarse meal Refrigeration will prevent premature rancidity	Wheat germ	Enriching doughs and cereals

TABLE 5.2 (*continued*)

NAME	PROCESSING	SAMPLES	APPLICATIONS
Flour	Most widespread market form of grain Whole or polished grains are ground into a fine powder	All-purpose flour Rye flour	Baking Thickening Crusts Binding
Starch	The pure, finely ground carbohydrate portion of the grain All protein, fiber, and fat removed	Cornstarch Wheat starch Rice starch	Thickening Binding

GRAIN PILAFS

Many cuisines include grains prepared and served as a pilaf. This method includes sweating or parching the whole or polished seeds in fat, and then simmering them in a distinct amount of a flavorful liquid. To ensure full hydration of the seeds during cooking, the proper grain-to-liquid ratio is imperative. Cooked in too much liquid, the grains will become mushy and soggy, resembling a porridge. Too little liquid will leave them hard and undercooked no matter how much time they spend on the fire. Stirring the pilaf should only be done before the liquid has come to a boil; excessively mixing the grains throughout the cooking will potentially result in a scorched, sticky, and mashed-up pilaf. Once a slow simmer has been established, the cooking vessel needs to be covered with a tight-fitting lid for the remainder of the cooking time. When the pilaf is done, it needs to rest for at least 15 minutes before it is gently loosened up with a fork or wooden spoon. See Table 5.3 for the ratios of grain cooking.

TABLE 5.3 Grain-to-Liquid Ratio and Approximate Cooking Times

GRAIN	GRAIN:LIQUID BY VOLUME	COOKING TIME
Amaranth	1 : 2	20–30 minutes
Barley	1 : 3	50 minutes–1 hour
Barley, pearled	1 : 2.5	35–45 minutes
Buckwheat	1 : 2	12–20 minutes
Bulgur wheat, pilaf	1 : 2.5	20 minutes, soaking in boiling liquid
Couscous	1 : 1.5	10 minutes, soaking in boiling liquid
Millet	1 : 2	30–35 minutes

(*continued*)

Grains **259**

TABLE 5.3 (*continued*)

GRAIN	GRAIN:LIQUID BY VOLUME	COOKING TIME
Oat groats	1 : 2	45 minutes–1 hour
Polenta/cornmeal	1 : 3	35–45 minutes
Quinoa	1 : 1.25	15 minutes
Rice, basmati	1 : 1.25	18 minutes
Rice, brown, long-grain	1 : 3	45 minutes
Rice, brown, short-grain	1 : 2.5	35–40 minutes
Rice, converted	1 : 1.5	18 minutes
Rice, East Asian short-grain	1 : 1.25	18 minutes
Rice, jasmine	1 : 1.25	18–20 minutes
Teff	1 : 3	15 minutes
Triticale	1 : 2.5	1 hour
Wheat berries	1 : 3.5	2 hours after soaking overnight
Wheat, Kamut	1 : 3	1 hour
Wheat, spelt	1 : 3	1 hour
Wild rice	1 : 3	1 hour

LEGUMES

Legumes or pulses, the seeds of pod-bearing leguminous plants, include beans, peas, and lentils. Their importance to the human diet is second only to that of grains. A long shelf life and unique nutritional makeup of high protein content, healthy fats, and complex carbohydrates have made them a staple in many cuisines all over the world. Their proteins, lacking one or more essential amino acids, are, in most cases, incomplete. To overcome this deficiency, many cuisines have created dishes combining grains and legumes with complementary nutritional profiles. Examples include the rice and bean dishes found in the southern United States or Latin America, and the Korean *bin dae dok*, a crispy pancake made from crushed soaked rice and mung beans. Soybeans, as an exception, are the only legume supplying all essential amino acids. Popular all over East Asia, soy is employed to produce soy milk, tofu, and other protein-rich foods. Fermenting soybeans into flavor-enhancing condiments like miso paste and soy sauce is another ingenious way to take advantage of their remarkably high protein content.

COOKING LEGUMES

In order to shorten the cooking time, the hard and dry legumes are often soaked in water before cooking. For smaller legumes, soaking is less critical; they cook relatively quickly. Additionally, soaking also helps to leach out some of the carbohydrates responsible for the gas often associated with eating beans.

To take advantage of legumes' high starch content, applying dry-heat cooking methods can result in interesting dishes. Falafel (page 317), popular in many Middle and Near Eastern cuisines, is prepared by deep-frying small patties made from coarsely ground soaked chickpeas, sometimes fava beans, and aromatics. Vadai, a comparable preparation from India, are crunchy doughnut-shaped fritters made from ground soaked white lentils and spices. In many South and East Asian cuisines, crêpe batters are made from puréed soaked legumes or their flours. The Italian province of Liguria is famous for farinata, a flatbread based on chickpea flour.

Aromatic bean spreads, like Hummus (page 322) or lima bean spread, can now be found in many food-service operations. Inexpensive and relatively easy to prepare and hold, they are used as sandwich spreads, on appetizer plates, or as healthy dips.

Edible raw or after only brief cooking, immature legumes are sold as green beans, edamame, green chickpeas, snow peas, or sugar snap peas. These popular vegetables have been harvested early in the growing season, before the plant converted the sugars into complex starches. See Table 5.4 for the characteristics of selected legumes.

TABLE 5.4 Characteristics and Applications of Legumes

NAME	CHARACTERISTICS	APPLICATIONS
Adzuki bean	Small, oval, dark red bean with a white ridge Grown and eaten in China and Japan	Paste for ice cream or other sweet dishes Mixed grain and legume porridges Sweet beverages
Black bean	Small, shiny, jet black bean Caribbean and Latin American cuisines	Soups Stews Salads Side dishes
Black-eyed pea	Small beige bean with a circular "eye" Popularized in the United States by African slaves Southern U.S. cuisine	Hopping John Salads Soups

(continued)

TABLE 5.4 *(continued)*

NAME	CHARACTERISTICS	APPLICATIONS
Cannellini bean	Large white kidney bean, originally from Argentina Excellent for minestrone and in Mediterranean dishes Smooth texture with a nutty flavor	Mediterranean cuisine Minestrone Bean spreads Sauces Stews
Chickpea	Also known as garbanzo Pale gold and round with a beet-like sprout Used worldwide	Falafel Hummus Salads Pasta dishes Soups Stews Curries Batters
Cranberry bean	Mottled, ivory colored with cranberry red markings Firm texture	Baked beans Stews
Fava bean	An ancient bean native to the Middle East Also known as broad bean or horse bean Outer seed coat needs to be removed	Spreads Falafel Soups Stews Salads Soaked and fried as a salty snack
Great Northern bean	Medium-size white bean grown commercially in Idaho, Colorado, Kansas, Wyoming, and Nebraska	Soups Stews
Kidney bean	Firm, medium-size bean with dark red skin and cream-colored flesh Full-bodied flavor	Chili con carne Rice and beans Stews
Lentils	Small, lens-shaped Grayish brown, green, reddish orange, yellow, or black Used throughout Europe, the Middle East, and India Green and black lentils hold their shape well when cooked; others turn mushy when cooked	Soups Stews Salads Side dishes
Mung bean	Small, round, ancient bean often used for mung bean sprouts Available husked or with the green hull attached	Sprouting Batters Beverages Soups Stews

TABLE 5.4 (*continued*)

NAME	CHARACTERISTICS	APPLICATIONS
Navy bean	Small white bean Also known as Yankee bean Named for the U.S. Navy, where it has been served as a staple since the 1800s	Pork and beans Boston baked beans Soups Bean spreads
Pinto bean	Small, flavorful, with reddish brown streaks on a pale pink background Northern Mexican dishes	Rice and beans Refried beans Soups Stews
Soybean	Beige Sweet, nutty flavor Low in carbohydrates, high in protein and fat Only legume containing all essential amino acids One of the most important legumes of East Asian cooking	Soy milk Tofu Soy sauce Fermented soy products Stews Pickled Soaked and deep-fried as soy nuts
Split peas	Green or yellow White opaque hull has been removed Distinct flavor Creamy when cooked	Soups Fritters Stews Purées

NOODLES

As soon as our ancestors understood how to mill grains or legumes, it was only a small step to process the resulting flour into strands or bite-size pieces of dough or paste and boil those in water. Noodles, starting off so humbly, have evolved into one of the most popular foods worldwide. Found in many cultures, they are the perfect vehicle for almost any accompaniment. Tossed in simple or complex sauces, swimming in an aromatic broth with morsels of meat and vegetables, or served cold as a salad, noodles possess a unique versatility that can be enhanced by a number of accompaniments. Though their origins are debated, most research suggests that noodle making was first refined to an art in China, where it evolved into the ultimate street food. In other regions, noodles were created much later. Contrary to popular belief, however, noodle making was well established in Italy and the Eastern Mediterranean long before Marco Polo's journeys.

The protein-rich durum wheat, common in Italy, provides pasta with its coveted sturdiness and chew. The strength of the dough allows for a great variety of shapes as well as industrial manufacturing. East Asian wheat has a significantly lower protein content, resulting in tender noodles with a slippery mouthfeel. In addition to wheat flour–based noodles, Asian cuisines offer a great variety of noodles made from other starchy ingredients. Examples include Chinese cellophane noodles made from mung bean starch, Korean glass noodles based on sweet potato starch, and rice noodles, which are common all over Southeast Asia. Unlike pasta, these noodles are not made from a stiff dough, but from a slurry or paste. This slurry is forced through a perforated disk into boiling water, where it instantly cooks into thin, long strands. For other varieties, the starch slurry is steamed into sheets and cut into fettuccine-like ribbons. Depending on the starch, these noodles can be crystal clear with a very smooth mouthfeel or opaque and slightly textured.

COOKING NOODLES

All noodles need to be cooked in a generous amount of water to prevent sticking, and fresh noodles cook significantly quicker than their dried counterparts. Many of the starch-based Asian varieties like cellophane, rice, or glass noodles only need to be rehydrated by soaking them in boiling water. Ideally, all noodles are finished and served immediately after cooking, and this is typical in food-service operations, especially those specializing in Asian noodle dishes. However, if this is not possible, care must be taken to keep noodles from clumping together after they are cooked. Italian pasta is best tossed in a small amount of oil, and most Asian noodles can be rinsed in water to remove excess starch. See Table 5.5 for the applications of noodles.

TABLE 5.5 Characteristics and Applications of Noodles

TYPE/NAME	CHARACTERISTICS	APPLICATIONS
Elbow pasta	Retain their shape Perfect for street food Can be eaten with only one utensil	Casserole dishes Salads Macaroni and cheese
Tubular pasta Penne, ziti, shells, bocconcini	Hollow interior soaks up sauce	Baking Casseroles
Flat pasta Tagliatelle, pappardelle, linguine	Sturdy Need to be coated with sauce or oil right after cooking to prevent sticking	Served hot in sauce
Cellophane noodles Fen si, fen tiao	China Thin strands or ribbons made from mung bean starch Crystal clear, very smooth, flavorless	Salads Stews Swimming in broth

TABLE 5.5 (*continued*)

TYPE/NAME	CHARACTERISTICS	APPLICATIONS
Soba noodles	Japan Thin strands made from buckwheat flour Gray color, distinct nutty flavor	Salads Served in broth
Somen noodles	Japan and China Very thin strands based on wheat flour	Pan-fried crispy noodle cakes Salads Served in broth
Hand-pulled noodles La mian	China Based on soft wheat flour Known as *ramen* in Japan A soft dough is manually pulled into thin strands right before cooking	Served in broth
Udon noodles	Japan Thick, white, wheat-based noodles	Served in broth
Sweet potato noodles Jap chae	Korea Translucent grayish spaghetti-like strands made from sweet potato starch	Stir-fried Served in broth
Rice noodles Mi fen, he fen	Southeast Asia Bright white, opaque Ribbons, vermicelli, or sheet	Served in broth Stir-fried Crispy fried
Chinese wheat-based noodles Mien	Off-white color Tender Thick noodles	Stir-fried Pan-steamed Served in broth
Chinese egg noodles Dan mian	Rich yellow Medium thick	Stir-fried Pan-steamed

BREAD

Few foods exemplify our culinary ingenuity like bread. Transforming solid, bland, and gritty seeds into aromatic, sometimes fluffy loaves, disks, and rolls suggests aspiration, skill, and inventiveness. Today, almost all culinary cultures embrace bread, even those where bread was not an indigenous element. It is a perfect intermediary for limitless toppings, condiments, and fillings, and bread's service to the street-food scene is immeasurable. Paired with breads, all types of food can be served on the go, without utensils. Bread hugs a hot dog, wraps taco fillings, and prevents flavorful sauces from dripping onto one's shirt. The triumphant culinary advance of the burger can in all probability be credited in part to the bun.

Depending on the place of origin, breads vary tremendously and are served in different contexts. Northern Europe is famous for dark and dense rye breads, and Sweden for crisp flatbreads. Thinly sliced, they are often topped with fried or cured fish or charcuterie meats. Crunchy baguettes, originating in France, can be found sliced thinly as Bruschetta (pages 301–304) or topped with sliced meats and cheese and then baked until hot, well browned, and deliciously gooey. The pocket in Middle Eastern pita bread simply asks for a stuffing, and roti prata, a flaky flatbread from South and Southeast Asia, is perfect for clutching morsels of stewed meat and vegetables, or cleaning the last drops of curry gravy from the bowl. Bread is truly breaking all cultural and culinary borders. Not long ago, a tandoor-baked flatbread from India, known as naan, was considered exotic in many parts of the world. Naan is now a mainstream item available in many supermarkets. Some restaurants and street-food vendors offer it baked with pizza toppings, calling it "nizza."

Depending on the layout of the business, some street-food stands cook their breads, especially flatbreads, on a grill or griddle on-site. For convenience reasons, the dough is often prepared and shaped at an off-site location and delivered frozen or refrigerated. Some dishes, like pizza, filled steamed buns, or chimichangas, include raw bread dough that is baked, steamed, or fried as part of the preparation. The limited infrastructure of most mobile vending situations, however, makes baking the bread on-site impractical. In order to provide fresh-tasting bread, it should be briefly toasted, grilled, or broiled at service. The resulting toasty aroma might attract more customers.

Grains and legumes, to this day, are unfortunately often seen as unglamorous plate or belly fillers. Prepared properly and with respect, however, they can be the base for amazingly diverse and delicious food. Without grains and legumes, our culinary world would look quite different, and many beloved dishes would simply not exist. Cultures of the world have been resourceful in developing ingenious vehicles for grains and beans. At times, the efforts and amounts of energy invested in the preparation of these dishes may seem unreasonable; however, the thought of all the good meals they continue to provide helps to justify that hard work.

BLACK BEAN SOUP

YIELD: 8 PORTIONS

1 lb/454 g dried black beans	1 tsp/2 g chili powder
1 lb/454 g smoked, meaty ham hocks	1 tsp/2 g chopped thyme
	Salt, as needed
3 qt/2.84 L chicken stock, plus as needed	Ground black pepper, as needed
	¼ habanero chile, seeded, minced
8 oz/227 g Spanish chorizo, cut into small dice	1 tbsp/15 mL cider vinegar
	1 tbsp/12 g sugar
2 fl oz/60 mL lard	8 oz/227 g small-dice plum tomatoes
8 oz/227 g small-dice onions	¼ cup/12 g coarsely cut cilantro
2 garlic cloves, minced	½ cup/120 mL sour cream
1 tsp/2 g ground cumin	

1. Fully submerge the black beans in cold water and allow to soak until doubled in size, at least 12 hours.

2. Simmer the ham hocks in the stock until very tender, 1½ to 3 hours, adding more stock as needed to maintain a level of 3 quarts. Remove the cooked ham hocks from the broth. Reserve the broth. Dice and reserve the meat from the ham hocks, discarding the bones and skin.

3. In a 1½-gal/5.76-L stockpot over medium heat, cook the beans in the ham hock broth until very tender. If desired, purée the soup or whisk heavily to partially break the beans.

4. In a skillet over medium heat, sauté the chorizo in the lard until browned slightly, 2 to 3 minutes. Add the onions and garlic to the pan, and continue to sauté until tender, 3 to 5 minutes. Add the cumin, chili powder, and thyme, and sweat briefly until fragrant, about 30 seconds.

5. Transfer the mixture to the pot of beans, and adjust the seasoning of the soup with salt and pepper. Add the habanero, vinegar, sugar, and diced tomatoes and simmer for about 5 minutes.

6. Serve in individual bowls with the cilantro and a dollop of sour cream.

SALAD OF BEAN STARCH SHEETS

YIELD: 8 PORTIONS

1 lb/454 g bean starch sheets

2 fl oz/60 mL vegetable oil

½ tsp/1 g Sichuan pepper

1 tsp/2 g red pepper flakes

2 tbsp/25 g sugar

1½ fl oz/45 mL black rice vinegar

2 European cucumbers, cut into julienne

1 cup/48 g coarsely cut cilantro

3 oz/85 g mung bean sprouts

1½ tbsp/22.5 mL sesame oil

Salt, as needed

1. Pour boiling water over the bean starch sheets until they are fully submerged. Allow to soak for 30 minutes.

2. In a sauté pan over high heat, heat the vegetable oil almost to its smoke point. Add the Sichuan pepper and the red pepper flakes to the oil and fry until they begin to turn brown, 5 to 10 seconds. Strain, discard the solids, and reserve the oil.

3. Drain the bean starch sheets thoroughly and rip them into bite-size pieces. Combine the sheets with the pepper oil, sugar, vinegar, cucumbers, cilantro, bean sprouts, and sesame oil. Season the salad with salt.

4. Serve in a soup bowl with chopsticks.

CHEF'S NOTE | Bean starch sheets, also known as *Tianjin green bean sheets*, are translucent sheets made from mung bean starch that visually resemble Vietnamese rice paper. The slippery texture of the bean starch sheets is comparable to cellophane noodles, another product made from mung bean starch.

SAVORY PORK SAUCE WITH NOODLES OR CORN PANCAKES

YIELD: 8 PORTIONS

2 fl oz/60 mL vegetable oil	5 fl oz/150 mL hoisin sauce
1 lb 8 oz/680 g ground pork	1 cup/240 mL water
2 tbsp/16 g minced ginger	
8 green onions, minced	2 lb/907 g Chinese, wheat, or lo mein noodles (or see Variation)
4 garlic cloves, minced	
1½ tbsp/22.5 mL Shaoxing wine, or sherry	1 lb 8 oz/680 g Kirby cucumbers, peeled, cut into 2- to 3-in/5- to 8-cm wedges
10 oz/284 g yellow soybean paste or dark miso paste	

1. For the sauce, heat the oil in a wok or similar pan over medium heat, add the ground pork, and stir fry until fully cooked, about 3 minutes. Add the ginger, half of the minced green onions, and garlic, and continue cooking until aromatic, 10 to 20 seconds. Add the wine and continue cooking over medium heat until fully evaporated, about 2 minutes. Add the soybean paste, hoisin sauce, and water. Bring to a boil and then simmer gently over medium heat until the mixture has reduced to a paste resembling a thick meat sauce, 2 to 4 minutes.

2. To cook the noodles, boil 2 gal/7.57 L of salted water. Add the noodles, and return to a boil. As soon as the water returns to a full boil, add 1 cup/240 mL of cold water, and allow the water to return to a boil. Repeat, adding cold water 1 cup/240 mL at a time, until the noodles are tender. The cooking time will depend on the variety of noodle that is used. Drain the noodles, and rinse with hot water.

3. Toss about 2 fl oz/60 mL of the sauce with each portion of noodles and transfer to a serving bowl. Sprinkle with the remaining green onions, and serve with cucumber wedges on the side.

CHEF'S NOTE

This dish, known as *zha jiang mian* in northern China, bears a strong resemblance to spaghetti in meat sauce. Be aware, however, that this sauce, unlike spaghetti sauce, is served in small amounts due to its pungency and saltiness. The cucumber accompaniment provides a nice flavor contrast to the very strong sauce.

VARIATION

Serve the Savory Pork Sauce on Corn Pancakes (page 322) instead of noodles; that way the dish can be served without utensils.

SPICY CHICKPEA SOUP

YIELD: 8 PORTIONS

1 lb/454 g dried chickpeas	**Condiments**
8 oz/227 g small-dice onions	
2 fl oz/60 mL extra-virgin olive oil	2 lemons, quartered
4 garlic cloves, minced	8 eggs, hard-cooked, coarsely chopped
Harissa (page 324), as needed	1 tbsp/6 g ground cumin
1½ tbsp/9 g ground cumin	Harissa (page 324), as needed
1 tbsp/6 g coriander	2 bunches green onions, sliced
2 tsp/4 g ground turmeric	Extra-virgin olive oil, as needed
2 tsp/4 g ground black pepper	Salt, as needed
Salt, as needed	Ground black pepper, as needed
8 oz/227 g canned tuna, drained and flaked	8 oz/227 g country-style bread, ripped into irregular pieces
2 oz/57 g capers, drained and chopped	

1. Soak the chickpeas in water until doubled in size, at least 12 hours.

2. Drain and rinse the chickpeas. Place them in a pot of unsalted water and simmer over low to medium heat until very tender, 45 to 90 minutes. Reserve in the cooking liquid.

3. In a saucepan or rondeau, sweat the onions in the olive oil over moderate heat until very tender, 10 to 15 minutes. Add the garlic, harissa, cumin, coriander, turmeric, and pepper, and sweat over medium heat until aromatic, 10 to 20 seconds.

4. Add the cooked chickpeas to the onion mixture along with enough of the chickpea cooking liquid to just cover them. Bring the mixture to a simmer over medium heat, and simmer until the mixture is the consistency of a stew, about 15 minutes. Adjust seasoning as needed with salt.

5. Arrange the condiments in serving bowls or in sectioned relish dishes. At service, offer the condiments, so that the guest can add them to the soup as desired.

CHEF'S NOTE

In Tunisia, this soup is called *lebilebi* and is a popular breakfast food. (This dish is not to be confused with the Turkish *lebilebi*, which is a roasted chickpea snack.) This soup is served out of a big pot with the condiments added as per guest request. Traditionally, the eggs are added raw to the very hot soup, which provides enough heat to at least partially cook them. The bread served with the soup should be stale—at least a day old.

SPLIT GREEN PEA STEW

Known as *Erbsensuppe*, this is a traditional and well-liked dish all over Germany. Its hearty appearance with cured and/or smoked meats makes this dish especially popular at outdoor events during the colder seasons. Additionally, it can be prepared ahead of time and kept warm for hours with little to no deterioration in quality.

YIELD: 8 PORTIONS

1 lb 8 oz/680 g pig tails, feet, or jowls, cured, not smoked	4 oz/113 g small-dice cauliflower
1 tbsp/7 g black peppercorns	4 oz/113 g small-dice celery
2 bay leaves	4 oz/113 g small-dice waxy potatoes
3 qt/2.84 L chicken stock	Salt, as needed
1 lb/454 g split green peas	Ground black pepper, as needed
4 oz/113 g small-dice onions	Maggi, as needed
4 oz/113 g small-dice carrots	8 knockwurst links
4 oz/113 g small-dice leeks	3 tbsp/3 g chopped parsley

1. In a large stockpot, simmer the pig tails, peppercorns, and bay leaves in the chicken stock until the pork is very tender, 60 to 90 minutes, adding water as needed to maintain the level of the cooking liquid. Remove the pork from the broth, and reserve. Strain the broth, and reserve.

2. Remove the meat from the pig tails, cut it into a small dice, and reserve it. Discard the bones and skin.

3. Add the peas to the reserved broth, and simmer over low to medium heat until the peas begin to fall apart, about 45 minutes, adding more water as needed to maintain the level of the cooking liquid. Add the onions, carrots, leeks, cauliflower, celery, and potatoes, and cook over medium heat until the vegetables are tender, 10 to 15 minutes. (The peas should be almost mush by this time.) Add the diced pork to the soup. Adjust seasoning with salt, pepper, and a few dashes of Maggi.

4. At service, heat the knockwurst gently in 180°F/82°C water and serve stew with knockwurst and a pinch of the parsley.

CHEF'S NOTES

When the green peas are harvested at full maturity, they are round, like any other pea. After drying, the membrane skin surrounding the cotyledon is removed, which allows the pea to split along its natural seam. This treatment is commonly done to expedite the cooking of the peas.

Maggi is a vegetable protein–based sauce that resembles soy sauce. It is popular in many cuisines of Central Europe as an all-purpose seasoning for soups and sauces. As an alternative, use light soy sauce or fresh lovage, a green herb with a flavor resembling Maggi.

PLAIN SOY MILK

YIELD: 1 GAL/3.84 L

1 lb 4 oz lb/567 g dried soybeans, rinsed

1. Cover the soybeans with water by 4 in/10 cm, and allow them to soak for 24 hours.

2. Drain the soybeans and discard the soaking liquid. Combine the soybeans with 1 gal/3.79 L cold water and purée into a very smooth slurry. If necessary, purée in batches.

3. Strain the purée through a fine-mesh strainer and then strain again through a cheesecloth-lined strainer, collecting the resulting liquid in a container below. Allow the soy bean purée to drain thoroughly, compressing it inside the cheesecloth in order to squeeze out any excess liquid.

4. Transfer the resulting soy milk to a saucepan, and bring to a boil over medium-high heat. Reduce to low or medium heat to establish a simmer and continue simmering, stirring often to prevent scorching, until the raw bean flavor has been cooked out, 10 to 12 minutes.

CURDLED SOY MILK WITH FRIED CRULLERS

YIELD: 8 PORTIONS

Plain Soy Milk (page 275)	3 tbsp/30 g kosher salt
4 fl oz/120 mL white vinegar	1½ tsp/7.5 mL sesame oil
1 tsp/2 g ground white pepper	1 cup/48 g coarsely cut cilantro
3 tbsp/21 g very small dried shrimp	1 fl oz/30 mL chili oil
1½ oz/43 g minced salted turnip	Fried Chinese Crullers (page 278)

1. In a saucepan over low to medium heat, bring the soy milk to a boil and hold hot. Stir the soy milk often to prevent scorching.

2. Meanwhile, equally distribute the vinegar, pepper, shrimp, turnip, salt, sesame oil, cilantro, and chili oil into 8 Asian noodle bowls that hold at least 1 pint/480 mL each.

3. Pour the hot soy milk into the bowls. The heat and the vinegar's acidity will curdle the soy milk. Should the soy milk not curdle, add a little more vinegar to each cup.

4. Serve immediately with the Fried Crullers on the side.

CHEF'S NOTE

This soup, known as *do jiang* in China, is a typical northern Chinese breakfast item. In this recipe, the vinegar causes the soy milk to curdle, giving the soup a texture resembling egg drop soup. Alternatively, the soy milk may be simply sweetened with sugar and served. Whether savory or sweet, the soy milk is a fantastic accompaniment to the crunchy fried crullers.

Cut the cruller dough into strips and press in the center with an oiled skewer.

Stretch the dough as you lower it into the hot oil, and deep-fry until golden.

Ladle the hot soy milk into bowls that have been prepared with the remaining ingredients.

Curdled Soy Milk with Fried Crullers

Recipes 277

FRIED CHINESE CRULLERS

Commonly served alongside wonton soup or curdled soy soup, these crullers can be found all over China, especially during breakfast hours.

YIELD: ABOUT 16 CRULLERS

1 tsp/5 g baking soda	1 tsp/3 g kosher salt
1 tbsp/12 g double-action baking powder	¼ tsp/0.5 g baker's ammonia
13 oz/369 g bread flour	9½ fl oz/285 mL water
1 tsp/3 g alum	Thin bamboo skewers
	Vegetable oil, as needed, for frying

1. In a bowl, combine the baking soda, baking powder, and flour.

2. In a separate bowl, combine the alum, salt, and ammonia. Add the water and stir until the mixture becomes frothy.

3. Combine the alum mixture with the baking soda mixture. Mix until it forms a smooth dough. Cover with plastic wrap, and allow to rest for 30 minutes.

4. After resting, punch the dough down several times and fold it over itself seven or eight times. Divide the dough into 2 equal pieces and wrap each piece in oiled plastic wrap. Refrigerate for 4 to 8 hours or overnight.

5. Place the rested dough on a lightly floured work surface and stretch each of the 2 pieces into a sheet 4 in/10 cm wide and ¼ to ½ in/½ to 1 cm thick.

6. Cover with plastic and allow the dough sheets to rest for 20 minutes.

7. Cut each of the sheets into 1-in/3-cm-wide strips. Place the strips on top of one another to create about 16 stacks of 2 strips each.

8. Dip a skewer in water. Holding the moistened skewer horizontally, firmly push it lengthwise onto the stacked dough strips to make an indentation, and press the strips together to join them securely.

9. Pick up a pressed strip of the dough and gently stretch it to a length of 6 to 8 in/15 to 20 cm. Immediately fry it in 400°F/204°C oil, moving and turning the strip constantly, until well puffed and golden brown on all sides, 1 to 2 minutes. Drain well, and serve hot.

CHEF'S NOTES

Alum, or sodium aluminum sulfate, is a chemical often used to produce white bread. In the case of this fried cruller, it provides a distinct flavor.

Baker's ammonia, often marketed as hartshorn, is pure ammonium carbonate. This classic leavener is the predecessor of today's chemical leaveners and is still used for many

CHEF'S NOTES *(continued)*

traditional recipes. The benefit of baker's ammonia is that it provides an extremely airy and crisp texture. Its strong odor makes it necessary to use caution.

The crullers can be fried ahead of time, and reheated in 425°F/218°C oven for about 2 minutes.

CORN TORTILLAS

YIELD: 16 TORTILLAS

14 oz/397 g masa harina	2 cups/480 mL warm water

1. Using a stand mixer, combine the masa harina and warm water, slowly adding the water. Knead the resulting dough for 5 to 8 minutes. It should feel like soft clay and be slightly above body temperature. Allow the dough to rest for 15 minutes and reevaluate the texture.

2. Divide the dough into 16 Ping-Pong–size balls. Using a tortilla press lined with plastic, press the balls into thin tortillas. Press once and rotate by 180 degrees before pressing again to achieve an even thickness of about ⅛ in/3 mm.

3. Preheat a well-seasoned comal or cast-iron skillet. To cook the tortilla, peel off the top sheet of plastic in which it was pressed and slide it off the other sheet onto the hot comal or cast-iron skillet. Cook for several seconds over medium-high heat, until the tortilla begins to cook on the outer edges.

4. Flip with a thin spatula and cook slightly longer on the other side. Flip again. The top layer of the tortilla should start separating from the bottom layer, creating a pocket.

5. Immediately transfer the tortillas to a kitchen towel and keep warm until serving time.

SPICY OR SWEET SOFT TOFU

Known as *do hua*, or "tofu blossom," in Chinese, this very soft bean curd is a common breakfast all over East Asia. In Northeast Asia, it is commonly served with a spicy topping and a fried pastry. In the southern parts of East Asia, sweet toppings are popular. You have the option of choosing either one of the topping recipes included here.

YIELD: 8 PORTIONS

---

2 qt/1.92 L Plain Soy Milk (page 275)

¾ oz/21 g food-grade gypsum powder

6 fl oz/180 mL cold water

Sweet Topping

7 oz/198 g sugar

1 cup/240 mL water

1 fl oz/30 mL lemon juice

1 tbsp/8 g minced ginger

Spicy Topping

4 oz/113 g dried wood ear mushrooms, soaked, cut into chiffonade

1 fl oz/30 mL vegetable oil

1 cup/240 mL water

1 tbsp/15 mL chili oil

2 fl oz/60 mL light soy sauce, not low-sodium

1 fl oz/30 mL dark rice vinegar

Cornstarch slurry, as needed

2 green onions, minced

---

1. Bring the soy milk to 180°F/82°C over low to medium heat. Stir often to prevent scorching.

2. Meanwhile, in a container large enough to hold 1 qt/960 mL, combine the gypsum and cold water to make a slurry.

3. When the soy milk reaches about 180°F/82°C, remove from the heat and pour it onto the gypsum slurry. Whisk vigorously to ensure even mixing. Cover the container, and hold warm for 30 minutes. The soy milk will coagulate into soft tofu with a texture resembling delicate custard.

4. If using the sweet topping, combine the sugar, water, lemon juice, and ginger in a saucepan. Bring to a boil over high heat, then reduce the heat to establish a gentle simmer. Simmer over medium heat until a maple syrup–like consistency is achieved, about 2 minutes. Strain and reserve.

5. If using the spicy topping, stir-fry the mushrooms in the vegetable oil for about 1 minute. Add the water, chili oil, soy sauce, and rice vinegar. Bring the mixture to a boil, and thicken with the cornstarch slurry to achieve a medium nappé. Add the green onions, and adjust the seasoning as necessary. Hold warm.

6. To serve, carefully ladle the soft tofu into a soup cup and top with the sweet or spicy topping, as desired.

| CHEF'S NOTES | In order to maintain its delicate texture, it is vitally important to handle the tofu very gently after coagulation.
Gypsum, the common term for calcium sulfate, is a common coagulant for tofu in Chinese cuisine, and food-grade gypsum is available in many Asian stores. Other cuisines use nigari salt, a coagulant based on either magnesium or calcium chloride. Acids will also coagulate the soy protein, but they also impact the flavor. |
|---|---|

To make fresh soy milk, purée the soybeans and water until very smooth, then strain through cheesecloth.

Heat the soy milk over medium heat, stirring to prevent scorching.

Pour the warm soy milk over the gypsum slurry. Whisk vigorously so that the mixture is thoroughly combined. Cover and let sit for 30 minutes or until the mixture coagulates.

Serve the tofu with either spicy or sweet topping.

Recipes 281

BRAISED LAMB RAVIOLI IN YOGURT SAUCE

YIELD: 8 PORTIONS

Pasta

1 lb 8 oz/680 g bread flour

1 tsp/3 g salt

6 eggs

Filling

1 lb 8 oz/680 g ground lamb

8 oz/227 g minced onions

¼ cup/12 g finely chopped parsley

1½ tsp/3 g ground coriander

½ tsp/3 g ground cumin

2 garlic cloves, minced

Salt, as needed

Ground black pepper, as needed

½ cup/120 mL extra-virgin olive oil

Sauce

3 garlic cloves, minced

1 pint/480 mL brown veal stock, or as needed

1 cup/240 mL drained Greek yogurt

3 oz/85 g butter

1½ tsp/3 g red pepper flakes

1. To make the pasta dough, combine the flour and salt in a food processor. Add the eggs and process until the mixture reaches the texture of coarse cornmeal. When pressed together, the dough should stick together and form a cohesive mass. If needed, add a little water or flour to adjust to the correct consistency.

2. Transfer the mixture to a work surface and knead it until it forms a smooth and pliable dough, 2 to 3 minutes. Place the dough in a mixing bowl, cover with plastic wrap, and allow to rest for 30 minutes.

3. To make the filling, thoroughly combine the lamb, onions, parsley, coriander, cumin, garlic, salt, and pepper. If needed, adjust the seasoning.

4. Using a pasta machine, roll the dough into thin sheets, between 1/16 in/2 mm and 1/8 in/3 mm. Brush half of the sheets lightly with water. Place 1-oz/28-g piles of the filling 1 in/3 cm apart on the sheets brushed with water. Top each of those sheets with another dough sheet. Press around each pile of filling to seal the top and bottom pieces of dough together, and cut out round ravioli about 1 in/3 cm in diameter.

5. Bring 2 gal/7.68 L of salted water to a boil. Precook the raviolis for 2 to 3 minutes and reserve.

6. In a skillet large enough to hold the ravioli in a single layer, sauté the ravioli in the olive oil over medium heat until well browned on both sides, 2 to 4 minutes. Work in batches if necessary to avoid overcrowding the pan.

7. Add the garlic and enough veal stock to halfway submerge the ravioli. Bring to a boil over high heat, then cover the pan with a tight-fitting lid and reduce the heat to establish a simmer. Slowly braise over medium heat until the ravioli are cooked through, 5 to 6 minutes.

(continued) →

Recipes **283**

8. Once the ravioli are fully cooked, remove the lid. Continue simmering over medium heat in order to reduce the stock to a glaze, 2 to 3 minutes. Stir in the yogurt, and toss over medium heat to combine well with the glaze and coat the ravioli, 2 to 3 minutes. Transfer to a serving dish and reserve.

9. In a skillet over medium heat, heat the butter until it begins to turn brown and develops a nutty aroma. Add the red pepper flakes and allow to brown slightly. Pour the butter mixture over the ravioli. Serve.

TURKISH WATER BÖREK

YIELD: 8 PORTIONS

Dough

1 lb/454 g all-purpose flour

1 lb/454 g cake flour

8 eggs

1 tbsp/15 mL lemon juice

1½ tsp/5 g salt

Filling

1 pint/480 mL milk, warmed

6 eggs

6 fl oz/180 mL extra-virgin olive oil

1 lb 2 oz/510 g crumbled feta cheese

¼ cup/12 g finely cut dill

¼ cup/12 g chopped flat-leaf parsley

1. To make the dough, combine the flours, eggs, lemon juice, and salt, and knead vigorously until the mixture forms a smooth, pliable dough, 2 to 3 minutes. Place in a tightly covered container and allow the dough to rest for 1 hour.

2. Roll the dough into a very thin sheet, 1/16 to 1/8 in/2 to 3 mm thick, and trim to fit into an oven-safe 9 by 13-in/23 by 33-cm casserole dish. Oil the dish.

3. Boil the dough in a generous amount of water until it is cooked through and firm, about 1 minute. Shock in an ice bath to cool. Remove the dough from the water bath and dry.

4. In a bowl, thoroughly combine the milk, eggs, and olive oil until homogenous.

5. Place the sheet of dough in the oiled casserole dish. Mix the cheese, dill, and parsley, then layer on top of the dough. Pour the egg mixture on top, and bake in a 375°F/191°C oven until the egg mixture is set and slightly browned, 10 to 15 minutes. Cut into 8 portions and serve on a plate.

CHEF'S NOTE | Börek, also known as *burek, briwat,* or *brik,* is a baked or fried, stuffed savory pastry commonly found in North Africa, the Middle East, the Balkans, and parts of western Central Asia. It can be prepared as individual pastries or as a multi-portion preparation in a large pan, like this version. The Greek version, spanakopita, has become a very popular cocktail snack.

MAC AND CHEESE WITH BACON

YIELD: 8 PORTIONS

2 lb/907 g elbow macaroni

2 oz/57 g unsalted butter

Cheese Sauce

1½ oz/43 g all-purpose flour

1 fl oz/30 mL vegetable oil

1.5 qt/1440 mL milk

4 oz/113 g Brie cheese, rind on, diced

4 oz/113 g grated Parmesan cheese

4 oz/113 g grated Gruyère cheese

2 tbsp/30 mL whole-grain Pommery mustard

Salt, as needed

Ground black pepper, as needed

Grated nutmeg, as needed

Crumbled cooked bacon, as needed

Grated mozzarella cheese, as needed

Bread crumbs, as needed

Unsalted butter, diced, as needed

1. Cook the elbow macaroni in 2 gal/7.57 L of well-salted water until tender, 5 to 7 minutes. Drain the macaroni, toss in the butter, and reserve.

2. To make the cheese sauce, combine the flour and oil in a saucepan and cook over low heat until it forms a pale paste and the raw flour aroma has dissipated, about 4 minutes. Gradually add the milk, whisking constantly. Bring to a boil, and then reduce the heat to establish a simmer. Slowly simmer, stirring frequently, until the sauce has reached medium nappé, about 20 minutes. Add the Brie, Parmesan, and Gruyère and allow to melt, stirring frequently, in the hot milk mixture. Transfer to a blender and purée until smooth. Add the mustard and adjust the seasoning as needed with salt, pepper, and nutmeg.

3. Toss the macaroni with the cheese sauce and pour into a lightly buttered hotel pan. Top with bacon, mozzarella cheese, bread crumbs, and diced butter as desired.

4. Bake in a 400°F/204°C oven until the cheese sauce is bubbling and the top is well browned, 10 to 15 minutes. Divide the macaroni and cheese into portions, and serve hot, directly from the pan.

CHILAQUILES WITH MUSHROOMS

YIELD: 8 PORTIONS

1 lb/454 g white mushrooms, sliced ¼ in/6 mm thick	Salt, as needed
2 fl oz/60 mL pure olive oil	Vegetable oil, as needed, to fry the tortillas
4 oz/113 g minced onions	8 oz/227 g Corn Tortillas (page 279), cut into 8 wedges each
2 garlic cloves, minced	½ cup/120 mL sour cream
1 cup/240 mL Cooked Tomatillo Salsa (page 325)	4 oz/113 g crumbled queso fresco
	½ cup/120 mL coarsely cut cilantro

1. In a very hot skillet, cook the mushrooms in the olive oil until slightly browned, 3 to 5 minutes. Add the onions and sweat for 1 minute. Add the garlic and cook until fragrant, 10 to 20 seconds. Add the salsa and simmer for about 2 minutes more. Adjust the seasoning as needed with salt.

2. Heat the oil to 325°F/163°C and deep-fry the corn tortilla wedges until crispy and very slightly browned, 1 to 2 minutes.

3. In a mixing bowl, combine the fried tortilla wedges with the mushroom mixture. The tortillas should soften slightly but not become mushy.

4. Transfer to a serving platter, the drizzle with sour cream, and sprinkle with the queso fresco. Bake in a 450°F/232°C oven until heated through, about 5 minutes.

5. Garnish with the cilantro and serve immediately.

CHEF'S NOTE Made from leftover corn tortillas and salsas mixed with eggs and other available ingredients, in Mexico chilaquiles are a traditional and very popular breakfast dish. Chilaquiles are often confused with Tex-Mex migas, which is a similar dish of scrambled eggs served with strips of corn tortillas and other garnishes.

BBQ HOMINY STEW

YIELD: 8 PORTIONS

8 oz/227 g minced onions	1½ cups/360 mL half-and-half
3 fl oz/90 mL vegetable oil	1 cup/240 mL barbecue sauce (from scratch or commercial)
8 oz/227 g Spanish chorizo, cut into small dice	Salt, as needed
8 oz/227 g small-dice red pepper	Ground black pepper, as needed
2 garlic cloves, minced	½ cup/24 g coarsely cut cilantro
8 oz/227 g poblano peppers, roasted, peeled, cut into small dice	1 fl oz/28 mL lemon juice
	6 oz/170 g finely grated Cheddar cheese
2 lb/907 g canned hominy, drained	

1. In a rondeau, sweat the onions in the vegetable oil over moderate heat until very tender, about 5 minutes. Add the chorizo and render over moderate heat for 3 minutes. Add the red pepper and garlic and continue to sweat until the pepper becomes tender, 1 to 2 minutes. Add the poblano pepper and sweat for 1 minute, until tender.

2. Add the hominy, half-and-half, and barbecue sauce, and simmer gently until the mixture resembles a stew, about 10 minutes. Adjust the seasoning as needed with salt and a generous amount of black pepper. Stir in the cilantro and lemon juice.

3. Transfer the mixture to a baking dish. Sprinkle the cheese on top, and bake in a 375°F/191°C convection oven until the stew is bubbly and the top is well browned, 10 to 15 minutes. Allow to rest for 10 minutes after baking, and serve in a bowl.

CHEF'S NOTE

To produce hominy, corn kernels are soaked and briefly boiled in a weak lye solution in order to remove the hull, a process known as *nixtamalization*. The traditional intent was to extend shelf life, but the process also imparts a unique flavor. There is also a nutritional benefit, since the process makes many of the corn's nutrients more easily accessible for the human metabolic system. Ground hominy is processed into hominy grits or into masa harina, a flour used to make tamales and corn tortillas.

STIR-FRIED SHREDDED FLATBREAD

YIELD: 8 PORTIONS

Flatbread

1 lb 8 oz/680 g all-purpose flour

9 fl oz/270 mL water, heated to boiling

4½ fl oz/135 mL cold water

Salt, as needed

1 cup/240 mL vegetable oil

Stir-Fry

2 fl oz/60 mL vegetable oil

2 garlic cloves, sliced

3 green onions, sliced

1 tsp/2 g red pepper flakes

4 oz/113 g julienne carrots

4 oz/113 g napa cabbage, cut into chiffonade

4 oz/113 g julienne leeks

Salt, as needed

Ground white pepper, as needed

2 fl oz/60 mL light soy sauce, not low-sodium

3 oz/85 g bean sprouts

½ bunch cilantro, coarsely cut

1 tbsp/15 mL sesame oil

1. To make the flatbread, combine the flour with the boiling water in the bowl of an electric mixer fitted with the dough hook. Mix on low speed until all the water is absorbed, about 30 seconds. Add the cold water and continue mixing until a pliable dough forms, about 30 seconds. Wrap the dough in plastic and allow the dough to rest for 30 minutes.

2. On a lightly floured surface, roll the dough into a ¼-in/6-mm-thick rectangle. Lightly sprinkle the dough with salt and generously brush with oil. Starting on the long side of the dough sheet, roll it up like a jelly roll. Roll the "jelly roll" into a coil (it should look like a snail shell) and gently press it together. Allow the dough to rest for 10 minutes.

3. Gently flatten the dough coil by hand, then roll it into a ¼-in/6-mm-thick round or rectangle.

4. In a lightly oiled skillet or griddle over moderate heat, cook the dough until cooked through and light golden brown on both sides, 3 to 5 minutes per side. Allow the flatbread to cool. Cut it into ½-in/1-cm-wide strips. Reserve.

5. At service, heat the vegetable oil in a wok over medium heat. Add the garlic, green onions, and red pepper flakes and stir-fry until fragrant, about 30 seconds. Add the carrots, cabbage, and leeks and stir-fry until tender. Add the shredded flatbread, toss well to combine, and adjust seasoning with salt, pepper, and soy sauce. Add the bean sprouts, cilantro, and sesame oil, toss well, and serve immediately on a plate with chopsticks.

| CHEF'S NOTE | Stir-fried flatbread, or *chao bing* in Chinese, is traditional in northern China, where products based on wheat are more common than those based on rice. Since this dish can be prepared without any special gadgets or equipment, it is oftentimes referred to as "poor man's noodles." |

Roll the dough thin, then roll into a log.

Roll the dough into a coil.

Cook the rolled flatbread in oil over moderate heat until browned on both sides.

Shred the flatbread before adding to the stir-fried vegetables in the wok.

MALAYSIAN STIR-FRIED RICE NOODLES

YIELD: 6 PORTIONS

2 lb/907 g dried rice noodles, wide ribbon–style

6 eggs

2 fl oz/60 mL vegetable oil, plus as needed

4 Chinese dry sausages (lap cheong), thinly sliced on the bias

3 garlic cloves, sliced

1 lb/454 g shrimp, peeled, deveined

2 fl oz/60 mL light soy sauce, not low-sodium

1 fl oz/30 mL thick, dark soy sauce

1 fl oz/30 mL chili paste or sriracha

4 oz/113 g bean sprouts

8 green onions, thinly sliced

1. Soak the rice noodles in boiling water until soft, about 10 minutes. Drain, rinse in cold water, and reserve.

2. Crack all the eggs in a bowl but do not beat. Reserve at room temperature.

3. In a wok or similar pan, heat the vegetable oil over medium to high heat. Add the sausages and stir-fry until lightly browned and some of the fat has rendered. Add the garlic and stir-fry until aromatic, 10 to 20 seconds. Add the shrimp and stir-fry until the shrimp turn bright orange, 20 to 30 seconds. Add the noodles and continue to stir-fry, tossing until the mixture is well combined. Add both soy sauces and chili paste, and toss to thoroughly combine.

4. Push all ingredients toward the sides of the wok to create a well in the center. Place a small amount of oil and the eggs into the well at the center. Cook until the eggs begin to set, 30 seconds to 1 minute, then start stirring them gently. Continue to cook, stirring gently, until the eggs are halfway cooked. Add the bean sprouts, and combine with everything that had been pushed to the sides of the wok. Continue to stir-fry until the eggs are fully cooked and dispersed in small pieces throughout the entire mixture, about 1 minute.

5. Garnish with the green onions and serve.

CHEF'S NOTE

Char kwey teow is probably one of the most iconic noodle dishes in Malaysia, Singapore, and Indonesia. Commonly sold at the hawker centers of the region, the recipes for *char kwey teow* vary from vendor to vendor. Most feature wide ribbon–style rice noodles, Chinese sausage, eggs, and shrimp. Traditionally it was a rather fatty preparation, using inexpensive cuts of pork as an economical source of sustenance for workers.

Recipes

CURRY UDON NOODLES

First-time travelers to Japan are commonly surprised by the popularity of curry. Curry was introduced to Japan by European chefs at the beginning of the twentieth century, which explains curry's similarity to goulash.

YIELD: 8 PORTIONS

Curry Sauce

8 oz/227 g sliced onions

2 fl oz/60 mL vegetable oil

4 garlic cloves, sliced

1 oz/28 g very fine julienne ginger

1 lb/454 g chicken breast, very thinly sliced

1 lb/454 g julienne turnip

½ oz/14 g sugar

Salt, as needed

2½ qt/2.4 L water

3 oz/85 g Japanese curry paste

1 fl oz/30 mL light soy sauce, not low-sodium

1 lb/454 g napa cabbage

2 lb/907 g dried udon noodles

4 green onions, sliced

2 cups/142 g radish sprouts

1. In a pan over medium heat, sweat the onions in the vegetable oil until tender, 5 to 8 minutes. Add the garlic and ginger and continue to sweat until aromatic, 10 to 20 seconds. Add the chicken breast and cook, turning as necessary, until opaque. Add the turnip and continue to cook over medium heat until tender, 3 to 5 minutes. Add the sugar and adjust the seasoning with salt. Remove the mixture from the pan and reserve.

2. Add the water to the pan and bring to a boil over high heat. Lower the heat to a gentle simmer, and add the Japanese curry paste and simmer until the curry paste is fully dispersed and the sauce is slightly thick, about 2 minutes. Add the soy sauce, the cooked chicken mixture, and the cabbage to the curry sauce and simmer until the cabbage is slightly tender, 3 to 5 minutes.

3. In a pot over high heat, cook the noodles in 2 gal/7.57 L of well-salted boiling water until tender, 3 to 5 minutes. Rinse with hot water, toss with the green onions, and divide into 8 Asian noodle bowls.

4. Top each bowl of noodles with the curry sauce and mix gently to combine. Garnish each bowl with radish sprouts.

CHEF'S NOTES

Udon noodles are thick white noodles made from wheat flour, water, and salt that have a unique slippery texture and are an integral component of Japanese cookery. Available fresh, dried, or parcooked, udon noodles are commonly served with a hot broth. During the hot summer months, chilled versions with various flavorings are very popular. As with other noodle dishes, in Japan it is a sign of good table manners to slurp the udon noodles while eating them.

Even the most accomplished chefs use commercial Japanese curry paste, essentially a curry-flavored roux, to prepare this dish.

294   CHAPTER 5   Grains, Legumes, Noodles, & Bread

PAELLA VALENCIANA

YIELD: 8 PORTIONS

½ tsp/0.5 g saffron threads	8 oz/227 g medium-dice green pepper
3 qt/2.84 L chicken stock	1 lb/454 g chicken breast, diced
Salt, as needed	2 lb 8 oz/1.13 kg Calasparra rice
8 oz/227 g Spanish chorizo, cut into small dice	8 clams
	8 mussels
6 fl oz/180 mL extra-virgin olive oil	8 shrimp, head on, deveined, not peeled
4 oz/113 g medium-dice yellow onions	4 oz/113 g green peas
2 garlic cloves, minced	2 lemons
8 oz/227 g medium-dice red pepper	

1. Add the saffron to the stock and gently simmer for 5 minutes. Adjust the seasoning with salt as needed. Reserve.

2. In a paella or similar pan over medium heat, cook the chorizo in the olive oil until it begins to brown, 1 to 2 minutes. Add the onions and continue to cook over medium heat until tender and translucent, 2 to 3 minutes. Add the garlic and sweat until it becomes aromatic, 10 to 20 seconds. Add the peppers and chicken and sauté for 2 minutes more.

3. Add the rice and mix well until all the rice grains are coated with oil. Add the stock, and, stirring occasionally, bring to a boil over high heat. Lower the heat to establish a gentle simmer. Simmer for 3 to 4 minutes. Press the clams into the rice with the hinge sides down, and simmer for an additional 3 minutes. Press the mussels into the rice with the hinge sides down. Arrange the shrimp and peas over the rice and continue to simmer until all the moisture has been absorbed by the rice and a crust has formed on the bottom of the pan, about 5 more minutes. Remove the pan from the heat. Discard any clams or mussels that have not opened.

4. Add the juice from 1 lemon, cover the pan, and allow it to rest for 10 minutes before serving.

5. Meanwhile, cut the remaining lemon into wedges.

6. Garnish with the lemon wedges, and serve the paella in the pan.

CHEF'S NOTE

Paella, a rice dish originating in the Valencia region of Spain, is one of the identifying dishes of Spanish cuisine. It is often served as a celebratory dish for a crowd, and the ingredients vary depending on seasonal and regional availability. A good paella has a crust on the bottom of the pan that is formed by the rice and just the right amount of heat and cooking time. Calasparra rice, a short-grain rice grown in the mountainous regions of Murcia, Spain, is paramount to a successful paella. It provides exactly the right texture for paella, because it absorbs large amounts of liquid without becoming sticky, too soft, or too creamy.

STIR-FRIED GLASS NOODLES

YIELD: 8 PORTIONS

8 dried shiitake mushrooms

1 oz/28 g dried wood ear mushrooms

1 lb/454 g Korean sweet potato noodles, also known as glass noodles

5 large eggs

Vegetable oil, as needed, for cooking the eggs

6 green onions, sliced thinly

½ cup/120 mL light soy sauce, not low-sodium

1 tbsp/15 mL sesame oil

2 tbsp/25 g sugar

8 oz/227 g thinly sliced onions

6 cloves minced garlic

4 fl oz/120 mL vegetable oil

8 oz/227 g julienne red peppers

8 oz/227 g napa cabbage, cut into thin chiffonade

8 oz/227 g julienne carrots

Salt, as needed

Ground black pepper, as needed

1. Soak the shiitake and the wood ear mushrooms, separately, in enough cold water to cover, overnight. Drain the mushrooms, reserving the shiitake soaking liquid.

2. De-stem the shiitake mushrooms. Slice the caps into thin strips and reserve. Remove and discard all hard parts of the wood ear mushrooms. Slice the mushrooms into thin strips.

3. Submerge the noodles in boiling water, remove the pot from the heat, and allow to soak until the noodles are soft and pliable, 8 to 10 minutes. Drain the noodles, rinse with cool water, and reserve.

4. Beat the eggs thoroughly. In a nonstick skillet over medium heat, cook the eggs in vegetable oil to create very thin egg crêpes that are cooked but not brown, 1 to 2 minutes. Allow the crêpes to cool, then cut them into very thin strips and reserve.

5. Combine the green onions, soy sauce, sesame oil, and sugar, and reserve.

6. Stir-fry the onions and garlic in the vegetable oil over high heat until translucent, 1 to 2 minutes. Add the peppers, cabbage, and carrots, and stir-fry until almost tender, 3 to 4 minutes. Add the soaked noodles and stir-fry to heat through, 2 to 3 minutes. Add the soy sauce mixture and 1 cup/240 mL of the shiitake soaking liquid. Cook over medium-high heat until the liquids have been absorbed. Adjust the seasoning with salt and pepper as needed.

7. Transfer to serving plates. Serve garnished with sliced egg crêpes.

CHEF'S NOTE — Known as *japchae* in Korea, this dish features transparent noodles made from sweet potato starch. Prized all over northeastern Asia for their unique chewiness and slipperiness, these noodles have a neutral flavor that makes them a fantastic vehicle for other flavors.

WHOLE WHEAT PASTA WITH SHARP PESTO

YIELD: 8 PORTIONS

Pasta

1 lb/454 g durum flour

1 lb/454 g whole wheat durum flour

1 fl oz/30 mL extra-virgin olive oil

1 tbsp/10 g salt

8 eggs

Pesto

1 bunch basil leaves

¼ cup/30 g walnuts, toasted

¼ cup/21 g grated Pecorino Romano cheese

3 fl oz/90 mL extra-virgin olive oil

2 garlic cloves

Salt, as needed

1 lb/454 g shredded green beans

1 lb/454 g yellow potatoes, cut into ¼-in/ 6-mm slices

Salt, as needed

1. To make the pasta, combine the durum flour, whole wheat durum flour, oil, and salt in a food processor. Add the eggs and process until the mixture resembles coarse meal. When pressed, the dough should form a cohesive mass. Add water or flour to adjust the consistency as needed.

2. Transfer the dough to a work surface and knead until the dough is very firm yet still pliable. Cover and allow the dough to rest at room temperature for at least 30 minutes.

3. To make the pesto, combine the basil, walnuts, cheese, olive oil, and garlic in a food processor and pulse into a slightly coarse paste. Adjust consistency as needed with olive oil. Season with salt as needed. Reserve.

4. Roll the pasta dough into sheets ⅛ in/3 mm thick. Cut the sheets into linguine or similar long thin strips, and reserve uncovered.

5. Cook the beans in rapidly boiling salted water until fork-tender, 3 to 5 minutes. Remove the beans from the water, and reserve.

6. In the same boiling salted water, cook the potatoes until fork-tender, 3 to 5 minutes. Remove from the water, and combine with the beans.

7. If necessary, add more salt to the boiling water, then add the pasta and cook until just done, 1 to 2 minutes. Drain the pasta, and in a large bowl, toss it with the pesto and green beans and potatoes. Serve immediately.

298 CHAPTER 5 Grains, Legumes, Noodles, & Bread

BRUSCHETTA WITH CAULIFLOWER AND PROSCIUTTO

YIELD: 8 PORTIONS

1 head cauliflower	Salt, as needed
½ cup/120 mL extra-virgin olive oil	Ground black pepper, as needed
	Lemon juice, as needed
6 garlic cloves, finely minced	16 slices baguette, cut on the bias ¼ in/6 mm thick
8 salted anchovy fillets	
¼ cup/33 g chopped capers	Olive oil, as needed, for brushing
¼ cup/12 g coarsely chopped flat-leaf parsley	16 very thin slices prosciutto

1. Divide the cauliflower into 2-in/5-cm florets. Toss the florets in a small amount of olive oil, place on a sheet pan, and roast in a 375°F/191°C oven until fully cooked and slightly caramelized, 10 to 15 minutes.

2. In a skillet, sweat the garlic in the remaining olive oil over moderate heat until fragrant, 10 to 20 seconds. Add the anchovies and capers and continue cooking for 1 minute more. Remove from the heat and set aside.

3. Once the cauliflower is tender, combine it with the anchovy mixture in the bowl of a food processor and purée into a coarse paste. Stir in the parsley and adjust the seasoning with salt, pepper, and lemon juice as needed.

4. Brush the baguette slices with olive oil and grill or toast them over medium-high heat until crisp and lightly charred, 1 to 2 minutes per side, and top with each piece with 1 slice of prosciutto. Top each piece of prosciutto with a dollop of the cauliflower spread. Serve.

BRUSCHETTA WITH ROASTED TOMATOES, GREEN ONIONS, AND PECORINO CHEESE

YIELD: 8 PORTIONS

16 roma tomatoes (3 lb 8 oz/ 1.59 kg), cut in half lengthwise, cored

1 bunch green onions, thinly sliced

¼ cup/60 mL extra-virgin olive oil

½ bunch basil leaves

1½ tbsp/22.5 mL balsamic vinegar

Salt, as needed

Ground black pepper, as needed

16 slices baguette, sliced on the bias ¼ in/6 mm thick

1 cup/84 g very finely grated pecorino cheese

1. Place the tomatoes cut side down on a sheet pan fitted with a wire rack. Roast the tomatoes under a broiler until the skin begins to char and blister, 3 to 5 minutes. Remove from the oven, remove the skins, and place the peeled tomatoes back on the wire rack. Bake in a 275°F/135°C convection oven until they have shrunk to half their original size, 1 to 2 hours.

2. Cook the green onions in the olive oil in a pan over moderate heat for 1 minute. Toss the green onions with the tomatoes.

3. Add the basil and balsamic vinegar to the tomato mixture. Adjust the seasoning with salt and pepper as needed.

4. Brush the baguette slices with olive oil and grill or toast them over medium-high heat until crisp and lightly charred, 1 to 2 minutes per side, and top each slice with 2 tomato halves and some of the green onions. Just before serving, top each portion with 1 tbsp of pecorino cheese.

BRUSCHETTA WITH EGGPLANT RELISH AND RICOTTA SALATA CHEESE

YIELD: 8 PORTIONS

3 lb/1.36 kg eggplant, peeled, cut into ½-in/1-cm cubes

½ oz/14 g salt, plus as needed

4 oz/113 g minced onions

4 fl oz/120 mL extra-virgin olive oil

4 oz/113 g small-dice celery

1½ cups/360 mL tomato purée

3 oz/85 g pitted green olives, cut into small dice

1½ oz/43 g capers, rinsed and drained

2 oz/57 g sugar

2½ fl oz/75 mL white wine vinegar

Ground black pepper, as needed

16 baguette slices, cut on the bias ¼ in/6 mm thick

1 cup/84 g ricotta salata cheese, crumbled

1. Toss the eggplant with the salt and allow to sit for 30 minutes.

2. Sweat the onions in 1 fl oz/30 mL of the olive oil in a sauté pan over medium heat until tender, 2 to 3 minutes. Add the celery and continue to cook until tender, 2 to 3 minutes. Add the tomato purée, and increase the heat to medium-high and bring the mixture to a boil. Add the olives, capers, sugar, and vinegar. Adjust the seasoning with salt and pepper and reserve.

3. Squeeze the eggplant cubes to remove any excess water. Rinse, and pat dry with paper towels.

4. In a rondeau, cook the eggplant over high heat in the remaining 3 fl oz/90 mL of olive oil until slightly caramelized, 2 to 3 minutes. Lower the heat to medium and add the reserved sauce. Increase the heat and bring to a boil, then lower the heat to medium and simmer until the mixture thickens, about 10 minutes. Adjust seasoning, if necessary.

5. Brush the baguette slices with olive oil and grill or toast them over medium-high heat until crisp and lightly charred, 1 to 2 minutes. At service, top the grilled baguette with a generous pile of the eggplant mixture and sprinkle with the ricotta salata.

Recipes 303

BRUSCHETTA WITH MUSTARD GREENS AND PARMESAN CHEESE

YIELD: 8 PORTIONS

3 lb/1.36 kg mustard greens	1 cup/240 mL chicken stock
5 garlic cloves, very thinly sliced	Salt, as needed
4 oz/113 g minced onions	Ground black pepper, as needed
1 pinch red pepper flakes	16 slices baguette, cut on the bias ¼ in/6 mm thick
3 fl oz/90 mL extra-virgin olive oil, plus as needed	1 cup/84 g grated Parmesan cheese

1. Wash the mustard greens thoroughly in several changes of water. Drain, and cut into bite-size pieces.

2. In rondeau over moderate heat, sweat the garlic, onions, and red pepper flakes in the olive oil until fragrant, 1 to 2 minutes. Add the greens and chicken stock, cover the pot with a lid, and braise slowly until the mustard greens are tender and all liquid has evaporated, 10 to 30 minutes, depending on the maturity of the mustard greens. Remove the pot from the heat, and adjust the seasoning with salt and pepper as needed.

3. Brush the baguette slices with olive oil and grill or toast them over medium-high heat until crisp and lightly charred, 1 to 2 minutes per side. At service, top the grilled baguette with a generous pile of the braised mustard greens and sprinkle with the Parmesan cheese. Drizzle with olive oil.

POTATO PARATHAS

YIELD: 8 PORTIONS

Filling

1 lb 8 oz/680 g waxy potatoes

1 oz/28 g very finely minced onions

1 serrano, minced

2 tbsp/6 g coarsely cut cilantro

½ tsp/1 g cayenne

½ tsp/1 g garam masala

1 tbsp/15 mL lime juice

Salt, as needed

Dough

1 lb/454 g atta flour (Indian whole wheat flour), plus as needed, for dusting

1 tsp/3 g salt

10 fl oz/300 mL water

Canola oil, as needed, for rolling and cooking

Butter, as needed, for serving

1. To make the filling, bake the potatoes at 375°F/191°C until thoroughly cooked, 30 to 45 minutes. Once cool enough to handle, cut the potatoes in half lengthwise and force each half, flesh side down, through a medium-size wire rack into a hotel pan (so that the skins stay behind on the wire rack). Discard the skins.

2. Mash the potatoes with your hands into a chunky, slightly cohesive mass. Add the onions, serrano, cilantro, cayenne, garam masala, and lime juice, and adjust the seasoning with salt. Reserve.

3. To make the dough, combine the atta flour, salt, and water, and knead the mixture into a smooth, pliable dough, 1 to 2 minutes. Add more flour or water as needed to adjust the consistency. Cover the dough with plastic wrap and allow it to rest for 30 minutes.

4. Divide the dough into pieces measuring 1½ to 2 oz/43 to 57 g and roll each out into a thin disk (about ⅛ in/3 mm thick) on a lightly floured work surface. Dust each dough disk with flour and place about ¼ cup/50 g of the potato mixture in the center. Bring the edges of the dough up to create a pouch around the filling. Gently press down on the center of the pouch to create a round disk that completely encloses the filling. Generously dust the disk with flour and roll it to a thickness of about ¼ in/6 mm. Brush off any excess flour, and reserve.

5. Brush each disk of paratha with oil and cook in an ungreased cast-iron skillet or similar pan over moderate heat until slightly brown on both sides, 1 to 2 minutes per side. To ensure even browning, press gently with a spoon or spatula on top of the paratha during cooking and flip the paratha over occasionally. At service, brush the paratha with butter and serve immediately.

CHINESE MUNG BEAN AND RICE CRÊPES

YIELD: 8 PORTIONS

Batter

10 oz/284 g husked mung beans

5 oz/142 g jasmine rice

28 fl oz/840 mL water

8 egg roll wrappers

Vegetable oil, as needed, for frying

1 cup/240 mL Korean soybean paste

½ cup/120 mL chili paste

Vegetable oil, as needed, to cook the crêpes

8 eggs

4 green onions, minced

½ cup/24 g coarsely cut cilantro

1. Combine the mung beans and rice in a bowl, cover with the water, and soak until fully hydrated, overnight.

2. In a blender, purée the rice, mung beans, and soaking water into a very smooth batter. Reserve.

3. Deep-fry the egg roll wrappers in 375°F/191°C oil until very crispy, 30 seconds to 1 minute. Reserve.

4. Purée the Korean soybean paste and the chili paste separately in a blender until each is very smooth with a viscosity resembling that of the crêpe batter.

5. To cook each crêpe, pour about 6 fl oz/180mL of the batter onto a preheated and well-oiled crêpe maker over high heat, and spread the batter as thin as possible with a crêpe spreader. Allow the crêpe to cook all the way through on one side, about 1 minute.

6. With the crêpe still on the crêpe maker, crack a raw egg onto the crêpe and spread it out evenly. Sprinkle with green onions and cilantro, and allow the egg to cook until almost fully set, about 1 minute. Once the egg is almost fully cooked, flip the crêpe over with a long spatula, and spread the other side of the crêpe with the soybean paste and chili paste.

7. Place a crispy egg roll wrapper on top and fold the edges of the crêpe over the egg roll wrapper to form a square shape. Fold the square in half. Serve immediately.

CHEF'S NOTES

For this dish, it is crucial to use a crêpe maker or a griddle. Skillets are often too small and due to the rim of the pan, it is very challenging to flip the crêpes.

Crêpes, although primarily associated with French cooking, are a popular dish in many cuisines. This version, made with a batter based on mung beans and rice, is a popular all-day snack on the streets of northern China. A comparable version known as *bánhxèo* is found in Vietnam. Made with a batter based on rice, coconut milk, and turmeric, *bánhxèo* is commonly stuffed with mung bean sprouts, fresh leafy greens, herbs, and sometimes meat and served with a traditional Vietnamese dipping sauce.

306 CHAPTER 5 Grains, Legumes, Noodles, & Bread

PAN-STEAMED CILANTRO AND PORK DUMPLINGS

YIELD: 8 PORTIONS (32 TO 40 DUMPLINGS)

Dough

1 lb 5 oz/595 g self-rising flour

14 oz/397 g water

Filling

1 lb/454 ground pork, 80% lean

8 oz/227 g coarsely cut cilantro

1 tbsp/8 g minced ginger

1 green onion, minced

½ tsp/1 g ground white pepper

1 tbsp/15 mL sesame oil

1 fl oz/30 mL light soy sauce, not low-sodium

1 tbsp/15 mL dark soy sauce

¼ cup/60 mL cold water

1 tsp/3 g salt, or as needed

Spicy Cucumbers (page 325)

1. Combine the flour and water, and knead by hand until the mixture forms a smooth dough, 1 to 2 minutes. Reserve.

2. To make the filling, combine the ground pork, cilantro, ginger, green onion, white pepper, sesame oil, soy sauces, cold water, and salt. Cook a sample and adjust seasoning, if needed.

3. Shape the dough into a log about 2 in/5 cm in diameter. Slice the log into 1-oz/28-g pieces. Roll the dough pieces into 4-in/10-cm rounds that are slightly thicker in the center than around the edges.

4. To achieve the classic steamed dumpling shape, place about 1 oz/28 g stuffing onto the center of each dough circle. Fold the edges of the dough over the filling and pinch small sections of the dough in a pleated fashion to create a closed pouch around the filling. Using your hands, gently press the dumpling on a level surface to achieve an even shape and to avoid a dome-like appearance of the dumpling after steaming.

5. Lightly oil a nonstick skillet and tightly arrange the dumplings in the skillet. Add enough water to come one-third to halfway up the side of the dumplings. Cover with a tight-fitting lid, and cook over high heat until all water has evaporated and the dumplings are well browned on the bottom, 8 to 10 minutes. Once the dumplings are done cooking, transfer them from the skillet to a wire rack and allow them to rest for 5 to 10 minutes.

6. Serve with Spicy Cucumbers.

While turning the dough in a circular motion, roll the dough from the edges toward the center so that the middle is significantly thicker than the edges.

Pinch the dough around the filling, pressing to seal.

Pan steam the dumplings, covered; the water should come one-third of the way up the dumplings.

Allowing the water to fully evaporate during the cooking will both steam the dumplings and encourage a golden brown crust to form on the bottom.

CHICKPEA STEW WITH KIMCHI IN PITA BREAD

YIELD: 8 PORTIONS

1 lb/454 g dried chickpeas

1 oz/28 g dried shiitake mushrooms

1 lb/454 g medium-dice onions

3 fl oz/90 mL vegetable oil

2½ floz/75 mL gochujang (Korean hot pepper paste)

Salt, as needed

2 tsp/8 g sugar

1 fl oz/30 mL light soy sauce, not low-sodium

½ tsp/1 g ground Korean chili powder

8 oz/227 g cabbage kimchi

4 pieces Pita Bread (page 111), cut in half

Radish sprouts, as needed

1. Sort and rinse the chickpeas. Cover with 4 to 5 in/10 to 13 cm cold water and allow to soak for at least 24 hours.

2. Cover the shiitake mushrooms with cold water and allow to soak for at least 24 hours.

3. Rinse the soaked chickpeas, and cook in a generous amount of unsalted simmering water until tender, 30 to 90 minutes.

4. Drain the soaked shiitake mushrooms and reserve the soaking liquid. De-stem the mushrooms, cut them into small dice, and reserve.

5. In a rondeau over low heat, sweat the onions in the vegetable oil until very tender, about 15 minutes. Add the ground Korean chili powder and continue to sweat until aromatic for about 20 to 30 seconds. Add the diced mushrooms along with their soaking liquid, the cooked chickpeas, and the gochujang. Adjust seasoning with salt, sugar, and soy sauce.

6. Simmer gently until vegetables are tender and the mixture looks like a thick stew, 30 to 40 minutes. Add the cabbage kimchi, and adjust seasoning, if necessary. Hold until ready to serve. Refrigerate if not serving within 4 hours.

7. At service, fill the pocket of each pita half with the chickpea stew. Top with the radish sprouts and serve immediately.

GRILLED TOAST WITH COCONUT JAM AND CODDLED EGGS

This grilled sandwich is known as *roti kaya* in Singapore and Malaysia and is a popular all-day snack often accompanied by a sweet and creamy hot tea or coffee. It is believed to have been created by Chinese cooks working in kitchens that catered to British colonists. Over time, the British jams and marmalades were replaced with the native coconut spread. Kaya can be obtained commercially in any Asian grocery store with a focus on Southeast Asian ingredients.

YIELD: 8 PORTIONS

Coconut Jam (Kaya)

1 cup/240 mL thick coconut milk

12 oz/340 g sugar

1 cup/240 mL eggs, beaten

¼ tsp/1 mL pandan extract

Grilled Toast

16 slices white bread

4 oz/113 g hard butter, thinly sliced

Coddled Eggs

8 eggs, at room temperature

2 tsp/4 g ground white pepper

1 fl oz/30 mL dark soy sauce

1. To make the coconut jam, simmer the coconut milk and sugar until the sugar dissolves. Temper the beaten eggs into the hot coconut milk.

2. Gently heat the mixture over a water bath until it thickens into jam and reaches heavy nappé, 2 to 3 minutes. Add the pandan extract, and allow to cool. Reserve.

3. Spread 1 tbsp/15 mL of the coconut jam onto each slice of bread and top with ¼ oz/7 g of the butter slices. Sandwich every 2 slices of bread together to produce 8 portions.

4. At service, grill each sandwich until the butter begins to melt and the bread is slightly charred, 1 to 3 minutes per side.

5. To make the coddled eggs, place the eggs in a bowl, cover with 1 qt/960 mL of boiling water, and allow to sit for 3 minutes.

6. At service, crack the eggs, which should be barely cooked, into individual soup cups. Distribute the white pepper and dark soy sauce evenly over the soup cups. Do not mix with the eggs.

7. Cut the grilled toast lengthwise into thirds, and serve with the coddled egg mixture on the side as a dip.

CHEF'S NOTE

Pandan, a member of the screw pine family, is a popular ingredient in Southeast Asian cooking, particularly in sweet dishes. Pandan's flavor is often described as sweet and floral, with citrus and vanilla notes. Pandan extract or frozen pandan leaves are available in most Asian grocery stores. Whole leaves are often boiled and pounded into a paste, or they are shaped into a knot and cooked together with the sauce to provide a subtle flavor.

CHINESE CHIVE POCKETS

YIELD: 8 PORTIONS (24 POCKETS)

Wrappers

1 lb 2 oz/510 g all-purpose flour

12 oz/340 g water

Stuffing

1½ oz/43 g thin bean thread noodles

3 large eggs, beaten

1 fl oz/30 mL vegetable oil, plus as needed for cooking the eggs

7 oz/198 g Chinese chives, cut into ¼-in/6-mm pieces

½ tsp/1 g ground white pepper

1½ tsp/2 g small dried shrimp, chopped

Salt, as needed

Dipping Sauce

1 cup/240 mL light soy sauce, not low-sodium

½ cup/120 mL dark rice vinegar

3 green onions, minced

1 tsp/5 mL chili paste

½ cup/120 mL water

1. To make the dough for the wrappers, combine the flour and water and knead into a smooth, soft dough, 1 to 2 minutes. Wrap the dough in plastic wrap and allow to rest at room temperature for 30 minutes.

2. Pour boiling water over the bean thread noodles, and allow to soak off the heat for about 10 minutes. Drain and reserve.

3. In a pan over medium-high heat, cook the beaten eggs in vegetable oil until they're relatively dry, small-curded scrambled eggs, 1 to 2 minutes.

4. Combine the bean thread noodles, scrambled eggs, 1 fl oz/30 mL vegetable oil, Chinese chives, white pepper, dried shrimp, and salt. If necessary, adjust seasoning. Reserve.

5. Portion the wrapper dough into 1¼-oz/35-g pieces. On a well-floured surface, roll each dough piece into a thin 5-in/13-cm round. Place about ¾ oz/21 g of the stuffing on top of each round of dough, and fold the round in half to completely enclose the stuffing.

6. Cook each pocket in a well-oiled, nonstick skillet or griddle over low heat until golden brown on both sides and heated through, 2 to 3 minutes per side.

7. To make the dipping sauce, combine the soy sauce, rice vinegar, green onions, chili paste, and water.

8. Serve chive pockets with the dipping sauce.

CHEF'S NOTE — Also known as *standard garlic chives,* Chinese chives have flat, broad leaves that are not hollow like other chives. They are often used in a stuffing or with eggs, but if Chinese chives are overcooked, the flavor becomes unpleasantly overpowering.

TAPIOCA CHEESE BREAD

YIELD: 8 PORTIONS (32 SMALL ROLLS)

2 lb/907 g *polvilhoazedo* (soured tapioca starch)	½ oz/14 g salt
1 pint/480 mL whole milk	6 eggs
1 oz/28 g butter	2 lb/907 g grated Parmesan cheese

1. Place the tapioca starch in a large bowl. Combine the milk, butter, and salt in a saucepan and bring to a boil over high heat, stirring to prevent scorching. Pour the boiling mixture over the tapioca starch. Allow the mixture to cool enough to handle, then rub the tapioca starch together with your fingertips until the mixture resembles coarse meal. Gradually add the eggs to the mixture, and knead into a smooth dough, 2 to 3 minutes. Add more milk to adjust the consistency if needed. Mix the cheese into the dough.

2. With oiled hands, form the dough into small balls, about 2 oz/57 g each. Arrange the rolls about 3 in/8 cm apart on an oiled sheet pan.

3. Bake in a 400°F/204°C oven for 5 minutes. Reduce the heat to 350°F/177°C and continue baking until the rolls are crisp and golden in color, about 15 minutes more. Serve.

CHEF'S NOTE

This popular and inexpensive bread, known as *pão de queijoin* in Brazil or as *chipa*, *cuñapé*, or *pan de yucca* throughout South America, can be found at street vendors in many regions of South America. Its unique chewy texture results from the use of tapioca, also known as *manioc starch*. Manioc starch is a refined starch made from the tuberous root of a shrub known as manioc, cassava, or yucca. In Brazilian cuisine, it is found in two forms: sweet manioc starch made from fresh manioc juice, and sour manioc starch that is a by-product of fermented manioc juice. The sour manioc starch, called *polvilhoazedo* in Brazil, is used in this recipe. Do not confuse manioc starch with manioc flour, which is unrefined ground yucca root.

CILANTRO AND CHICKPEA FRITTERS

YIELD: 8 PORTIONS (24 FRITTERS)

1 bunch cilantro, coarsely cut

6 oz/170 g atta flour (Indian whole wheat flour)

6 oz/170 g chickpea flour

4 oz/113 g roasted peanuts, finely chopped

1 tbsp/9 g sesame seeds

½ tsp/1 g cayenne

1 tbsp/12 g sugar

1 tsp/3 g salt

1 tsp/2 g finely minced ginger

1 tsp/3 g finely minced garlic

½ tsp/1 g garam masala

½ tsp/1 g ground turmeric

¼ tsp/1 g baking soda

1 pint/480 mL water

Vegetable oil, as needed, for deep-frying

Cucumber Raita (page 326), as needed

1. For the batter, combine the cilantro, both flours, peanuts, sesame seeds, cayenne, sugar, salt, ginger, garlic, garam masala, turmeric, and baking soda in a bowl. Gradually add the water until the mixture is a thick but pourable batter. If needed, adjust the consistency by adding more flour or water.

2. Pour the batter into an oiled baking dish to a thickness of 1 to 2 in/3 to 5 cm. Cook in a steamer until cooked through, about 15 minutes. Remove the steamed dough from the baking dish and allow to cool completely.

3. Cut the steamed dough into diamond-shaped pieces (1 by 2 in/3 by 5 cm) and deep-fry in 350°F/177°C vegetable oil until golden brown, 3 to 5 minutes. Serve fritters on a plate, accompanied by Cucumber Raita.

FALAFEL

Falafel is popular in all the cuisines of the Middle East and Egypt. It is made by grinding raw chickpeas, fava beans, or a mixture of both along with spices and aromatics into a coarse paste. The patties or balls of that paste are then deep-fried.

YIELD: 8 PORTIONS

1 lb/454 g dried chickpeas	6 garlic cloves, peeled
½ bunch flat-leaf parsley	Salt, as needed
½ bunch cilantro	Pure olive oil, as needed, for deep-frying
8 green onions	4 pieces Pita Bread (page 111), cut in half
1 tsp/2 g cayenne	1 cucumber, peeled, cut into small dice
1 tbsp/6 g ground cumin	2 tomatoes, cut into small dice
2 tsp/4 g ground coriander	1 lb/454 g Hummus (page 322)

1. Pour enough boiling water over the chickpeas to cover by 4 to 5 in/10 to 13 cm. Allow to soak for at least 8 hours in the refrigerator.

2. Drain the chickpeas thoroughly, and combine with the parsley, cilantro, green onions, cayenne, cumin, coriander, garlic, and salt. Grind the mixture through the ¼-in/6-mm die of a meat grinder. See Chef's Notes for more information about grinding.

3. Shape a small ball of the chickpea mixture to test it. Fry the test piece in 350°F/177°C olive oil until golden brown and cooked through. Taste it, and adjust seasoning if needed. Shape the remainder of the chickpea mixture into 1½-oz/43-g flattened patties. Deep-fry each patty in 350°F/177°C olive oil until golden brown and cooked through, 2 to 3 minutes.

4. To serve, place 2 falafel patties into each pita half. Garnish with cucumbers, tomatoes, and hummus. The falafel can be served as a handheld item or on a plate.

CHEF'S NOTES

Pouring boiling water over the chickpeas to soak them not only expedites the soaking, it also partially cooks a part of the chickpea's starch, resulting in a more pliable raw fritter. Some recipes suggest adding baking soda to the soaking water, since the alkalinity of baking soda helps to expedite the soaking process. The disadvantage is that the baking soda can leave a residual soapy taste, and it neutralizes some of the chickpeas' nutritionally beneficial acids.

When grinding the soaked legumes, the fine disk of a meat grinder is preferable to a food processor. If using a food processor, it's easy to over- or under-process the ingredients, which results in an unpleasant texture either way.

Recipes 317

PEANUT BUTTER–STUFFED STEAMED FLOWER ROLLS

YIELD: 8 PORTIONS (16 ROLLS)

Dough

2 lb/907 g self-rising flour

19 fl oz/570 mL cold water

Filling

3½ oz/99 g creamy peanut butter

1 tsp/2 g coarsely ground black pepper

2½ fl oz/75 g water

Salt, as needed

1. To make the dough, combine the flour and cold water in a stand mixer and mix on low speed until it forms a pliable dough that is no longer sticky, 1 to 2 minutes. Cover with plastic wrap and rest at room temperature for 30 minutes.

2. To make the filling, combine the peanut butter with the pepper, and add the water. The mixture should have the consistency of sour cream. Adjust seasoning with salt as needed.

3. To shape the flower rolls, on a floured surface roll the dough into a rectangle about ¼ in/6 mm thick. Spread the filling evenly over the entire surface of the dough, leaving a margin of about ½ in/1 cm on all sides.

4. Starting from the short side, roll the dough up as you would a jelly roll. Allow the dough to rest for about 10 minutes.

5. Cut the rolled dough into 1½-in slices and press down the middle of each with a chopstick.

6. Place the rolls into a steamer lined with cheesecloth. Steam the rolls for 10 minutes. Serve warm, on a plate.

MUNG BEAN AND SCALLION PANCAKES

YIELD: 8 PORTIONS

6 oz/170 g short-grain rice

14 oz/397 g husked yellow mung beans

4 green onions, finely minced

8 oz/227 g mixed seafood, cooked, finely chopped (see Chef's Note)

4 oz/113 g finely minced red pepper

4 oz/113 g finely chopped napa cabbage

4 oz/113 g finely minced turnip kimchi

Salt, as needed

Dipping Sauce

4 oz/113 g gochujang (Korean hot pepper paste)

4 oz/113 g water

4 green onions, minced

2 oz/57 g sesame seeds, toasted

1. Soak the rice and mung beans separately in cold water to cover until they have doubled in size, at least 4 hours.

2. Drain the rice and mung beans thoroughly. In a food processor, purée the rice into a fine paste, adding water as needed to facilitate the blending. Add the drained mung beans. Continue to blend with until the mixture is a slightly coarse paste resembling the consistency of pancake batter, adding water as needed to adjust the consistency. Add the green onions, seafood, red pepper, cabbage, and kimchi, and adjust seasoning with salt.

3. Prepare a griddle or skillet over medium heat with a moderate amount of fat, and spread the batter into pancakes measuring 2 to 3 in/5 to 8 cm in diameter and about ¼ in/6 mm thick. Fry the pancakes until cooked through and golden brown on both sides, 2 to 4 minutes per side.

4. To make the dipping sauce, combine the gochujang, water, green onions, and sesame seeds.

5. Serve the pancakes with the dipping sauce.

CHEF'S NOTES

These pancakes, known as *bin daedok* in Korea, are made using a combination of falafel-making and pancake-making techniques. The seafood suggested in this recipe can be shrimp, mussels, clams, or anything similar. Optionally, the pancakes can be prepared without any seafood as a vegetarian version.

It is important to use husked yellow mung beans, not the unhusked green mung beans, because the green mung beans will make the pancakes taste unpleasantly astringent. An interesting alternative to mung beans is green split peas; using them will change the pancakes' color from a bright yellow to a striking green.

CORN PANCAKES

YIELD: 8 PORTIONS

1 lb/454 g self-rising cornmeal
2 eggs
4 fl oz/120 mL g milk
6 fl oz/180 mL water
2 green onions, minced
1½ tsp/3 g ground black pepper
Vegetable oil, as needed, for cooking

1. Combine the cornmeal, eggs, milk, water, green onions, and pepper to form a thick batter.
2. In a skillet over low to medium heat, cook the pancakes in enough hot vegetable oil to reach ¼ in/6 mm up the sides of each pancake until golden brown on both sides, 2 to 3 minutes per side. Make 1½-oz/43-g or 3-oz/85-g pancakes.

CHEF'S NOTE | The recipe for these popular northern Chinese corn pancakes is actually very similar to the hoecakes that are popular in the Deep South of the United States. Similarly, they can be used as a great vehicle for barbecued meats.

HUMMUS

YIELD: 1 LB/454 G

4 oz/113 g sliced onions
3 garlic cloves, peeled
2½ fl oz/75 mL extra-virgin olive oil
10 oz/284 g cooked chickpeas, with some cooking liquid reserved
4 oz/113 g Greek yogurt
1 oz/28 g tahini
1 tbsp/8 g capers
½ fl oz/15 mL lemon juice
Salt, as needed
Ground black pepper, as needed

1. Cook the onions and garlic in the olive oil in a pan over moderate heat until very tender but not browned, about 15 minutes.
2. In a blender, combine the onions and garlic with the chickpeas, yogurt, tahini, capers, and lemon juice, and purée until smooth. If needed, adjust the consistency of the hummus with the chickpea cooking liquid. Adjust the seasoning with salt and pepper as needed.
3. For the best results, allow the hummus to rest overnight in the refrigerator and adjust seasoning the next day if needed. Serve in a bowl as a condiment.

CHICKPEA FLATBREAD

YIELD: 8 PORTIONS

Batter

- 1 lb/454 g chickpea flour
- 3 cups/720 mL cold water
- Salt, as needed

- 4 green onions, minced
- 1½ oz/43 g minced black olives
- 3 fl oz/90 mL extra-virgin olive oil

- ¼ cup/120 mL chopped flat-leaf parsley
- 2 tbsp/6 g sage, cut into chiffonade
- 1 tbsp/3 g chopped rosemary
- 1 tbsp/3 g coarsely cracked black pepper

- Vegetable oil, as needed, for cooking
- Sweet and Sour Zucchini (page 324)

1. Combine the chickpea flour, cold water, and salt and whisk until smooth. Allow to rest for about 1 hour. The batter's consistency should resemble that of pancake batter. Adjust the consistency with flour or water, if needed.

2. In a skillet over high heat, cook the green onions and olives in the very hot olive oil until fragrant, about 10 seconds. Remove from the heat, and add the parsley, sage, rosemary, and black pepper. Set aside and allow to cool completely.

3. Add the herb oil mix to the chickpea batter, and mix until thoroughly combined.

4. Preheat a cast-iron skillet in a 550°F/288°C oven. When the pan is hot, oil it with vegetable oil and pour enough of the chickpea batter into the skillet to create a ¼-in/6-mm layer of the batter. Bake in the oven until the sides are lightly browned and crispy, 5 to 10 minutes. Repeat until all batter is used.

5. Transfer the flatbread from the pan to a wire rack and allow to cool for 5 minutes. Cut the flatbread into eight 3-oz/85-g pieces, and serve with the Sweet and Sour Zucchini.

SWEET AND SOUR ZUCCHINI

YIELD: 8 PORTIONS

2 lb/907 g zucchini	1 tbsp/15 mL honey
2 fl oz/60 mL extra-virgin olive oil	1 oz/28 g pine nuts, toasted
1 clove garlic, minced	1 oz/28 g golden raisins
2 salted anchovy fillets, minced	Salt, as needed
1 fl oz/30 mL white wine vinegar	

1. Quarter the zucchini lengthwise and remove the seeds. Cut the quarters on a drastic bias in 1-in/3-cm diamonds.

2. In a skillet over high heat, sauté the zucchini in the olive oil until slightly browned, 1 to 2 minutes. Add the garlic and anchovy and continue cooking until aromatic, 5 to 10 seconds. Add the vinegar and honey and 1 fl oz/30 mL water, and simmer for 5 minutes.

3. Add the pine nuts and golden raisins. Season with salt, and serve.

HARISSA

YIELD: 1 PINT/480 ML

6 oz/170 g ancho chiles, stemmed, seeded	1 tsp/2 g ground coriander
2 oz/57 g chiles de árbol, seeded	2 tsp/4 g ground caraway seeds
3 garlic cloves, sliced	4 fl oz/120 mL olive oil
	Salt, as needed

1. Soak the chiles in cold water for 15 minutes. Drain well, and squeeze out excess moisture.

2. Combine the chiles, garlic, coriander, caraway seeds, and oil in a blender, and blend into a fine purée, adding water as needed to facilitate blending.

3. Adjust seasoning with salt as needed. Serve in a small bowl as a condiment.

CHEF'S NOTE | Harissa is a chili paste very popular in northwestern Africa, specifically Tunisia and Morocco. It is commonly used to boost the flavor of stews, tagines, and soups.

COOKED TOMATILLO SALSA

YIELD: 1½ CUPS/360 ML

2 lb/907 g tomatillos, husks removed, rinsed	1 small (6 oz/170 g) white onion
¾ oz/21 g jalapeños, stems removed	¼ bunch cilantro
	1 fl oz/30 mL canola oil
2 garlic cloves, peeled	Salt, as needed

1. Place the tomatillos, jalapeños, garlic, and onion in a saucepan, and add enough water to completely cover the vegetables. Gently simmer over medium heat until the tomatillos and jalapeños turn an olive green color, 5 to 10 minutes.

2. Drain the vegetables, and combine with the cilantro in a blender. Process until the mixture is a slightly coarse texture.

3. Heat the oil in a saucepan over high heat. Add the puréed salsa, and allow to simmer until the salsa begins to thicken, about 10 minutes. Adjust seasoning with salt as needed. Serve in a bowl as a condiment.

SPICY CUCUMBERS

YIELD: 8 PORTIONS

2 lb/907 g Kirby cucumbers, peeled	3 garlic cloves, thinly sliced
Salt, as needed	½ cup/120 mL vegetable oil
1 tbsp/12 g sugar	1½ tsp/3 g Sichuan pepper
¼ cup/60 mL white vinegar	1 tbsp/6 g red pepper flakes

1. Cut the cucumbers into wedges about 3 in/8 cm in length. Toss with the salt, sugar, and vinegar. If needed, adjust seasoning to taste. Place the sliced garlic on top but do not mix it in.

2. In a skillet, combine the oil with the Sichuan pepper and red pepper flakes. Slowly heat the oil over medium to high heat until the pepper begins to turn brown and a slight haze of smoke develops. Immediately pour the smoking hot oil through a fine-mesh strainer over the cucumber mixture.

3. Toss well. Adjust seasoning as needed. Serve in a bowl as an accompaniment.

CUCUMBER RAITA

YIELD: 1 QT/960 ML

1 qt/960 mL Bulgarian yogurt

1 cup/240 mL mint leaves

2 cucumbers, peeled, seeded, grated (1 lb/454 g)

Salt, as needed

1. Combine the yogurt and mint in a blender and purée until frothy.
2. Add the cucumbers to the yogurt and adjust seasoning with salt. Serve in a bowl as a condiment.

MINT CHUTNEY

YIELD: 8 PORTIONS

7 oz/198 g black lentils (urad dal), husked

2 tsp/8 g black mustard seeds

3 fl oz/90 mL vegetable oil

1 tsp/2 g red pepper flakes

1 oz/28 g mint leaves, cut into chiffonade

1 cup/240 mL Bulgarian yogurt

2 tbsp/30 mL tamarind pulp

1 tbsp/12 g sugar

1 tsp/4 mL asafetida

Salt, as needed

1. Cook the black lentils in salted water over low to medium heat until very tender, 15 to 30 minutes. Drain the lentils and reserve.
2. In a skillet over medium to high heat, fry the mustard seeds in the vegetable oil until they begin to pop, 10 to 30 seconds. Add the red pepper flakes and mint, and continue cooking until the mint leaves wilt slightly, 10 to 30 seconds.
3. In a food processor, combine the mint mixture with the yogurt, tamarind pulp, sugar, asafetida, and salt. Purée the mixture into a paste, and adjust seasoning if needed.

TABBOULEH

YIELD: 8 PORTIONS

8 oz/227 g bulgur wheat

Salt, as needed

1 lb/454 g tomatoes, peeled, cut into small dice

10 oz/284 g European cucumber, peeled, cut into small dice

3 green onions, sliced

1 bunch flat-leaf parsley, coarsely chopped

½ bunch mint, coarsely chopped

½ cup/120 mL extra-virgin olive oil

1½ fl oz/45 mL lemon juice

Salt, as needed

Ground black pepper, as needed

1. Rinse the bulgur in cold water and place it in a bowl. Add enough boiling water to cover the bulgur by 1 in/3 cm, and add a pinch of salt. Allow it to sit, covered, until the bulgur is tender, about 20 minutes. If necessary, drain any excess water.

2. Combine the bulgur with the tomatoes, cucumber, green onions, parsley, and mint. Season with the olive oil, lemon juice, salt, and pepper. Allow to rest for 30 minutes before serving. Serve in a bowl as a condiment.

CHEF'S NOTE | Bulgur wheat, very popular in the cuisines of the Middle East, Turkey, and Iran, is made by parboiling, dehydrating, and cracking whole wheat berries. Bulgur can be simply soaked with hot water, as in this recipe, or it can be cooked into a pilaf or soup.

CHAPTER 6

SWEETS &

BEVERAGES

Most street food is bought on impulse. Delectable aromas from mobile kitchens will grab attention and trigger an appetite. A stroll on the boardwalk, even after a filling meal, is often accompanied by an ice cream cone. Sweet foods, like the perfect ice cream cone, crunchy Beignets (page 358), or freshly squeezed lemonade, are especially difficult to resist. A preference for all things sweet is hardwired into our brain.

Sweet snacks are not designed for satiation; they are a treat, satisfying our sweet tooth or catering to our desires and cravings, sometimes even vicariously. When parents hand a large cloud of cotton candy to their cheerful children, gratification is instant—for kids as well as for Mom and Dad. The emotional aspect of sweet food is especially evident when time-honored and well-remembered sweets bring immediate flashbacks of happy memories, even from the most distant childhood.

NUTRITIONAL CONCERNS

Concerns about our diet, especially the high intake of refined sugar, are leaving their marks. Unsurprisingly, sweet foods are high on the agenda of health-food advocates. Reacting to the growing demand for natural and wholesome food, manufacturers and vendors reformulate their products and change their menus. Sugar and the hotly contested high-fructose corn syrup might be reduced or replaced with alternative sweeteners. Industrial soft-serve ice cream, loaded with controversial additives, is gradually giving way to all-natural ice cream and ice pops. Even snow cones, infamous for their artificial syrups, can now be found using flavored honey, natural fruit syrups, or other natural sweeteners derived from agave, maple, or birch.

Enjoying a stellar nutritional reputation, fresh fruits have become a common item on many street-food stands and food trucks. Available at good quality year-round, fruits are offered in many different ways, including whole or sliced, raw or cooked, or as freshly extracted juice.

NEW SWEETS ON THE BLOCK

An increasing desire for something unusual or innovative is creating a market for foods beyond our traditional horizon. Some of those novelties blur the dividing line between sweet and savory. Sometimes inspired by international recipes, salt and chile–flavored fruit ice pops, maple-bacon ice cream, and Sweet and Spicy Fruit Salad (page 340) are pushing the envelope for the inexperienced. Other preparations, like Grilled Pineapple with Green Peppercorns and Orange (page 332), smoothies (page 368), or compotes with basil or lavender, are suddenly considered less exotic. In recent years, legumes or grains made their way onto the sweet stage. Ice cream featuring mung beans or adzuki beans can be found next to funnel cakes made from chickpea flour. Rice pudding, a traditional all-time favorite, is dressed up with spices like cardamom or saffron, like in Cardamom-Flavored Cream of Rice with Saffron (page 333), or made from different grains including barley, quinoa, and cracked wheat.

Developments in technology and cooking methodology have also had an impact on mobile sweets. In addition to the traditional methods of churning, still-freezing, or shaving, some producers of frozen treats employ liquid nitrogen. Mainly found in high-end restaurants, freezing with liquid nitrogen allows chefs to produce ice cream or similar dishes at a moment's notice—an exciting show for the customer. The relative high cost and logistical challenges associated with this method limit its application mainly to restaurateurs using a street-food outlet as a promotional stage for their business. However, industrial cryogenically frozen ice cream can actually be found in quite a few places; small ice cream pebbles served in cups have become quite popular.

BEVERAGES

Just like food, street beverages are a direct reflection of a society's culture and a region's *terroir*. In Italy, a coffee to go is an unusual request. Most people take the time to sit down in a street café and enjoy the beverage and the view. Germans take great pleasure in their favorite beer in one of the many famous biergartens, and many Mexicans like to start the day with Hot Chocolate with Masa (page 375), known as *champurrado*, accompanied by a Churro (page 356).

Despite all cultural differences, the time of the day universally determines beverage preferences. Energizing drinks like coffee, tea, or yerba maté are in high demand during the morning hours or late afternoon. Popular cold beverages for the early hours include fresh juices or smoothies. Throughout the day, refreshing beverages like lemonade; Peruvian Purple Corn Drink (page 373), known as *chicha morada*; or a Mexican fruit drink, like Lime Agua Fresca with Chia Seeds (page 370), are appreciated. Alcoholic beverages are often part of celebrations or distinct seasons. Mulled red wine is a popular hot drink to keep warm at open-air Christmas fairs in Northern and Central Europe. During the hot summer in Portugal and Spain, sangria, a fruit-flavored wine punch, can be found at public events and gatherings. Caution is advised, however; in many regions, serving as well as consuming alcoholic beverages in public is regulated by very strict governmental rules, with hefty fines for violators.

Hot or cold drinks embellished with chewy tapioca pearls, known as bubble teas, have become very trendy in recent years. Other additions to beverages include chia seeds, soft legumes, or bits of firm jelly. The sole purpose of these enhancements is to stimulate the senses with an intriguing chewy or slippery mouthfeel.

Sweets and beverages stand witness that we don't eat just to fill up with nutrients or drink merely to hydrate ourselves. Sweets and beverages provide the guilty pleasures in which we indulge. We enjoy them in company to solidify friendships, we give them to our children to take pleasure in their joy, and we raise our glasses to pay respect or to make a point. After all, a good meal accompanied by a great beverage and followed by a sweet treat is not just a collection of calories; it is truly more than just the sum of its nutrients.

GRILLED PINEAPPLE WITH GREEN PEPPERCORNS AND ORANGE

YIELD: 8 PORTIONS

1 large pineapple (2 to 2½ lb/ 907 g to 1.13 kg)

2 tsp/4 g minced green peppercorns

Glaze

¼ cup/60 mL honey

½ cups/360 mL orange juice

½ tsp/1 g minced green peppercorns

1 pint/480 mL vanilla ice cream

1. Remove the top and bottom from the pineapple and peel generously, making sure to remove all the eyes. Cut the pineapple into ¾-in/2-cm slices and remove the core with a round cutter. Rub the sliced pineapple with the peppercorns on both sides.

2. In a saucepan, combine the honey, orange juice, and peppercorns and simmer over medium heat until the liquid has reduced to a viscosity resembling maple syrup, 15 to 20 minutes.

3. Grill the pineapple slices over high heat on both sides until they are well caramelized, 1 to 2 minutes per side. Brush with the reduced syrup and allow to caramelize a little more, 10 to 30 seconds.

4. Serve immediately with a scoop of ice cream.

CARDAMOM-FLAVORED CREAM OF RICE WITH SAFFRON

YIELD: 8 PORTIONS

½ cup/90 g basmati rice	5 green cardamom pods
2 qt/1.92 L cold water	1 tsp/1 g saffron threads
2 qt/1.92 L half-and-half	½ cup/120 mL heavy cream
12 oz/340 g jaggery	

1. Submerge the rice in the cold water, covered 4 to 5 in/10 to 13 cm, until the rice doubles in size, at least 8 hours.

2. Drain the rice, and purée it with 1 pint/480 mL of the half-and-half in a blender until very smooth, adding more half-and-half as needed to facilitate blending. Combine with the remaining half-and-half in a saucepan and bring to a boil over moderate heat, stirring constantly. Add the jaggery and cardamom pods and continue to simmer over low heat for 15 to 20 minutes, until it has reached a light to medium nappé.

3. Remove the cardamom pods and divide the mixture between eight 5-oz/150-mL ramekins. Cover with plastic wrap and allow to cool for at least 4 hours.

4. In a dry skillet, heat the saffron over low heat until fragrant and slightly darker, 10 to 30 seconds. Grind it with the back of a teaspoon or a pestle until powdery, then add the heavy cream and bring to a boil.

5. Drizzle the saffron cream over each ramekin of the rice cream and serve.

CHEF'S NOTE

Jaggery is one of the ingredients in this classical rice-based dessert. Also known as *panela* or *piloncillo,* jaggery is an unrefined sugar made from cane juice that lends a sweetness and a distinct flavor to any dish.

CRISPY CHOCOLATE WAFFLES WITH MINT SYRUP AND WHIPPED CREAM

YIELD: 8 PORTIONS

Mint Syrup

14 oz/397 g sugar

1½ cups/360 mL water

2 fl oz/60 mL lime juice

½ cup/120 mL mint leaves

9 oz/255 g all-purpose flour

1 oz/28 g unsweetened cocoa powder

3 oz/85 g cornstarch

1 oz/28 g sugar

2 tsp/6 g salt

2 tbsp/24 g baking powder

1 pint/480 mL milk

2 eggs, separated

1 fl oz/30 mL vanilla essence

3 oz/85 g dark chocolate, melted

2 oz/57 g unsalted butter, melted

1 pint/480 mL heavy cream, whipped to medium peaks

1. For the mint syrup, combine the sugar and water and bring to a boil over medium heat, until the sugar is fully dissolved. Remove from the heat, and combine the resulting sugar syrup with the lime juice and mint in a blender. Purée until smooth, and set aside.

2. For the batter, thoroughly combine the flour, cocoa powder, cornstarch, sugar, salt, and baking powder in a mixing bowl.

3. Combine the milk, egg yolks, and vanilla thoroughly.

4. Beat the egg whites to medium peaks.

5. In a bowl, combine the flour-cornstarch mix with the milk and egg yolk mix into a batter with hazelnut-size lumps, then fold in the beaten egg whites. Add the melted chocolate and melted butter to the batter and combine well.

6. Cook on a waffle iron per the manufacturer's instructions and serve waffle topped with whipped cream and drizzled with the mint syrup.

SHREDDED CARAMELIZED PANCAKE

There are many tales about the roots of the native name *kaiserschmarrn*, which literally translates into "emperor's nonsense." One popular account is that the Austrian emperor Franz Josef was once very upset about a dessert that was served to his wife, but after calling it a *schmarrn*, meaning "nonsense," he tasted it and, to everyone's surprise, he actually enjoyed it. Since it found the emperor's approval, this dish was from then on known as *kaiserschmarrn*.

YIELD: 8 PORTIONS

6 eggs, separated

1 cup/240 mL milk

1 tbsp/15 mL vanilla extract

2 fl oz/60 mL kirschwasser

8 oz/227 g all-purpose flour

2 oz/57 g sugar

½ tsp/2 g salt

Vegetable oil, as needed, for cooking

Garnish

Confectioners' sugar, as needed

Apple Compote (page 361)

1. Thoroughly combine the egg yolks, milk, vanilla extract, and kirschwasser. Combine the flour, sugar, and salt and mix with the egg yolk and milk mixture to create a smooth batter.

2. Whip the egg whites to medium peaks and carefully fold into the batter.

3. Pour a ¼-in/6-mm-thick layer of the batter into a preheated and oiled skillet and cook over moderate heat until golden brown on the underside, 2 to 3 minutes. Flip the pancake and cook until the other side is golden brown and the pancake is fully cooked, 2 to 3 minutes.

4. In the skillet, shred the fully cooked pancake with two wooden spoons or spatulas into bite-size pieces. Dust the shredded pancake with confectioners' sugar and toss until the pieces are well caramelized and aromatic, 30 seconds to 1 minute.

5. Pile on a plate and dust with more confectioners' sugar. Serve with Apple Compote.

CHEF'S NOTE

This dish is one of the most popular desserts in Austria and southern Germany. It features a pancake made from a rich batter of eggs without any chemical leavener. These dense pancakes are cooked in a 10- to 12-in/25- to 30-cm skillet over low heat rather than on a griddle. Accomplished culinarians are revered for their ability to gracefully flip the pancake without the help of any tools. It is important to fully cook the pancake on both sides before shredding it with two forks or a spatula and to caramelize the pancake after dusting it with sugar.

Recipes 337

RED BERRY PUDDING WITH VANILLA SAUCE

YIELD: 8 PORTIONS

8 oz/227 g strawberries	7 oz/198 g sugar
8 oz/227 g raspberries	One 2-in/5-cm cinnamon stick
8 oz/227 g pitted cherries	1 oz/28 g cornstarch
8 oz/227 g blackberries	Vanilla Sauce (page 361)
1 cup/240 mL red wine	

1. Combine the strawberries, raspberries, cherries, and blackberries with the wine, sugar, and cinnamon stick and simmer over medium heat until the fruit starts disintegrating, 1 to 3 minutes.

2. Combine the cornstarch with a small amount of water into a slurry with the consistency of heavy cream. Add the slurry to the simmering berries and thicken to a medium to heavy viscosity. Stir liberally to avoid lumps.

3. Remove the cinnamon stick and divide the berry pudding into portion-size cups (5 to 6 oz/ 142 to 170 g). Refrigerate and serve cold with the Vanilla Sauce.

CHEF'S NOTE

Known as *rødgrød* in Denmark and *rote grütze* in Germany, this classic Northern European dessert features mixed fresh berries cooked and thickened with cornstarch or tapioca pearls. It is traditionally served with a vanilla sauce, vanilla ice cream, or simply chilled heavy cream. During the cold winter months, hot variations of this dessert are served as an accompaniment to vanilla ice cream.

SWEET AND SPICY FRUIT SALAD

YIELD: 8 PORTIONS

Flavoring Mix

2 tbsp/24 g sugar

2 tbsp/30 mL raisin powder

1 tsp/3 g fleur de sel or similar
sea salt

½ tsp/1 g cayenne

1 lb/454 g jícama

10 oz/284 g green apples

10 oz/284 g Asian pears

1 lb/454 g peeled pineapple

10 oz/284 g yellow bananas

½ cup/120 mL verjus

1. Mix the sugar, raisin powder, salt, and cayenne.

2. Peel all fruits and core as necessary.

3. Cut all fruits into bite-size pieces, and, at service, toss with the verjus and the Flavoring Mix. Adjust seasoning as desired and serve immediately.

CHEF'S NOTES

Raisin powder, available in health-food stores or at wholesale food manufacturers, is a versatile ingredient often employed as a thickening agent or a fat substitute in batters. In this unique fruit salad, it provides an interesting texture and mouthfeel, plus flavor and sweetness.

Verjus, a common ingredient in French and Italian cooking, is an acidic juice made from unripe grapes. Known as *husroum* in Syria and Lebanon and *abgooreh* in Iran, it is a popular condiment in the Middle East and Central and Southern Asia. It is often used as a dressing or as a glaze for grilled meats. If verjus is not available, pomegranate molasses is an adequate substitute.

Fleur de sel, an artisan sea salt hand-harvested on the coast of Brittany, is a very popular seasoning. With residual moisture of 5 to 8 percent, fleur de sel's uniquely shaped salt crystals dissolve very slowly, giving a slight crunch to the food as well as the sensory perception of gradual seasoning.

340 CHAPTER 6 Sweets & Beverages

CREAMY CITRUS RICE

YIELD: 8 PORTIONS

2 oz/57 g unsalted butter	1 tbsp/9 g finely grated orange zest
1 tbsp/8 g minced ginger	1 to 2 cups/240 to 480 mL buttermilk
8 oz/227 g Arborio rice	Salt, as needed
7 cups/1.68 L whole milk	
4 oz/113 g light brown sugar	8 oz/227 g mandarin orange suprêmes
1 cup/240 mL orange juice	Cinnamon-sugar mix (1:10), as needed

1. In a rondeau or similar pan over medium heat, melt the butter and allow to brown until golden, about 30 seconds. Add the ginger and sweat for 10 seconds. Add the Arborio rice and continue sweating until every grain is evenly coated with the brown butter. Add the milk and brown sugar to the rice, and bring to a boil over moderate heat, stirring occasionally.

2. Adjust the sweetness and seasoning as desired, cover the pot with a tight-fitting lid, and cook in the oven at 350°F/177°C for about 20 minutes, until the rice has absorbed all the liquid.

3. Remove from the heat and add the orange juice and zest and enough buttermilk to adjust the viscosity and consistency. Stir for about 30 seconds to achieve a thick yet pourable creamy consistency. Adjust the sweetness and seasoning as desired. As the creamy rice is held warm, it will continue to thicken. This can be counteracted with the addition of more liquid, as desired.

4. At service, ladle into a bowl and top with mandarin segments and sprinkle with cinnamon-sugar mix as desired.

BLACK RICE PUDDING WITH COCONUT MILK AND DRIED MANGO

YIELD: 8 PORTIONS

1½ qt/1.44 L water	3 cups/720 mL coconut milk
2 cups/440 g Thai purple rice	Juice of 2 limes
7 oz/198 g palm sugar	Kosher salt, as needed
1 stalk lemongrass, very finely minced (¾ oz/21 g)	4 oz/113 g small-dice dried mangos
	2 oz/57 g desiccated coconut

1. In a rondeau or similar pan, bring the water to boil, and add the rice, palm sugar, and lemongrass. Bring back to a boil over high heat, cover with a lid, and cook in an oven at 350°F/177°C for 30 minutes.

2. Once the rice has absorbed all the water, add the coconut milk, bring back to a simmer over medium heat, and return the pot to the oven. Continue to cook until the coconut milk has been absorbed and the rice is creamy.

3. Add the lime juice and adjust seasoning as needed. If necessary, add more liquid to adjust viscosity.

4. At service, pour the rice into bowls and top with some diced mango and desiccated coconut.

CHEF'S NOTE | Known as *forbidden rice,* this rice has a rich, deep purple color due to its high concentration of anthocyanin pigments. It is most commonly served for breakfast as a hot cereal.

FUNNEL CAKE SANDWICH WITH ICE CREAM AND MAPLE SYRUP

Believed to have originated in the Pennsylvania Dutch region, funnel cakes are standard fare at many carnivals, public events, and seaside resorts.

YIELD: 8 PORTIONS

Batter

24 fl oz/720 mL milk, at room temperature

⅔ oz/19 g dry yeast

1 lb 5 oz/595 g all-purpose flour

¼ tsp/0.5 g kosher salt

1 egg

Vegetable oil, as needed, for deep-frying

Maple syrup, as needed

Serve with

Pistachio Ice Cream (page 362), as needed

or

Frozen Almond Ricotta (page 363), as needed

or

Bananas in Cardamom Syrup (page 366), as needed

1. Combine the milk, yeast, flour, salt, and egg in a bowl, cover with a lid, and allow to proof until doubled in size, about 1 hour.

2. Once doubled in size, mix thoroughly, and allow to proof again until doubled in volume, about 45 minutes.

3. Using a squirt bottle with a ¼-in/6-mm-wide nozzle or a funnel cake pitcher, carefully squirt the batter in a tight circular pattern into 350°F/177°C hot vegetable oil to form 16 individual funnel cakes.

4. Fry, turning once, until crispy and golden brown on both sides, 2 to 3 minutes. Once done, remove the funnel cakes from the hot oil and allow to drain on wire racks.

5. At service, drizzle some maple syrup onto 2 funnel cakes and sandwich a scoop of ice cream between them. Alternatively, serve with a condiment of your choice.

CHEF'S NOTE

Funnel cakes are most commonly served dusted with confectioners' sugar, cinnamon and sugar, or sweet cocoa powder or drizzled with syrup. They can also be served with different toppings, like stewed fruits, preserves, or other sweet spreads.

SWEET TAMALES

YIELD: 8 PORTIONS (24 SMALL TAMALES)

24 corn husks

1 lb/454 g masa harina for tamales

1½ cups/370 mL water

10 oz/284 g sugar

1 tsp/2 g ground cinnamon

Red food coloring, as needed

1 tsp/5 mL vanilla extract

6 oz/170 g lard

2 tsp/8 g baking powder

3 oz/85 g dark raisins

1. Submerge the corn husks in tepid water and allow to soak for 30 minutes, and then allow to drain in a colander.

2. Combine the masa harina with the water, sugar, cinnamon, food coloring, and vanilla in a mixing bowl until it forms a soft dough. Cover and allow to rest for 20 minutes.

3. In a stand mixer, whip the lard until airy. Add the baking powder and, on low speed, gradually add the masa mix to achieve a smooth dough.

4. To assemble the tamales, place 2 to 3 tbsp/30 to 45 mL of masa mix onto the center of a corn husk. Add the raisins and enclose the tamale by folding the sides together and then both ends toward the center. Tie with threads of corn husks, if desired.

5. In a steamer or a tamalera, steam the tamales for 45 minutes to 1 hour, until they are cooked completely. Serve tamales on a plate.

CHEF'S NOTE

Found all over Latin America, tamales are quintessential street and celebratory food. Traditionally, they are made by wrapping banana leaves or soaked corn husks around slightly coarse ground masa. More often than not, tamales are filled with aromatic preparations based on meat, seafood, cheese, fruits, or vegetables.

BAKLAVA

YIELD: 48 PIECES

1 lb/454 g shelled walnuts	**Syrup**
3½ oz/99 g sugar	14 oz/397 g sugar
1 tsp/2 g ground cinnamon	1½ cups/360 mL water
½ tsp/1 g ground cardamom	½ cup/120 mL honey
¼ tsp/0.5 g ground cloves	1 tbsp/9 g grated lemon zest
1 lb/454 g phyllo sheets, thawed	1 clove
1½ cups/360 mL melted butter	

1. Toast the walnuts at 325°F/163°C until very lightly browned, 5 to 10 minutes. Chop the walnuts finely and combine with the sugar, cinnamon, cardamom, and cloves; set aside.

2. Layer 8 sheets of phyllo pastry onto a half sheet pan (13 by 18 in/33 by 46 cm), brushing melted butter between each layer. Sprinkle one-third of the nut mixture over the phyllo sheets and place 4 more sheets of phyllo on top of the nuts, brushing melted butter between each sheet. Place the next one-third of the nut mixture on the phyllo dough and top with 4 more sheets of phyllo, brushing melted butter between each sheet. Continue the same process with the remaining walnuts and phyllo dough.

3. If necessary, trim the edges so that they do not stand above the level of the pan. Using a pizza cutter or similar tool, score the pastry into 2-in/5-cm squares, making sure not to slice through the bottom layer of the phyllo dough. Leaving the bottom layer uncut will allow the syrup to soak in more efficiently.

4. Bake at 375°F/191°C until the top layer of the phyllo takes on a light golden brown color, 25 to 30 minutes.

5. For the syrup, combine the sugar, water, honey, lemon zest, and clove, and bring to a boil over medium heat. Simmer gently for about 3 minutes, and strain through a fine-mesh strainer.

6. Remove the baklava from the oven and immediately pour the hot syrup over the top, making sure it is evenly saturated. Allow the baklava to cool to room temperature, and cut into 3 by 3-in/8 by 8-cm portions and serve.

CHEF'S NOTE

Baklava, a sweet and sticky layered pastry that originated in Central Asia, can be found in various forms throughout the Middle East and Central and South Asia. To make baklava, paper-thin pastry sheets are layered with crushed nuts and soaked with aromatic sugar syrup flavored with cardamom, rose water, honey, cloves, or other spices.

BAKED CHERRY PANCAKE

YIELD: ONE 9-IN/23-CM PANCAKE

Batter

3 eggs

4 oz/113 g all-purpose flour

1 oz/28 g sugar

1 pinch salt

6 fl oz/180 mL heavy cream

6 fl oz/180 mL milk

1 tsp/5 mL vanilla extract

Butter, as needed, for greasing the baking dish

Sugar, as needed, for dusting the baking dish

1 lb/454 g pitted black cherries

Confectioners' sugar, as needed

1 cup/240 mL crème fraîche

1. In a mixing bowl, combine the eggs, flour, sugar, salt, heavy cream, milk, and vanilla until mixed homogenously. Butter a 9-in/23-cm round baking dish or skillet and sprinkle with sugar until evenly coated.

2. Arrange the cherries tightly in the prepared baking dish, pour the batter over the cherries, and sprinkle with additional sugar.

3. Bake at 350°F/177°C for about 30 minutes, until a knife inserted in the center of the custard comes out dry. As it bakes, the pancake will rise in the oven and fall immediately when removed.

4. Serve warm or at room temperature, sprinkled with confectioners' sugar and accompanied by a dollop of crème fraîche.

CHEF'S NOTE | Known as *clafoutis* in the Limousin region of central France, this pancake is made from an almost custard-like batter that is traditionally made with unpitted cherries. Culinary purists feel that the pits lend a strong flavor to the pancake and do not allow the cherries to release as much juice during baking. Other fruits, such as plums, apples, pears, and berries, are popular alternatives to the cherries.

ROTI PRATA WITH BANANAS AND HONEY

YIELD: 8 PORTIONS

Dough

2 lb/907 g all-purpose flour

1 oz/28 g sugar

2 tsp/6 g salt

2 eggs, beaten

3½ fl oz/105 mL ghee or vegetable shortening, melted but cool

1 pint/480 mL water

1 fl oz/30 mL unsweetened condensed milk

8 bananas, thinly sliced

1 cup/240 mL honey

1. For the dough, combine the flour, sugar, and salt in a bowl. Add the eggs, ghee, water, and milk. Combine well and knead until the dough is smooth and homogenous, about 2 minutes. Return the dough into the mixing bowl, cover with plastic, and allow to rest for about 30 minutes.

2. Divide the dough into sixteen 2½-oz/71-g balls. Coat each dough ball in ghee or shortening, cover, and set aside to rest until the dough is relaxed and very flexible, at least 2 hours.

3. With greased hands, flatten the dough balls into rounds thicker in the center than on the perimeter. Stretch the dough as far as possible, or fling the dough like a fisherman's net to achieve the ultra-thin dough sheet.

4. Place about half a banana onto each piece of dough, drizzle with honey, and enclose the filling by folding over the dough to form a packet.

5. Cook the pratas on a preheated and well-oiled griddle over medium heat with the folded side down until golden brown, 1 to 2 minutes, then flip and continue to cook the other side until golden brown, 1 to 2 minutes. Serve immediately.

Working on a well-oiled surface, thin the edges of the dough by pressing with your hands.

Repeatedly tossing the dough in a quick, smooth motion, similar to using a fisherman's net, will create a paper-thin dough sheet.

Place the filling in the center of the dough, and fold the dough around it.

Cook the prata in a hot skillet until golden on both sides.

Recipes 351

BUCKWHEAT CRÊPES

YIELD: 8 PORTIONS

Crêpe Batter

8 oz/227 g buckwheat flour

8 oz/227 g all-purpose flour

3 eggs, well beaten

1½ pints/720 mL milk

1 tsp/3 g kosher salt

1½ cups/360 mL water

1 fl oz/30 mL vegetable oil

Clarified butter, as needed,
for cooking

Filling

Apple Compote (page 361)

or

Frozen Almond Ricotta (page 363)

or

Melons in Basil-Lime Syrup (page 366)

or

Bananas in Cardamom Syrup (page 366)

or

Applesauce, as needed

or

Fresh berries, as needed

or

Cooked ham, as needed

Shredded cheese, such as Cheddar, Gouda, or Fontina, as needed

1. For the batter, combine the flours, eggs, milk, salt, water, and oil in a blender and process until very smooth.

2. Pour 5 fl oz/150 mL of crêpe batter onto a preheated and well-buttered crêpe maker or griddle and spread with a crêpe spreader into a thin crêpe. Cook on one side until lightly browned, 1 to 2 minutes, and flip and finish on the other side, about 1 minute.

3. Fill with the stuffing of your choice on the griddle or crêpe maker, fold over, and serve.

CHEF'S NOTE

This crêpe from the Breton region of France stands out with its intense, nutty flavor. This recipe features a batter made with buckwheat flour. Buckwheat, even though very starchy, is not related to wheat and isn't actually a grain. Buckwheat is very popular in northern cuisines, because it thrives in colder climates. In Central Europe, it is used for crêpes and cakes, whereas in Eastern Europe and Russia, it is popular for hot cereals, for blinis, or as an accompaniment to caviar. In Japan and Korea, noodles based on buckwheat flour are common fare.

RUM BABAS

YIELD: 8 PORTIONS

Dough

4 fl oz/120 mL milk, warm

1½ tsp/5 g active dry yeast

12 oz/340 g bread flour

1 pinch salt

6 fl oz/180 mL melted butter, cooled

1 tsp/5 mL vanilla extract

Rum Soak

11 fl oz/330 mL water

1 lb/454 g sugar

4 fl oz/120 mL dark rum

2 fl oz/60 mL lemon juice

1 lb/454 g apricot jam, heated, strained

1. For the dough, combine the milk and the yeast in a stand mixer with a paddle and allow to rehydrate for 10 seconds. Add 3 oz/85 g of the bread flour and allow the mixture to proof until frothy, 10 to 15 minutes.

2. Add the remaining flour, the salt, butter, and vanilla and mix into a very soft, almost batter-like dough. Cover with plastic and allow to rest in a warm place until doubled in size, 30 minutes to 1 hour.

3. Butter baba molds or small muffin pans and fill halfway with the baba dough. Cover and allow to proof until they are 1½ times their original size, about 20 minutes.

4. Bake the babas at 400°F/204°C for 20 minutes, then lower the temperature to 350°F/177°C and continue to bake for another 10 minutes, until the babas are golden brown and baked through.

5. Unmold the babas onto a wire rack and allow to cool completely. Once cool, keep the babas uncovered to dry slightly, another 30 minutes.

6. For the Rum Soak, combine the water and sugar in a saucepan over medium heat and bring to a boil to dissolve the sugar. Immediately remove from the heat, allow to cool to about 160°F/71°C, and add the rum and lemon juice.

7. Submerge the babas individually in the rum until saturated. Arrange on a dish and brush with the apricot jam. Serve.

CHEF'S NOTE

Babas, especially popular in both Italy and France, are very rich small yeast cakes, comparable to a brioche, that are soaked in rum-lemon syrup. Babas are similar to a small French cake known as *savarin*. However, a savarin is more commonly served as a plated dessert and is baked in a ring mold, which gives it a doughnut-like shape. In stores in Italy, babas can oftentimes be found in glass jars, soaked in limoncello, a traditional lemon-flavored liqueur.

Recipes 353

MINT-LIME ICE CREAM SANDWICHES WITH COCONUT MERINGUE

YIELD: 8 PORTIONS

Coconut Meringues

6 oz/170 g egg whites

12 oz/340 g sugar

1 tsp/3 g salt

2 oz/57 g desiccated coconut, finely ground

Mint-Lime Ice Cream

4 egg yolks

6 oz/170 g sugar

¼ tsp/0.5 g kosher salt

1 tbsp/15 mL lime juice

Zest of 3 limes

½ oz/14 g mint, cut into chiffonade

3 cups/720 mL heavy cream

1 cup/240 mL whole milk

1. For the coconut meringue, combine the egg whites, sugar, and salt in a mixing bowl and gently heat over a water bath to a temperature of 115°F/46°C.

2. Transfer to a mixer with a whisk attachment and whip to very firm peaks. Gently fold in the ground coconut and spread or pipe into circles measuring ¼ in/6 mm thick and 2 in/5 cm in diameter on a sheet pan lined with parchment paper or a silicone mat.

3. Bake in an oven without convection at 180°F/82°C until completely dried, 2 to 3 hours. Make sure to vent the oven well to allow the evaporated moisture to escape.

4. For the Mint-Lime Ice Cream, combine the egg yolks, sugar, salt, lime juice, zest, and mint in a mixing bowl. Over moderate heat, heat the cream and milk to a near boil and temper with the egg mix. Stirring constantly, heat the mix gently until it reaches 170°F/77°C and it begins to thicken.

5. Once the mix has thickened, strain it through a fine-mesh strainer and cool it instantly over an ice bath to about 40°F/4°C. Refrigerate for at least 4 hours or overnight.

6. Freeze in an ice cream maker according to the manufacturer's instructions and allow to harden in a freezer. At service, sandwich a scoop of the ice cream between 2 coconut meringues.

CHURROS

YIELD: 8 PORTIONS (24 CHURROS)

1 cup/240 mL water	4½ oz/128 g all-purpose flour
4 oz/113 g butter	3 eggs, beaten
¼ tsp/1 g kosher salt	Vegetable oil, as needed, for frying

1. Combine the water, butter, and salt in a 2-qt/1.92-L saucepan and bring to a rolling boil. Add the flour to the boiling water, stirring vigorously with a wooden spoon over low heat until the mixture forms a ball and a white layer is appearing on the bottom of the pan, 1 to 3 minutes.

2. Transfer the hot dough ball to a dough mixer with a paddle attachment and mix on low speed for about 30 seconds. Gradually add the beaten eggs to the running mixer, making sure the eggs get fully absorbed by the dough. Transfer the batter into a piping bag with large star tip.

3. Squeeze 4-in/10-cm strips of the batter into vegetable oil at 360°F/182°C and fry until golden brown, turning once, about 2 minutes on each side.

4. Once done, remove from the oil and allow to drain on a wire rack and blot gently with a paper towel. Serve.

CHEF'S NOTES

Churros, deep-fried rods of pâte à choux, originated in Spain and are found at street-food stands all over Latin America. Churros are traditionally served with a thick hot chocolate or, in Mexico, a big bowl of Hot Chocolate with Masa (see page 375).

The churros can be served rolled in cinnamon and sugar. Combine ¼ cup/60 mL sugar and 1 tsp/2 g Mexican cinnamon in a mixing bowl and roll the fried churros in the mixture as soon as they are out of the fryer.

RICOTTA FRITTERS

YIELD: 8 PORTIONS (32 TO 40 FRITTERS)

Batter

1 lb/454 g drained ricotta cheese

8 eggs

5 oz/142 g sugar

1 fl oz/30 mL dark rum

3 fl oz/90 mL orange juice

2 tbsp/18 g grated orange zest

1 tsp/4 g baking powder

Salt, as needed

6 oz/170 g all-purpose flour

Confectioners' or granulated sugar, as needed, for dusting

1. For the batter, combine the ricotta, eggs, sugar, rum, orange juice, zest, baking powder, salt, and flour thoroughly, adding more flour as needed.

2. In a deep-fryer at 350°F/177°C, fry 1-tbsp/15-mL fritters until lightly browned and cooked through, 2 to 3 minutes.

3. Remove the fritters from the oil, allow to drain on a wire rack, and blot them gently with a paper towel. Dust with confectioners' or granulated sugar and serve while hot.

FRIED BANANAS IN MANIOC CRUST

YIELD: 8 PORTIONS

8 just-ripe yellow bananas

1 pint/480 mL buttermilk

8 oz/227 g manioc flour

Vegetable oil, as needed, for frying

¼ cup/50 g sugar

½ tsp/1 g fleur de sel

1 tsp/2 g ground cinnamon

Bamboo skewers

1. Peel the bananas and cut them in half.

2. Dip the bananas in the buttermilk and, without wiping off the buttermilk, dredge in the manioc flour until coated all around.

3. Immediately deep-fry in vegetable oil at 350°F/177°C until golden brown, 2 to 3 minutes.

4. Combine the sugar, fleur de sel, and cinnamon and sprinkle over the fried bananas. Put 2 banana halves on each skewer. Serve immediately.

BEIGNETS

YIELD: 8 PORTIONS

Dough

1 lb/454 g all-purpose flour

½ tsp/1.5 g kosher salt

1 tbsp/10 g dry yeast

1 cup/240 mL milk

2 eggs, beaten

2 fl oz/60 mL melted butter

Vegetable oil, as needed, for deep-frying

Confectioners' sugar, as needed, for dusting

1. In a large mixing bowl, combine the flour, salt, yeast, milk, eggs, and butter until smooth and elastic, 2 to 3 minutes. Add more flour as needed to adjust the dough. Place the dough in a bowl with a tight-fitting lid or cover with plastic wrap and allow to proof in a warm place until it has doubled in size, about 1 hour.

2. On a well-floured surface, roll the dough to a ¼-in/6-mm thickness, cut into rectangular shapes, and place on a lightly floured pan. Dust gently with flour, cover with a plastic wrap, and allow to double in size again, about 30 minutes.

3. Right before frying, stipple the dough with your fingers and gently stretch each dough sheet to 1½ times its original length.

4. Deep-fry the beignets in vegetable oil at 325°F/163°F, turning once, until golden brown, 2 to 3 minutes. Drain, and dust generously with confectioners' sugar. Serve.

CHEF'S NOTE | Beignets and similar fried dough preparations are found in many culinary cultures. It is interesting to note that in France or Germany, the word *beignet* is oftentimes used to describe a sweet or savory preparation of a batter-fried fruit or vegetable.

QUARK FRITTERS

YIELD: 8 PORTIONS

Dough

2 fl oz/60 mL whole milk, warmed to 100°F/38°C

1 tsp/3 g active dry yeast

1½ oz/43 g butter, melted

2½ oz/71 g sugar, plus as needed, for finishing

1 tsp/5 mL vanilla extract

1 egg

½ tsp/2 g kosher salt

8 oz/227 g all-purpose flour

7 oz/198 g quark, drained in cheesecloth

1½ tsp/5 g finely grated lemon zest

1½ tsp/7.5 mL lemon juice

Canola oil, as needed, for deep-frying

1. For the dough, combine the milk and yeast. Allow to hydrate for 20 seconds, and add the butter, sugar, vanilla, egg, salt, flour, quark, lemon zest, and lemon juice. Work into a very soft dough, adding more flour or milk as needed. In a container with a tight-fitting lid, in a warm space, allow the dough to double in size, about 1 hour.

2. Once the dough has doubled, use an oiled tablespoon or similar tool to shape the dough into balls the size of Ping-Pong balls. Deep-fry in canola oil at 325°F/163°C until puffed up and golden brown, 2 to 4 minutes.

3. Remove from the fat, allow to drain on a wire rack, and roll the fritters in sugar until thoroughly coated. Allow the fritters to cool for 10 to 15 minutes before serving.

CHEF'S NOTES

Quark fritters are a popular snack at Christmas fairs and markets all over Germany. They are often found on stands next to fried dough and glazed nuts.

The featured ingredient is quark, a fresh cheese with a uniquely tangy flavor and slightly chalky mouthfeel that is relatively unknown in the United States. Quark can be compared to ricotta or puréed cottage cheese, and like its Italian and American counterparts, quark is suitable for sweet or savory preparations.

Quark can be obtained online or from the dairy shelves of well-stocked grocery stores. If it is not available, an adequate substitute for quark can be produced in a few simple steps. In a mixing bowl over a water bath not exceeding 145°F/63°C, heat buttermilk without stirring until a soft curd separates from the whey. Depending on the amount and the initial temperature of the buttermilk, the time it takes can vary from 1 to several hours. The curd needs to be carefully drained from the whey through cheesecloth until a consistency resembling ricotta is reached. Store refrigerated in a tightly closed container for up to 1 week.

APPLE COMPOTE

YIELD: 8 PORTIONS

2 lb/907 g firm, moderately sweet apples	4 oz/113 g sugar
2 fl oz/60 mL lemon juice	1 stick cinnamon
12 fl oz/360 mL water	1 cup/90 g raisins
	1 tsp/5 mL vanilla extract

1. Peel and core the apples, cut them into fine wedges, and toss in the lemon juice to prevent browning.

2. In a saucepan over medium heat, combine the water, sugar, and cinnamon and bring to a boil. Add the apples and raisins, cover with a tight-fitting lid, and continue to cook over high heat for 1 minute. After 1 minute, check the doneness of the apples and continue cooking as needed; they should be tender yet not mushy.

3. Once the apples are done, add the vanilla, and transfer the apples, raisins, and cooking liquid to a storage container and allow to cool to room temperature. Serve well chilled in a bowl.

VANILLA SAUCE

YIELD: 8 PORTIONS

1 vanilla bean	4 oz/113 g sugar
2 cups/480 mL half-and-half	4 egg yolks

1. Split the vanilla bean lengthwise, scrape out the interior, and combine with the half-and-half in a saucepan. Add half of the sugar and bring to a simmer over medium heat.

2. In a mixing bowl, combine the egg yolks and the remaining sugar with about 1 cup of the simmering half-and-half and stir well to combine thoroughly. Add this egg yolk–half-and-half mix to the simmering half-and-half in the pot, stirring constantly until the mixture reaches 180°F/82°C and becomes slightly thick, 2 to 5 minutes.

3. Immediately strain the mixture through a fine-mesh strainer into a metal bowl over an ice bath and cool down to 40°F/4°C. Serve well chilled, in a bowl as a condiment.

PISTACHIO ICE CREAM

YIELD: 3 LB/1.36 KG

1 qt/960 mL half-and-half	7 oz/198 g sugar
4 oz/113 g shelled pistachios	6 egg yolks
½ tsp/2 g salt	

1. In a saucepan over medium heat, bring the half-and-half, pistachios, salt, and half of the sugar to a boil, stirring constantly.

2. Allow to sit for 5 minutes, then purée in a blender until very smooth and strain through a fine-mesh strainer if necessary.

3. Combine the egg yolks and the remaining sugar and temper with the pistachio cream. Place over moderate heat and cook, stirring constantly, until the mixture reaches 180°F/82°C and begins to thicken.

4. Immediately strain the mixture through a fine-mesh strainer into a metal bowl over an ice bath and cool down to 40°F/4°C. Refrigerate the mixture for at least 4 hours or overnight.

5. Churn the mixture to the desired consistency according to the manufacturer's instructions and harden in the freezer for at least 2 hours.

FROZEN ALMOND RICOTTA

YIELD: 8 PORTIONS

1 lb 4 oz/567 g ricotta cheese

7 oz/198 g sugar

2 fl oz/60 mL amaretto liqueur

1 tsp/5 mL vanilla extract

1 tbsp/9 g finely grated orange zest

1 cup/240 mL heavy cream

1 oz/28 g amaretti cookies or macaroons, crushed

1. Combine the ricotta, sugar, amaretto, vanilla, orange zest, and cream in a blender and purée until smooth.

2. Freeze in an ice cream maker according to manufacturer's instructions. If necessary, allow to firm in a freezer to the desired consistency.

3. Fold in the crushed cookies and serve.

CHEF'S NOTE

Ricotta-based frozen desserts provide a great flavor and mouthfeel and give you the option of serving a creamy dessert with lower fat content. The drawback is that, due to their low fat content, these types of frozen desserts will crystallize relatively quickly and will not stay creamy for a long time. Therefore, they need to be made fresh daily and kept in a designated ice cream freezer, which commonly is not as cold as a regular freezer.

FROZEN MINT LIMEADE

YIELD: 8 PORTIONS

7 oz/198 g sugar

6 fl oz/180 mL water

10 fl oz/300 mL lime juice

3 lb/1.36 kg crushed ice

1 cup/48 g mint leaves

1. In a saucepan over medium heat, combine the sugar and water and simmer to dissolve the sugar.

2. Combine the sugar water with the remaining ingredients in a blender and purée until smooth, adding liquid as needed to facilitate the blending. Serve in a cup or glass with a straw or spoon.

MANGO LASSI

YIELD: 8 PORTIONS

1½ qt/1.44 L Bulgarian or similar yogurt

1 cup/240 mL crushed ice

1 cup/240 mL whole milk

4 very ripe mangos, peeled, pitted, chopped (2 lb/907 g)

½ tsp/1 g ground cardamom

1 fl oz/30 mL lime juice

Sugar, as needed in case mangoes are not ripe enough

1. Combine the yogurt, ice, milk, mangos, cardamom, lime juice, and sugar thoroughly in a blender and purée until smooth.

2. Serve well chilled over ice.

CHEF'S NOTE | Mango lassi, a sweet and refreshing yogurt drink originating in India and Pakistan, has now gained popularity in many places outside the Indian subcontinent. It is important to use very ripe mangos or mango purée when making this drink, which is comparable to a mango smoothie. Traditionally, lassis have been made by blending yogurt with water, salt, and spices, making something very similar to the Turkish and Middle Eastern ayran (see page 377).

BANANAS IN CARDAMOM SYRUP

YIELD: 8 PORTIONS

4 just-ripe yellow bananas

½ cup/100 g sugar

2 cardamom pods

¾ cup/180 mL water

2 tsp/10 mL lime juice

1. Peel the banana and cut into bite-size pieces.

2. In an appropriate-size, heavy-bottomed stainless-steel skillet, combine the sugar and cardamom with about ¼ cup/60 mL water. Over moderate heat, bring the water to a boil and allow the sugar to melt, then caramelize until golden brown and the cardamom becomes fragrant, 5 to 10 minutes.

3. Add the remaining water and simmer over medium heat until the caramelized sugar is completely dissolved, 1 to 2 minutes.

4. Add the bananas and simmer over medium heat until the syrup evenly coats the bananas. Add the lime juice and adjust flavor as needed. Serve in a bowl as a condiment.

MELONS IN BASIL-LIME SYRUP

YIELD: 8 PORTIONS

4 lb/1.81 kg honeydew melons

4 lb/1.81 kg cantaloupe melons

1 cup/240 mL water

1 cup/198 g sugar

¼ cup/60 mL lime juice

½ cup/21 g basil leaves

4 oz/113 g macadamia nuts, toasted, chopped

1. Peel the melons thoroughly, remove all seeds, and cut into large dice.

2. For the syrup, combine the water and sugar, bring to a boil over medium heat, and simmer until the sugar is completely dissolved, about 1 minute. Allow to cool to room temperature, combine in a blender with the lime juice and basil leaves, and purée until smooth.

3. Toss the melons in the syrup and top with the chopped macadamia nuts.

366 CHAPTER 6 Sweets & Beverages

CAIPIRINHA

YIELD: 8 PORTIONS

16 limes

7 oz/198 g sugar

1 pint/480 mL cachaça

Crushed ice, as needed

Garnish

1 lime, thinly sliced

1. Cut the limes in half lengthwise, remove the white pith in the center, and cut into wedges. Divide the limes and sugar between 8 cocktail glasses and, using a wooden pestle or similar tool, crush the sugar and limes together until the sugar dissolves.

2. Add 2 fl oz/60 mL of cachaça to each glass. Fill each glass with ice and cover with the lid of a cocktail shaker. Vigorously shake each cocktail individually for several seconds and pour the contents into a new glass.

3. Garnish with a lime wedge and serve immediately.

CHEF'S NOTES

Known as *Brazilian rum,* cachaça is a distilled liquor made from fermented sugarcane juice, whereas standard rum is made from molasses.

Caipirinha, classically made with limes, sugar, and cachaça, is probably the most prominent cocktail in Brazil. Over the years, bartenders around the world have created new variations using fruits, different alcohols, and sweeteners.

AÇAI AND BANANA SMOOTHIE

YIELD: 8 PORTIONS

1 lb/454 g açai pulp, frozen

1 lb/454 g ripe bananas, frozen

1½ qt/1.44 L unsweetened
almond milk

1 pint/480 mL Greek yogurt
or similar yogurt

In a blender, purée the açai pulp, bananas, almond milk, and yogurt until smooth. Serve in a
glass.

CHEF'S NOTE	Açai berries from Central and South America are available in the United States as frozen pulp, juice, or powder. Their flavor is often described as a unique mix of berry and chocolate. Açai berries are commonly used for hot and cold cereals, beverages, sauces, and baked goods. Perceived health benefits and strong marketing in recent years have made açai berries very popular as a nutritional supplement.

AVOCADO-APPLE SMOOTHIE

YIELD: 8 PORTIONS

2 ripe Hass avocados, peeled,
pitted (1 lb/454 g)

4 Granny Smith or similar apples,
peeled, cored, diced (1 lb 8 oz/
680 g)

Honey, as needed

1 lb/454 g ice cubes

1 pint/480 mL Bulgarian or similar yogurt

1 fl oz/30 mL lemon juice

In a blender, purée the avocados, apples, honey, ice, yogurt, and lemon juice until very smooth.
Adjust viscosity, sweetness, and acidity as needed. Serve in a glass or cup.

LIME AGUA FRESCA WITH CHIA SEEDS

YIELD: 8 PORTIONS

2 oz/57 g chia seeds	2 qt/1.92 L water
½ cup/100 g sugar	4 fl oz/120 mL lime juice

1. Soak the chia seeds in 1 qt/960 mL of 100°F/38°C water for 10 minutes.

2. Combine the sugar and 1 cup/240 mL of water and simmer to dissolve the sugar. Add the remaining 3 cups of water and the lime juice. Add this liquid to the water with the soaked chia seeds and refrigerate until very cold. Serve well chilled but not over ice.

CHEF'S NOTES

Originating in Latin America, agua fresca is a refreshing nonalcoholic beverage based on fruits, hibiscus flowers, or, in some regions, cereals, along with sugar and water.

Chia seeds, the seeds of flowering mint, provide agua frescas and other beverages with an interesting, gelatinous texture. Chia seeds can also be found in hot cereals, baked goods, sandwiches, and salads. The seeds' ability to sprout and grow on porous rock gave rise to the popular clay figures known as Chia Pets.

PURPLE CORN DRINK

This beverage, known as *chicha morada* in Peru, is an unfermented refreshment made by simmering Peruvian purple corn with other fruits and aromatics. Chicha morada was enjoyed by the indigenous peoples of South America well before colonization.

YIELD: 8 PORTIONS

3 dried Peruvian purple corncobs (6 oz/170 g)	2 oz/57 g dried cherries
1 pineapple rind	4 allspice berries
2 Granny Smith or similar apples (10 to 12 oz/184 to 340 g)	4 cloves
	1 gal/3.84 L water
8 oz/227 g piloncillo or light brown sugar	Lime juice, as needed
	Sugar, as needed
Two 2-in/5-cm cinnamon sticks	Ground cinnamon, as needed, for dusting

1. Combine the corncobs, pineapple rind, apples, piloncillo, cinnamon sticks, dried cherries, allspice berries, cloves, and water in a stockpot and simmer over medium heat for about 2 hours, until the kernels on the purple corn begin to split.

2. Strain the liquid into a bowl in an ice bath and chill rapidly.

3. Once chilled, adjust sweetness and acidity with lime juice and sugar. At service, sprinkle with a very small amount of ground cinnamon. Serve in a glass over ice.

CHEF'S NOTE | Purple corn, native to the Andes Mountains, has traditionally been grown for use in beverages and for its strong coloring properties. Rich in antioxidants and other beneficial nutrients, purple corn is believed to have health benefits and the potential to help fight diseases.

HOT OR ICED MINT TEA

YIELD: 8 PORTIONS

2 cups/480 mL mint leaves	3 oz/85 g sugar
2 tbsp/30 mL green tea leaves	2 qt/1.92 L boiling water

1. Bruise the mint leaves slightly and combine with the tea leaves and sugar in a pot.

2. Add the boiling water and allow to steep for at least 10 minutes.

3. Strain the tea and serve in a glass, hot or over ice.

CHEF'S NOTE

Commonly served hot, strong, and very sweet, mint tea is probably the ultimate sign of hospitality in Morocco. It seems counterintuitive to modern Western culture to serve a hot beverage during elevated summer temperatures. However, the cuisines of hotter climate zones feature deliberately developed foods and beverages that embrace ingredients that heat up the body temperature in order to bring about the desired evaporative cooling.

CARROT-APPLE SMOOTHIE WITH GINGER

YIELD: 8 PORTIONS

1 lb/454 g Fuji or similar apples	1½ tsp/4 g finely minced or grated ginger
1 pint/480 mL fresh carrot juice	1 lb/454 g crushed ice
1 fl oz/30 mL honey	8 oz/227 g bananas
1 pint/480 mL buttermilk	

1. Peel and core the apples and cut into large dice.

2. Combine with the carrot juice, honey, buttermilk, ginger, ice, and bananas in a blender and purée until very smooth. Serve in a glass.

CHEF'S NOTE

Always be sure to peel the carrots before juicing, because the skins will give the juice an undesirable earthy flavor. Fresh carrot juice is best made using a juicer. If a juicer is not available, use a blender to purée the peeled and chopped carrots with just enough water to facilitate the blending, and then drain the purée through a piece of cheesecloth.

HOT CHOCOLATE WITH MASA

YIELD: 8 PORTIONS

2½ oz/71 g masa harina

1 qt/960 mL warm water

1 qt/960 mL milk

8 oz/227 g grated Mexican sweet chocolate

6 oz/170 g piloncillo

1 pinch ground anise seed

1 pinch salt

1. In a large pot, thoroughly combine the masa harina and the warm water. Add the milk, chocolate, piloncillo, anise, and salt. Bring to a simmer and whisk with a molinillo or an immersion blender until the chocolate is melted and the sugar is dissolved, 30 seconds to 1 minute.

2. Serve hot with Churros (page 356).

CHEF'S NOTE

This hot beverage, known as *champurrado*, is served with Churros (page 356) as a popular breakfast throughout Mexico. Champurrado is a variation of atole, a popular warm beverage thickened with masa and/or cornstarch and sweetened with piloncillo, an unrefined brown sugar, and aromatics.

A molinillo is a wooden whisk used in traditional Mexican cooking that is essential to creating this frothy hot beverage. It is used by holding it between the palms of both hands and rubbing both hands back and forth against each other to rotate the whisk.

SALTED YOGURT DRINK

YIELD: 8 PORTIONS

2 qt/1.92 L Bulgarian or similar yogurt, well chilled

8 oz/227 g crushed ice

1 pinch salt

1 pint/480 mL mineral water, chilled

Process the yogurt and ice in a blender until smooth and frothy. Add salt as desired. Add the water and immediately serve in a glass or cup.

CHEF'S NOTE | Variations of this slightly salted yogurt beverage are known as *ayran* in Turkey and the Middle East, as *doogh* in Iran and Afghanistan, and as the popular *lassi* in India. Often enjoyed on hot days after strenuous work, these drinks help to quench thirst and recharge the body with minerals and electrolytes.

HOT TEA PUNCH

YIELD: 8 PORTIONS

1 qt/960 mL brewed black, Darjeeling, Assam, or similar tea

1 qt/960 mL dry red wine

¼ cup/57 g brown sugar

One 2-in/5-cm cinnamon stick

4 cloves

1 tbsp/9 g grated lemon zest

2 star anise

5 fl oz/150 mL dark rum

5 fl oz/150 mL kirschwasser

1. Combine the tea, red wine, brown sugar, cinnamon stick, cloves, lemon zest, and star anise in a pot and bring to a near simmer. Allow to steep for about 5 minutes, then strain.

2. Add the rum and kirschwasser and serve in a mug or large cup, while hot.

CHEF'S NOTE

This hot tea punch, known as *jagertee* in Austria, is a popular beverage among tourists skiing in the Alps. The relatively high alcohol content makes it advisable, however, not to consume it before hitting the slopes.

SOUTHEAST ASIAN ICED BUBBLE TEA

YIELD: 8 PORTIONS

12 oz/340 g large tapioca pearls for bubble tea, about ¼ in/6 mm in diameter

Iced Tea

1 stalk lemongrass, bruised, coarsely chopped

5 kaffir lime leaves, bruised

½ oz/14 g mint leaves

½ oz/14 g galangal, peeled, very thinly sliced

½ oz/14 g ginger, peeled, very thinly sliced

¾ oz/21 g jasmine tea leaves

1 gal/3.84 L boiling water

4 oz/113 g palm sugar

2 fl oz/60 mL lime juice

1. Simmer the tapioca pearls in about 2 qt/1.92 L water over medium heat for about 5 minutes, until the pearls have a pleasant chewiness. Drain and rinse with cold water. Set aside.

2. For the tea, combine the lemongrass, lime leaves, mint, galangal, ginger, and jasmine tea leaves in a pot and add the boiling water. Allow to steep off the heat for about 15 minutes.

3. Add the palm sugar and lime juice and adjust sweetness and acidity as desired.

4. Strain the tea and refrigerate until very cold. At service, add the cooked tapioca pearls to a glass and top with the very cold tea. Serve with an extra-wide straw designed for bubble tea.

CHEF'S NOTES

Originating in Taiwan, bubble tea has become very popular all over East Asia as well as in Asian communities abroad. The bubbles are large tapioca pearls designed to provide a unique, chewy textural experience. Tapioca pearls for bubble tea are available online or at well-stocked Asian grocery stores.

Bubble tea is always served with an extra-wide straw in order to accommodate the width of the tapioca pearls. As with any tea, bubble tea is served both hot and cold in many flavors. Sometimes milk tea, made with fresh or condensed milk, is used as the liquid for bubble tea.

GLOSSARY

A

Acid A substance having a sour or sharp flavor. A substance's degree of acidity is measured on the pH scale; acids have a pH of less than 7. Most foods are somewhat acidic. Foods generally referred to as acids include citrus juice, vinegar, and wine. *See also* Alkali.

Active dry yeast A dehydrated form of yeast that needs to be hydrated in warm water (105°F/41°C) before use. It contains about one-tenth the moisture of compressed yeast.

Aioli Garlic mayonnaise, often used as a condiment with fish and meat. In Italian, *allioli*; in Spanish, *aliolio*.

À la carte A menu from which the patron makes individual selections in various menu categories; each item is priced separately.

Al dente Literally, Italian for "to the tooth"; refers to an item, such as pasta or vegetables, cooked until it is tender but still firm, not soft.

Alkali A substance with a bitter, sometimes soapy flavor. Alkalinity is measured on the pH scale; alkaline substances have a pH higher than 7. The few alkaline substances used in food production include baking soda or powder, calcium hydroxide for the nixtamalization of corn in Mexican cuisine, or sodium hydroxide for color enhancement in pretzels.

Andouille A spicy pork sausage that is French in origin but is now more often associated with Cajun cooking. There are hundreds of varieties of this regional specialty.

Antioxidants Naturally occurring substances that retard the breakdown of tissues in the presence of oxygen. May be added to food during processing or may occur naturally. They help to prevent food from becoming rancid or discolored due to oxidation.

Appetizer One or more of the initial courses in a meal. These may be hot or cold, plated or served as finger food. They should stimulate the appetite and go well with the remainder of the meal.

Aromatics Plant ingredients, such as herbs and spices, used to enhance the flavor and fragrance of food.

B

Baguette A loaf of bread of French origin, made with 12 to 16 oz/340 to 454 g of dough, shaped into a long, skinny loaf that ranges from 2 to 3 in/5 to 8 cm in diameter and 18 to 24 in/46 to 61 cm in length. The dough, made of flour, water, salt, and yeast, yields a paper-thin, crisp crust and a light, airy crumb.

Bake To cook food by surrounding it with dry heat in a closed environment, as in an oven.

Baking powder A chemical leavener made with an alkaline and an acidic ingredient, most commonly sodium bicarbonate (baking soda) and cream of tartar. When exposed to liquid, it produces carbon dioxide gas, which leavens doughs and batters. Double-acting baking powder contains ingredients that produce two leavening reactions: one upon exposure to liquid, the second when heated.

Baking soda Sodium bicarbonate, a leavening agent that, when combined with an acidic ingredient and moisture, releases carbon dioxide gas and leavens baked goods.

Barbecue A variation of a roasting method involving smoke-roasting food over an indirect wood or charcoal fire. In some instances, a dry rub, marinade, or sauce is brushed on the item before or during cooking.

Batter A mixture of flour and liquid, sometimes with the inclusion of other ingredients. Batters vary in thickness but are generally semiliquid and thinner than doughs. Used in such preparations as cakes, quick breads, pancakes, and crêpes. Also, a liquid mixture used to coat foods before deep-frying.

Béchamel A white sauce made of milk thickened with a pale roux and flavored with white mirepoix. One of the "grand" sauces.

Binder An ingredient or appareil used to thicken a sauce or hold together another mixture of ingredients.

Blanch   To cook an item briefly in boiling water or hot fat before finishing or storing it. Blanching preserves the color, lessens strong flavors, and aids in removing the peels of some fruits and vegetables.

Blend   A mixture of two or more flavors combined to achieve a particular flavor or quality. Also, to mix two or more ingredients together until combined.

Boil   A cooking method in which items are immersed in liquid at or above the boiling point of water (212°F/100°C).

Bouillabaisse   A hearty fish and shellfish stew flavored with tomatoes, onions, garlic, white wine, and saffron. A traditional specialty of Marseille, France.

Bowl foods   Meals that are served in bowls as individual portions. Can include soups, stews, noodles, and salads, among others.

Braise   A cooking method in which the main item, usually a tough cut of meat, is seared in fat, then simmered in a specific quantity of stock or another liquid in a covered vessel, slowly tenderizing it by breaking down collagen.

Bran   The outer layer of a cereal grain; the part highest in fiber.

Brandy   Spirit made by distilling wine or the fermented mash of fruit. May be aged in oak barrels.

Bread   A product made of flour, sugar, shortening, salt, and liquid, leavened by the action of yeast. Also, to coat food with flour, eggs, and crumbs before frying or baking.

Brine   A solution of salt, water, and seasonings used to flavor and preserve foods.

Brisket   A cut of beef from the lower forequarter, best suited for long-cooking preparations such as braising. Corned beef is cured beef brisket.

Broil   A cooking method in which items are cooked by a radiant heat source placed above the food.

Broth   A flavorful, aromatic liquid made by simmering water or stock with meat, vegetables, and/or spices and herbs.

Bruise   To partially crush a food item in order to release its flavor.

Butcher   A chef or purveyor responsible for butchering meats, poultry, and occasionally fish. In the brigade system, the butcher may also be responsible for breading meat and fish items and other mise en place operations involving meat.

Buttermilk   A dairy beverage with a slightly sour flavor similar to that of yogurt. Traditionally the liquid by-product of butter churning, now usually made by culturing skim milk.

C

Cajun   A hearty cuisine of the southern United States based on French influences; signature ingredients include spices, dark roux, pork fat, filé powder, green peppers, onions, and celery. Jambalaya is a traditional Cajun dish.

Caramelization   The process of browning sugar in the presence of heat. The temperature range in which sugar begins to caramelize is approximately 320° to 360°F/160° to 182°C.

Cassoulet   A stew of beans baked with pork or other meats, duck or goose confit, and seasonings.

Cephalopod   Marine creatures whose tentacles and arms are attached directly to their heads, such as squid and octopus.

Charcuterie   The preparation of pork and other meat items, such as hams, terrines, sausages, pâtés, and other forcemeats, that are usually preserved in some manner, such as smoking, brining, and curing.

Cheesecloth   A light, fine-mesh gauze used for straining liquids and making sachets.

Chiffonade   Fine shreds of leafy vegetables or herbs; often used as a garnish.

Chile   The fruit of certain types of capsicum peppers (not related to black pepper), used fresh or dry as a seasoning. Chiles come in many types (for example, jalapeño, serrano, poblano) and varying degrees of spiciness and heat, measured in Scoville units.

Chili powder   Dried, ground, or crushed chiles, often including other ground spices and herbs.

Chop   To cut into pieces of roughly the same size. Also, a small cut of meat including part of the rib.

GLOSSARY   **383**

Choucroute Sauerkraut; preserved cabbage with a sour flavor. Choucroute garni is sauerkraut garnished with various meats such as cured meats and sausages.

Cioppino A fish stew usually made with white wine and tomatoes, believed to have originated in Genoa and popularized by Italian immigrants in San Francisco.

Clarified butter Butter from which the milk solids and water have been removed, leaving pure butterfat. Has a higher smoking point than whole butter but less butter flavor. Also known as *ghee.*

Coarse chop To cut into pieces of roughly the same size; used for items such as mirepoix, where appearance is not important.

Cold smoking A procedure used to give smoked flavor to products without cooking them.

Collagen A fibrous protein found in the connective tissue of animals, which is used to make sausage casings as well as glue and gelatin. Breaks down into gelatin when cooked in a moist environment for an extended period.

Complete protein A food source that provides all of the essential amino acids in the correct ratio so they can be used in the body for protein synthesis. May require more than one ingredient (such as beans and rice together).

Compote A dish of fruit (fresh or dried) cooked in syrup flavored with spices or liqueur.

Compound butter Whole butter combined with herbs or other seasonings and usually used to sauce grilled or broiled items, vegetables, or pastas, or as a spread for sandwiches and canapés.

Condiment An aromatic mixture, such as pickles, chutney, and some sauces and relishes, that accompanies food; usually kept on the table throughout service.

Confit Preserved meat (usually goose, duck, or pork) cooked and preserved in its own fat.

Corned beef Beef brisket preserved with salt and spices. The term *corned* refers to the corn kernel–like appearance of chunks of salt spread over the brisket during the corning process.

Cornichon A small, sour pickled cucumber.

Cornstarch A fine white powder milled from dried corn; used primarily as a thickener for sauces and occasionally as an ingredient in batters. Viscous when hot, gelatinous when cold.

Coulis A thick purée, usually of vegetables or fruit.

Creaming Blending fats and sugar together to incorporate air.

Cream of tartar A salt of tartaric acid used extensively in baking; found in wine barrels after fermentation. Used to give stability and volume in whipping egg whites. Often serves as the acid component in baking powder.

Crème fraîche Heavy cream cultured to give it a thick consistency and a slightly tangy flavor; used in hot preparations, as it is less likely to curdle when heated than sour cream or yogurt.

Creole This sophisticated type of cooking is a combination of French, Spanish, and African cuisines; signature ingredients include butter, cream, tomatoes, filé powder, green peppers, onions, and celery. Gumbo is a traditional Creole dish.

Crustacean A class of hard-shelled arthropods with elongated bodies, primarily aquatic, which includes edible species such as lobster, crab, shrimp, and crayfish.

Cure To preserve a food by salting. Also, the ingredients used to cure an item.

Curry A mixture of spices used primarily in Indian cuisine; may include turmeric, coriander, cumin, cayenne or other chiles, cardamom, cinnamon, clove, fennel, fenugreek, ginger, and garlic. Also, a dish seasoned with curry.

D

Debeard To remove the shaggy, inedible fibers from a mussel. These fibers anchor the mussel to its mooring.

Deep-fry To cook food by immersion in hot fat; deep-fried foods are often coated with bread crumbs or batter before cooking.

Deep poach To cook food gently in enough simmering liquid to completely submerge the food.

Deglaze/Déglacer   To use a liquid, such as wine, water, or stock, to dissolve food particles and/or caramelized drippings left in a pan after roasting or sautéing.

Degrease/Dégraisser   To skim the fat off the surface of a liquid, such as a stock or sauce, or to pour off excess fat from a sauté pan before deglazing.

Dice   To cut ingredients into small cubes (⅛ in/3 mm for small or fine; ¼ in/6 mm for medium; ¾ in/2 cm for large are standard measures for these cuts).

Direct heat   A method of heat transfer in which heat waves radiate from a source (such as an open burner or grill) and travel directly to the item being heated with no conductor between heat source and food. Examples are grilling, broiling, and toasting. Also known as *radiant heat.*

Drawn   A whole fish that has been scaled and gutted but still has its head, fins, and tail.

Dressed   Prepared for cooking or service; a dressed fish is gutted and scaled, and its head, tail, and fins are removed (same as pan-dressed). Dressed poultry is plucked, drawn, singed, trimmed, and trussed. Also, coated with dressing, as in a salad.

Dry cure   A combination of salts and spices usually used before smoking to process meats and forcemeats.

Dumpling   Any of a number of small soft dough or batter items that are steamed, poached, or simmered (possibly on top of a stew); may be filled or plain.

Durum   A very hard wheat typically milled into semolina, primarily used in making pasta.

E

Egg wash   A mixture of beaten eggs (whole eggs, yolks, or whites) and a liquid, usually milk or water, used to coat baked goods before or during baking to give them a sheen or to enhance browning.

Emulsion   A mixture of two or more liquids, one of which is a fat or oil and the other of which is water based, so that tiny globules of one are suspended in the other. This may involve the use of stabilizers, such as egg or mustard. Emulsions may be temporary, permanent, or semipermanent.

En croûte   Encased in a bread or pastry crust.

Étouffée   Literally, French for "smothered." Refers to food cooked by a method similar to braising, except that items are cooked with little or no added liquid in a pan with a tight-fitting lid (also *étuver, à l'étuvée*). Also, a Cajun dish made with a dark roux, crayfish, vegetables, and seasonings, served over a bed of white rice.

F

Fabrication   The butchering, cutting, and trimming of meat, poultry, fish, and game (large pieces or whole) into smaller cuts to prepare them to be cooked.

Fat   One of the basic nutrients used by the body to provide energy. Fats also provide flavor in food and give a feeling of fullness.

Fatback   Pork fat from the back of the pig, used primarily for barding.

Fermentation   The breakdown of carbohydrates into carbon dioxide gas and alcohol, usually through the action of yeast on sugar.

Fillet/Filet   A boneless cut of meat, fish, or poultry.

Fine-mesh strainer   A conical sieve made from fine-metal mesh screen, used for straining and puréeing foods.

Finger foods   Items intended to be consumed in two or three bites that are easily and cleanly eaten out of hand.

Five-spice powder   A mixture of equal parts ground cinnamon, clove, fennel seed, star anise, and Szechwan peppercorns.

Flatfish   A type of fish characterized by its flat body and having both eyes on one side of its head (such as sole, plaice, flounder, and halibut).

Flattop   A thick plate of cast iron or steel set over the heat source on a range; diffuses heat, creating a more even heat than an open burner.

Food mill   A type of strainer with a crank-operated, curved blade; used to purée soft foods.

Food on a stick   Food that is cooked or served or both on a skewer or stick, typically as a means of portability.

GLOSSARY   **385**

Food processor   A machine with interchangeable blades and disks and a removable bowl and lid separate from the motor housing. It can be used for a variety of tasks, including chopping, grinding, puréeing, emulsifying, kneading, slicing, shredding, and cutting julienne.

Forcemeat   A mixture of chopped or ground meat or seafood and other ingredients used for pâté, sausages, and other preparations.

Fritter   Sweet or savory food coated or mixed into batter and deep-fried. Also called *beignet*.

Fumet   A type of stock in which the main flavoring ingredient is smothered with wine and aromatics; fish fumet is the most common type.

G

Garnish   An edible decoration or accompaniment to a dish.

Gelatin   A protein-based substance found in animal bones and connective tissue. When dissolved in hot liquid and then cooled, it can be used as a thickener or stabilizer.

Glaze   To give an item a shiny surface by brushing it with sauce, aspic, icing, or another appareil. For meat, to coat with sauce and then brown in an oven or salamander.

Gluten   A protein present in wheat flour that develops through hydration and mixing to form elastic strands that build structure and aid in leavening.

Gravlax   Raw salmon cured with salt, sugar, and fresh dill. A regional dish of Scandinavian origin.

Griddle   A heavy metal cooking surface, which may be fitted with handles, built into a stove, or heated by its own gas or electric element. Cooking is done directly on the griddle.

Grill   A technique in which foods are cooked by a radiant heat source placed below the food. Also, the piece of equipment on which grilling is done. Grills may be fueled by gas, electricity, charcoal, or wood.

Grill pan   An iron skillet with ridges that is used on the stovetop to simulate grilling.

Grinder   A machine used to grind meat; ranges from small hand-operated models to large-capacity motor-driven models. Meat or other foods are fed through a hopper into the grinder, where the worm or auger pushes them into a blade. The blade cuts and forces the item through different-size grinder plates. Care should be taken to keep the machine as clean as possible to lessen the chances of cross contamination.

Gumbo   A Creole soup-stew thickened with filé or okra.

H

Haricot   French for "bean." Haricots verts are thin green beans.

Hock   The lowest part of an animal's leg; could be considered the ankle. The most familiar example is ham hock.

Hominy   Corn that has been milled or treated with a lye solution to remove the bran and germ. Ground hominy is known as grits.

Hors d'oeuvre   Literally, French for "outside the work." Typically a small, one- or two-bite-size item that precedes the meal.

Hotel pan   A rectangular metal pan, in a number of standard sizes, with a lip that allows it to rest on a storage shelf or in a steam table.

Hot smoking   A technique used when a fully cooked smoked item is desired. Both cured and uncured items can be hot smoked. Smoking temperature and time will depend on the product.

Hydrate   To combine ingredients with water.

Hygiene   Conditions and practices followed to maintain health, including sanitation and personal cleanliness.

I

Indirect heat   A method of heat transfer in which the heat is transferred to the product by the heated air instead of the heat source.

Induction burner   A type of heating unit that relies on magnetic attraction between the cooktop and metals in the pot to generate the heat that cooks the foods in the pan. Reaction time is significantly faster than with traditional burners.

Infusion Steeping an aromatic or other item in liquid to extract its flavor. Also, the liquid resulting from this process.

Instant-read thermometer A thermometer used to measure the internal temperature of foods. The stem is inserted in the food, producing an instant temperature readout.

J

Julienne Vegetables, potatoes, or other items cut into thin strips; ⅛ by ⅛ in by 1 to 2 in/3 by 3 mm by 3 to 5 cm is the standard measure for this cut. Fine julienne is ¹⁄₁₆ by ¹⁄₁₆ in by 1 to 2 in/1.5 by 1.5 mm by 3 to 5 cm.

Jus French for "juice." *Jus de viande* is "meat juice." Meat served *au jus* is served with its own juice.

K

Kasha Buckwheat groats that have been hulled, crushed, and roasted; usually prepared by boiling.

Knead To work or mix a dough by hand to soften it to working consistency, or to stretch yeasted doughs to expand their gluten.

Kosher Prepared in accordance with Jewish dietary laws.

Kosher salt Pure, refined rock salt often preferred for pickling because it does not contain magnesium carbonate and thus it does not cloud brine solutions. Also used to kosher items. Also known as coarse salt or pickling salt.

L

Lard Rendered pork fat used for pastry and frying. Also, the process of inserting strips of fat into meat before roasting or braising to add flavor and succulence.

Liqueur A spirit flavored with fruit, spices, nuts, herbs, and/or seeds and usually sweetened. Also known as

cordials, liqueurs often have a high alcohol content, a viscous body, and a slightly sticky feel.

Littleneck Small hard-shell clams, often eaten raw on the half-shell; smaller than a cherrystone clam (less than 2 in/5 cm in diameter).

M

Maillard reaction A complex browning reaction that results in the distinctive flavor and color of foods that do not contain much sugar, including roasted meats. The reaction, which involves carbohydrates and amino acids, is named after the French scientist who first discovered it. There are low-temperature and high-temperature Maillard reactions; high temperature is considered to be 310°F/154°C and above.

Mandoline A slicing device of stainless steel with carbon-steel blades. The blades may be adjusted to cut items into various cuts and thicknesses.

Marbling The intramuscular fat found in meat that makes it tender and juicy when cooked.

Marinade An appareil used before cooking to flavor and moisten foods; may be liquid or dry. Liquid marinades are usually based on an acidic ingredient, such as wine or vinegar; dry marinades are usually salt based or spice based.

Mark on a grill To turn a food (without flipping it over) 90 degrees after it has been on the grill for several seconds, to create the cross-hatching associated with grilled foods.

Mayonnaise A cold emulsion sauce made of oil, egg yolks, vinegar, mustard, and seasonings.

Medallion A small, round, disk-shaped cut of meat.

Meringue Egg whites beaten with sugar until they stiffen. Types include regular or common/French, Italian, and Swiss.

Microgreens Seedlings of various herbs, greens, and vegetables that are typically used in salads or as a garnish.

Millet A small, round grain containing no gluten. May be boiled or ground into flour.

GLOSSARY **387**

Milling   The process by which grain is separated into germ/husk, bran, and endosperm and ground into flour or meal.

Mince   To chop into very small pieces.

Minestrone   A hearty vegetable soup; typically includes dried beans and pasta.

Mirepoix   A combination of chopped aromatic vegetables—usually two parts onion, one part carrot, and one part celery—used to flavor stocks, soups, braises, and stews.

Mise en place   Literally, French for "put in place." The preparation and assembly of ingredients, pans, utensils, and plates or serving pieces needed for a particular dish or service period.

Mole   A spiced Mexican sauce made from chiles, vegetables, and sometimes chocolate.

Mollusk   Any of a number of invertebrate animals with soft, unsegmented bodies usually enclosed in a hard shell. Mollusks include gastropods (univalves), bivalves, and cephalopods; examples include clams, oysters, snails, octopus, and squid.

N

Napper/Nappé   To coat with sauce. Also, a word to describe a sauce that is thick enough to coat.

New potato   A young potato harvested early in the growing season before the aboveground stems and leaves wither away. A new potato is characterized by its sweet flavor and low starch content. New potatoes should be consumed within days of harvest because the sugar content of the potatoes will convert into starch during storage.

Nixtamalization   Process whereby maize (corn) is soaked and cooked in an alkaline solution, and then hulled.

Nonbony fish   Fish whose skeletons are made of cartilage rather than hard bone (such as shark and skate). Also called *cartilaginous fish*.

O

Offal   Variety meats including head meat, tail, and feet as well as organs such as brain, heart, kidneys, lights (lungs), sweetbreads, tripe, and tongue.

Organ meat   Meat from an organ rather than from the muscle tissue of an animal.

P

Pan-broiling   A cooking method similar to dry sautéing that simulates broiling by cooking an item in a hot pan with little or no fat.

Pan fry   To cook in fat in a skillet; generally involves more fat than sautéing or stir-frying but less than deep-frying.

Parchment   Heat-resistant paper used to line baking pans, cook items en papillote, construct pastry cones, and cover items during shallow poaching.

Parcook   To partially cook an item before storing or finishing by another method; may be the same as blanching.

Pasta   Literally, Italian for "dough" or "paste." Noodles are made from a dough of flour (often semolina) and water or eggs that is kneaded, rolled, and cut or extruded, and then cooked by boiling.

Pâte à choux   Cream-puff paste, made by boiling a mixture of water, butter, and flour, then beating in whole eggs. Also known as choux paste.

Phyllo/filo dough   Pastry made with very thin sheets of a flour-and-water dough layered with butter and/or bread or cake crumbs; similar to strudel.

Pickling spice   A mixture of herbs and spices used to season pickles; often includes dill seeds, coriander seeds, cinnamon sticks, peppercorns, and bay leaves.

Pilaf   A technique for cooking grains in which the grain is sautéed briefly in butter, then simmered in stock or water with various seasonings. Also known as pilau, pilaw, pullao, and pilav.

Poach   A method in which items are cooked gently in liquid at 150° to 180°F/71° to 80°C.

Polenta   Cornmeal mush cooked in simmering liquid until the grains soften and the liquid is absorbed. Can be eaten hot or cold, firm or soft.

Prawn   A crustacean that closely resembles shrimp; often used as a general term for large shrimp.

Prosciutto   A dry-cured ham. True prosciutto comes from Parma, Italy, although variations can be found throughout the world.

Protein   One of the basic nutrients needed by the body to maintain life, supply energy, build and repair tissues, form enzymes and hormones, and perform other essential functions. Protein can be obtained from animal and vegetable sources.

Purée   To process food by mashing, straining, or chopping very finely in order to make it into a smooth paste. Also, a product made using this technique.

R

Ramekin   A small, ovenproof dish, usually ceramic (in French, *ramequin*).

Ratios   A general formula of ingredients that can be varied.

Reduce   To decrease the volume of a liquid by simmering or boiling; used to provide a thicker consistency and/or concentrated flavors and color.

Reduction   The product that results when a liquid is reduced.

Refresh   To plunge an item into or run it under cold water after blanching to prevent further cooking. Also referred to as shocking.

Rempah   A Malaysian blend of spices and vegetables used primarily to season braised dishes.

Render   To melt fat and clarify the drippings for use in sautéing or pan frying.

Rest   To allow food to sit undisturbed after roasting and before carving; this allows the juices to seep back into the meat fibers.

Roast   A dry-heat cooking method in which items are cooked in an oven or on a spit over a fire.

Roe   Fish or shellfish eggs.

Rondeau   A shallow, wide, straight-sided pot with two loop handles; often used for braising.

Round   A cut of beef from the hindquarter that includes the top and bottom round, eye, and top sirloin. It is lean and usually braised or roasted. Also, in baking, to shape pieces of yeast dough into balls; this process stretches and relaxes the gluten and ensures even rising and a smooth crust.

Roundfish   A classification of fish based on skeletal type, characterized by a rounded body and eyes on opposite sides of the head. Roundfish are usually cut by the up and over method.

Roux   An appareil containing equal parts flour and fat (usually butter), used to thicken liquids. Roux is cooked to varying degrees (white, blond, brown, or dark) depending on its intended use. The darker the roux, the less thickening power it has but the fuller the taste.

Rub   A combination of spices and herbs applied to foods as a marinade or flavorful crust. Dry rubs are generally based upon spices; wet rubs (sometimes known as mops) may include moist ingredients such as fresh herbs, vegetables, and fruit juice or broth, if necessary, to make a pasty consistency. Rubs are absorbed into the meat to create a greater depth of flavor.

S

Sachet d'épices   Literally, French for "bag of spices." Aromatic ingredients encased in cheesecloth that are used to flavor stocks and other liquids. A standard sachet contains parsley stems, cracked peppercorns, dried thyme, bay leaf, and sometimes garlic.

Salt cod   Cod that has been salted and dried to preserve it. Also referred to as baccalà or bacalao.

Sanitation   The practice of preparation and distribution of food in a clean environment by healthy food workers.

Sashimi   Sliced raw fish, served with such condiments as a julienne of daikon radish, pickled ginger, wasabi, and soy sauce.

Sauce   A liquid accompaniment to food, used to enhance the flavor of the food.

Sauté   A cooking method in which naturally tender items are cooked quickly in a small amount of fat in a pan on the stovetop.

Sauteuse   A shallow skillet with sloping sides and a single long handle; used for sautéing. Often referred to as a sauté pan.

GLOSSARY   **389**

Savory Not sweet. Also, the name of a course served after dessert and before port in traditional British meals. Also, a family of herbs (including summer and winter varieties).

Score To cut the surface of an item at regular intervals to allow it to cook or cure evenly.

Sear To brown the surface of food in fat over high heat to add color and flavor. Searing is also applied as a part of other methods such as braising and stewing.

Sea salt Salt produced by evaporating seawater. Available refined or unrefined, crystallized or ground. Also, *sel gris*, French for "gray salt."

Shallow poach A method in which items are cooked gently in a shallow covered pan of simmering liquid. The liquid can then be reduced and used as the basis of a sauce.

Sieve A container made of a perforated material, such as wire mesh, used to drain, rice, or purée foods. Also known as a tamis.

Silverskin The tough, connective tissue that surrounds certain muscles.

Simmer To maintain the temperature of a liquid just below boiling. Also, a cooking method in which items are cooked in simmering liquid.

Slurry Starch (flour, cornstarch, or arrowroot) dispersed in cold liquid to prevent it from forming lumps when added to hot liquid as a thickener.

Smoking Any of several methods for preserving and flavoring foods by exposing them to smoke. Methods include cold smoking (in which smoked items are not fully cooked), hot smoking (in which the items are cooked), and smoke-roasting.

Smoking point The temperature at which a fat begins to smoke when heated.

Sodium An alkaline metal element necessary in small quantities for human nutrition; one of the components of most salts used in cooking.

Spice An aromatic vegetable substance from numerous plant parts, usually dried and used as seasoning.

Stabilizer An ingredient (usually a protein or plant product) that is added to an emulsion to prevent it from separating (for example, egg yolk, cream, or mustard). Also, an ingredient, such as gelatin, that is used in various desserts to prevent them from separating (for example, in Bavarian creams).

Standard breading procedure The procedure in which items are dredged in flour, dipped in beaten egg, then coated with crumbs before being pan fried or deep-fried.

Steam To cook items in a vapor bath created by boiling water or other liquids.

Steamer A set of stacked pots with perforations in the bottom of each pot. They fit over a larger pot filled with boiling or simmering water. Also, a perforated insert made of metal or bamboo, used in a pot to steam foods.

Stir-frying A cooking method similar to sautéing, in which items are cooked over very high heat using little fat and kept moving constantly. Usually done in a wok.

Stock A flavorful liquid prepared by simmering bones and/or vegetables in water with aromatics until their flavor is extracted. It is used as a base for soups, sauces, and other preparations.

Street food Snacks or whole meals prepared and sold from a nonpermanent structure, mainly for immediate consumption. Trucks, carts, small booths in public places, or floating markets are the most common venues.

Sweat To cook an item, usually vegetable(s), in a covered pan in a small amount of fat until it softens and releases moisture but does not brown.

T

Table salt Refined, granulated rock salt. May be fortified with iodine and treated with magnesium carbonate to prevent clumping.

Tapas Small hors d'oeuvre that are thought to have originated in Spain. The varieties of tapas are numerous and are meant to give just a taste of the dish.

Tart A shallow pie without a top crust; may be sweet or savory.

Tartlet A small, single-serving tart.

Temper To heat gently and gradually. May refer to the process of incorporating hot liquid into a liaison to gradually raise its temperature. May also refer to the proper method for working with chocolate.

Tempura Seafood and/or vegetables coated with a light batter and deep-fried, usually accompanied by a sauce.

Tenderloin A cut of tender, expensive meat from the loin or hindquarter, usually beef or pork.

Tripe The edible stomach lining of a cow or other ruminant. Honeycomb tripe, the most popular, comes from the second stomach and has a honeycomb-like texture.

Truss To tie up meat or poultry with string before cooking it in order to give it a compact shape for more even cooking and a better appearance.

Tuber The fleshy root, stem, or rhizome of a plant, able to grow into a new plant. Some, such as potatoes, are eaten as vegetables.

U

Univalve A single-shelled, single-muscle mollusk, such as abalone and sea urchin.

V

Variety meat Meat from a part of an animal other than the muscle; for example, organs.

Vegetarian An individual who has adopted a specific diet that eliminates meat and fish and products derived from meat and fish but not all animal products. Lacto-ovo-vegetarians include dairy products and eggs in their diet; ovo-vegetarians include eggs. Vegans eat no foods derived in any way from animals.

Vinaigrette A cold sauce of oil and vinegar, usually with flavorings; it is a temporary emulsion sauce. The standard proportion is three parts oil to one part vinegar.

W

Waffle A crisp, pancake-like batter product, cooked on a specialized griddle that gives the finished product a textured pattern, usually a grid. Also, a special vegetable cut that produces a grid or basket-weave pattern. Also known as *gaufrette.*

Whip To beat an item, such as cream or egg whites, to incorporate air. Also, a special tool, namely, a whisk for whipping made of looped wire attached to a handle.

Wok A round-bottomed pan, usually made of rolled steel, used in Asian cuisine for nearly all cooking methods. Its shape allows for even heat distribution and easy tossing of ingredients.

Y

Yeast Microscopic fungus whose metabolic processes are responsible for fermentation; used for leavening bread and in making cheese, beer, and wine.

Yogurt Milk cultured with bacteria to give it a slightly thick consistency and sour flavor.

Z

Zest The thin, brightly colored outer part of citrus rind. It contains volatile oils, making it ideal for use as a flavoring.

BIBLIOGRAPHY

Ainsworth, Mark, and The Culinary Institute of America. *Fish and Seafood*. Clifton Park, NY: Delmar Cengage Learning, 2009.

Bergerson, Sephi. *Street Foods of India*. London, England: I.B. Tauris & Co., 2010.

Bhumichitr, Vatcharin. *Vatch's Thai Street Food*. London, England: Kyle Books, 2002.

Biçer, Ali. *Orientalisches Finger Food, 101 Rezepte aus Tausendundeiner Nacht*. Lenzburg, Switzerland: Fona Verlag AG, 2009.

Cost, Bruce. *Asian Ingredients: A Guide to the Foodstuffs of China, Japan, Korea, Thailand, and Vietnam*. New York, NY: Harper Perennial, 2000.

Costner, Susan. *Great Sandwiches*. New York, NY: Crown, 1990.

Danhi, Robert. *Southeast Asian Flavors: Adventures in Cooking the Foods of Thailand, Vietnam, Malaysia, and Singapore*. El Segundo, CA: Mortar and Press, 2008.

Durack, Ted. *Noodle*. San Francisco, CA: Soma Books, 1999.

Ferguson, Claire. *Street Food*. London, England: Time Life Books, 1999.

Gisslen, Wayne. *Professional Baking*, 6th edition. Hoboken, NJ: John Wiley & Sons, 2012.

Halici, Nevin. *Turkish Cook Book*. London, England: Dorling Kindersley, 1989.

Helou, Anissa. *Mediterranean Street Food: Stories, Soups, Snacks, Sandwiches, Barbecues, Sweets and More from Europe, North Africa and the Middle East*. New York, NY: Harper Collins, 2002.

Hutton, Wendy. *Singapore Food*. Singapore: Marshall Cavendish Publishing, 2007.

Kamp, David. *The United States of Arugula*. New York, NY: Broadway Books, 2006.

Kazuko, Emi. *Japanese Cooking: The Traditions, Techniques, Ingredients and Recipes*. New York, NY: Hermes House Anness Publishing, 2002.

Kime, Tom. *Street Food: Exploring the World's Most Authentic Tastes*. New York, NY: DK Publishing, 2007.

Kowalski, John, and The Culinary Institute of America. *The Art of Charcuterie*. Hoboken, NJ: John Wiley & Sons, 2011.

McGee, Harold. *On Food and Cooking: The Science and Lore of the Kitchen*. New York, NY: Scribner, 2004.

Millon, Marc and Kim. *Flavors of Korea: With Stories and Recipes from a Grandmother's Kitchen*. London, England: Andre Deutsch, 1991.

Piras, Claudia. *Culinaria: Italy*. Potsdam, Germany: Tandem Verlag, 2008.

Schneller, Thomas, and The Culinary Institute of America. *Meat*. Clifton Park, NY: Delmar Cengage Learning, 2009.

Shaw, Steven A. *Asian Dining Rules: Essential Strategies for Eating Out at Japanese, Chinese, Southeast Asian, Korean, and Indian Restaurants*. New York, NY: Harper Collins, 2008.

The Culinary Institute of America. *Baking and Pastry: Mastering the Art and Craft*, 2nd edition. Hoboken, NJ: John Wiley & Sons, 2009.

———. *The Professional Chef*, 9th edition. Hoboken, NJ: John Wiley & Sons, 2011.

The Culinary Institute of America with text by Martha Rose Shulman. *Spain and the World Table*. New York, NY: DK Publishing, 2008.

This, Hervé. *The Science of the Oven*. New York, NY: Columbia University Press, 2007, translation 2009.

Thompson, David. *Thai Street Food: Authentic Recipes, Vibrant Traditions*. New York, NY: Ten Speed Press, 2009.

Toussaint-Samat, Maguelonne. *A History of Food*, 2nd edition. Chichester, UK: John Wiley & Sons, 2009.

Tung Lok Restaurants. *New Chinese Cuisine*. Singapore: Tung Lok Restaurants, 2002.

Wells, Troth. *The World of Street Food: Easy Quick Meals to Cook at Home*. Oxford, UK: New Internationalist Publications, 2006.

Wong, Julie. *Nonya Flavours: A Complete Guide to Penang Straits Chinese Cuisine*. Selangor, Malaysia: Star Publications, 2003.

Zibart, Eve. *The Ethnic Food Lover's Companion: Understanding the Cuisines of the World*. Birmingham, AL: Menasha Ridge Press, 2001.

INDEX

Note: Numbers in *italic* indicate recipe illustrations.

A

Açai (berries), 368
    Smoothie, Banana and, 368
Agua fresca, 370
    Lime, with Chia Seeds, 370, *371*
Aioli, 182
Alcoholic beverages, 9
Almond(s)
    -Honey-Tomato Chutney, 250
    Picada, 183
    Ricotta, Frozen, 363
Alsace and Lorraine culinary culture, 27
Alsatian Bäckeoffe, 5
Alum, 278
Amazonian cuisines, 35
The Americas. *See also specific regions*
    Central and South America, 33–37
    common tools of, 31
    United States, 30–33
Antojitos, 35
Apple(s)
    -Avocado Smoothie, 368
    -Carrot Smoothie with Ginger, 374
    Compote, 361
Arab culture, 18
Arab Levant, 20. *See also* Middle East
Aromatic Fish Escabeche, *172,* 173
Asia, 10. *See also* East and South;
    Southeast Asia; individual countries
Atmosphere of street food, 7
Atta flour, 115
Austin, Texas, 31
Avocado
    -Apple Smoothie, 368
    Salsa, Raw Tomatillo and, 118

B

Babas, 353
    Rum, 353
Bäckeoffe, 5
Bacon, Mac and Cheese with, 285
Bahia cuisine, 34–35
Baked Cherry Pancake, *348,* 349
Baked Phyllo Pocket with Spinach and Feta, 244
Baker's ammonia, 278–279
Baklava, 347
Bamboo mats, 12
Bamboo steamers, 12
Banana(s)
    in Cardamom Syrup, 366
    Fried, in Manioc Crust, 357
    Roti Prata with Honey and, 350–351
    Smoothie, Açai and, 368
Barbecue, 50–51
    BBQ Hominy Stew, *288,* 289
    Churrasco, 34
    cooking method, 51
Barley, 254

Barreado, 5
Basil-Lime Syrup, Melons in, 366
Batter, Beer, 176
BBQ Hominy Stew, *288,* 289
Bean starch sheets, 269
    Salad of, *268,* 269
Beef
    Cheeks, Tripe and, with Spanish Chorizo, *58,* 59
    cooking methods for, 48
    Cured with Lime and Onions, *66,* 67
    Marinade, 64
    Mixed Vegetables and, with Rice (Bibimbap), 64, *65*
    Patties, Jamaican, 94
    Rendang, *72,* 73–74
    Reuben Sandwich, *96,* 97
    Skewers, with Green Chili Sauce, 85
Beer Batter, 176
Beignets, 358, *359*
Belacan, 183
Berlin, 24
Beverages, 9, 331–332
    Açai and Banana Smoothie, 368
    Avocado-Apple Smoothie, 368
    Caipirinha, 367
    Carrot-Apple Smoothie with Ginger, 374
    Frozen Mint Limeade, *364,* 365
    Hot Chocolate with Masa, 375
    Hot or Iced Mint Tea, 374
    Hot Tea Punch, 378, *379*
    Lime Agua Fresca with Chia Seeds, 370, *371*
    Mango Lassi, 365
    Purple Corn Drink, *372,* 373
    Salted Yogurt Drink, *376,* 377
    Southeast Asian Iced Bubble Tea, *380,* 381
Bibimbap (Mixed Vegetables and Beef with Rice), 64, *65*
Black Bean Soup, 267
Black Ink Sauce, Squid in, 168
Black Rice Pudding with Coconut Milk and Dried Mango, *342,* 343
Black rice vinegar, 200
Boiling, 52–53
Börek, Turkish Water, 284
Bouillabaisse, *130,* 131
    Fish Stock for, 174
Bowl foods, 7–8
Braised Lamb Ravioli in Yogurt Sauce, *282,* 283–284
Braised Pork Belly with Dried Mustard Greens and Lily Buds in Fermented Tofu Sauce, *92,* 93
Braised Pork Knuckle Bun, 91
Braised Swordfish Kebob in Sweet and Savory Sauce, 150, *151*
Braising, 51
Brandade of Salt Cod, 161
Bratwurst, Currywurst, 54

Brazil, 34–35
    barreado, 5
    regional cuisines, 34–35
Brazilian rum, 367
Bread(s), 8–9, 265–266. *See also related entries, e.g.:* Flatbread
    Caribbean Roti, with Guyanese Filling, 102
    Chapati, 115
    Flaky (Roti Prata), 110
    Garlic, Grilled, 248
    Peanut Butter-Stuffed Steamed Flower Rolls, *318,* 319
    Pita, 111
    Roti, 102
    with spit-roasted foods, 51
    Tapioca Cheese, 314
    Tomato and Lamb, 230, *231*
Brie, Portobello Sandwich with Madeira-Glazed Onions and, 229
Browning, 47
Bruschetta
    with Cauliflower and Prosciutto, *300,* 301
    with Eggplant Relish and Ricotta Salata Cheese, 303
    with Mustard Greens and Parmesan Cheese, 304
    with Roasted Tomatoes, Green Onions, and Pecorino Cheese, 302
Bubble tea, 381
    Southeast Asian Iced, *380,* 381
Buckwheat, 352
    Crêpes, 352
Bulgur, 254, 327

C

Cabbage, Savoy, Creamed, for Seafood Hot Dog, 180
Caçik, 112
Caipirinha, 367
Cajun cuisine, 31
Cantonese cuisine, 13
Caramelized Pancake, Shredded, *336,* 337
Cardamom
    -Flavored Cream of Rice with Saffron, 333
    Syrup, Bananas in, 366
Caribbean, 31, 34
    Roti Bread with Guyanese Filling, 102
    tostonera, 31
    Vegetable Kebob, 213
Carrot-Apple Smoothie with Ginger, 374
Cashew-Cilantro Chutney, 116
Catalonia ratatouille, 195
Cauliflower
    Bruschetta with Prosciutto and, *300,* 301
    Tomato-Braised, 194
Causa, 34
Central and South America, 33–37. *See also specific countries or regions*
    Brazil, 34–35
    Caribbean, 34

INDEX   **393**

Central and South America (continued)
common tools of, 31
Mexico, 35, 37
Peru, 34
Ceviche, 34, 49
Chilean Tuna, 145
Colombian, with Coconut Milk, 148
Green Mexican, *146, 147*
Champurrado, 375
Chapati Bread, 115
Charmoula, 211
Cheese
Goat, and Tuna Empanadas, 156, *157*
Grilled East Mediterranean, with Tomatoes, *242, 243*
Mac and, with Bacon, 285
Manchego, Vegetable Sandwich with, *222, 223*
Parmesan, Bruschetta with Mustard Greens and, 304
Pecorino, Bruschetta with Roasted Tomatoes, Green Onions, and, 302
Ricotta Salata, Bruschetta with Eggplant Relish and, 303
Tapioca Bread, 314
Cherry Pancake, Baked, *348, 349*
Chia seeds, 370
Lime Agua Fresca with, 370, *371*
Chicago, Illinois, 31
Chicken
Curry, 75
Flautas, 99
fried, 49
Hainanese, Rice, 60, *61*
holding, 60
Köfte Kebob, 79
Satay, Malaysian, 80
Skewers, Jerk, 81
Thighs, with Green Olives, *76, 77*
Tikka, 89
Wings, Orange-Glazed, 108, *109*
Yakitori, 82, *83*
Chickpea(s)
Flatbread, 323
Fritters, Cilantro and, 315
Hummus, 322
soaking and grinding, 317
Soup, Spicy, 272, *273*
Stew, with Kimchi in Pita Bread, 311
Chilaquiles, 286
with Mushrooms, 286, *287*
Chilean Tuna Ceviche, 145
Chili
Crab, 140, *141*
Dipping Sauce, 107
Sauce, Green, 85
Sauce, Green, Beef Skewers with, 85
Chili bean paste, 200
China, 12–13
grains in, 12–13
Revolutionary Cuisine, 6
Chinese Chive Pockets, 313
Chinese Crispy Spring Rolls, 106
Chinese Crullers, Fried, 278–279
Chinese Mung Bean and Rice Crêpes, 306, *307*
Chips, Fish and, 143
Chive(s)
Chinese, 313
Pockets, Chinese, 313
Chorizo
Spanish, Beef Cheeks and Tripe with, *58, 59*
Spanish, Steamed Mussels with, 135

Chowder, 5
Coconut Seafood, 133
Churrasco, 34
Churros, 356
Chutney(s), 116
Cilantro-Cashew, 116
Honey-Tomato-Almond, 250
Mint, 326
Cilantro
-Cashew Chutney, 116
and Chickpea Fritters, 315
Cioppino, 132
Citrus Rice, Creamy, 341
Clams, Cioppino, 132
Coconut
Jam, 312
Jam, Grilled Toast with Coddled Eggs and, 312
Meringue, Mint-Lime Ice Cream Sandwiches with, *354, 355*
Seafood Chowder, 133
Coconut Milk
Black Rice Pudding with Dried Mango and, *342, 343*
Colombian Ceviche with, 148
Mild, Fish in, 144
Spicy, Vegetables in, 205
Coddled Eggs, Grilled Toast with Coconut Jam and, 312
Cold foods, 6
Cold holding, 7
Colombian Ceviche with Coconut Milk, 148
Comfort foods, 49, 51
Communal cooking and eating, 5, 6
Compote, Apple, 361
Condiments
Caribbean cuisine, 34
Chinese cuisine, 13
French cuisine, 27
Greek or Turkish cuisine, 19
Italian cuisine, 28
Japanese cuisine, 14
Korean cuisine, 15
Mexican cuisine, 37
Middle Eastern cuisine, 21
Midwestern U.S. cuisine, 32
North African cuisine, 21
northeastern European cuisine, 30
Northeastern U.S. cuisine, 32
Northwestern U.S. cuisine, 33
Southern U.S. cuisine, 32
Southwestern U.S. cuisine, 33
Spanish cuisine, 25
Thai or Vietnamese cuisine, 18
Cooked Tomatillo Salsa, 325
Cooking methods
the Americas, 31
East and South Asia, 12
eastern Mediterranean and North Africa, 19, 22
Europe, 25
for fish and seafood, 123–129
for grains, 257–260
Italy, 28
for legumes, 261–263
for meat and poultry, 47–53
Middle East, 21
native American, 31
for noodles, 264–265
Thailand, 18
Turkey, 20

for vegetables, 187–189
Vietnam, 16
Corn
on the Cob, Grilled, 212
nixtamalization, 35
Pancakes, 322
Pancakes, Savory Pork Sauce with Noodles or, 270, *271*
purple, 373
Purple Corn Drink, *372, 373*
Tortillas, 279
Corn Dog, 103
Coulis, Poblano, 250
Couscous, 19
Couscousière, 19
Crab
Chili, 140, *141*
Coconut Seafood Chowder, 133
Crabmeat, Vietnamese Crispy Spring Rolls, 105
Cream, Mexican, 119
Creamed Savoy Cabbage for Seafood Hot Dog, 180
Cream of Rice with Saffron, Cardamom-Flavored, 333
Creamy Citrus Rice, 341
Creole cuisine, 31
Crêpes, 28, 306
Buckwheat, 352
Chinese Mung Bean and Rice, 306, *307*
Crispy Chocolate Waffles with Mint Syrup and Whipped Cream, *334, 335*
Crispy Fried Shallots, 181
Croquettes, Serrano Ham and Manchego, 104
Crullers
Fried, Curdled Soy Milk with, 276–277
Fried Chinese, 278–279
Crustaceans, 122–124
Cryogenically frozen ice cream, 331
Cucina povera, 28
Cucumber(s)
Raita, 326
Salad, Fried Fish Cakes with, 136, *137*
Salad, Spicy Thai, 175
Spicy, 325
Tzatziki, or Caçik, 112
Culinary tools
The Americas, 31
Central and South America, 31
East and South Asia, 12
eastern Mediterranean and North Africa, 19
Europe, 25
North Africa, 18–19
the United States, 31
Cultural Revolution (China), 6
Curdled Soy Milk with Fried Crullers, 276–277
Curry, 24
Chicken, 75
Eggs in, 208, *209*
Goat, with Green Papaya Slaw, *100, 101*
Udon Noodles, 294, *295*
Curry powder, 22
Currywurst, 54

D

Dairy foods. *See also specific foods, e.g.:* Cheese
Dalpuri roti, 102
Dark rice vinegar, 200
Deep-Fried Potato Balls, 239

Deep-frying, 49
Deglazing, 50
Dip, Tzatziki, or Caçik, 112
Dipping Sauce
    Chili, 107
    Soy, 107
    Vietnamese, 178
Disposable serving ware, 8
Dog
    Corn, 103
    Italian Sausage, 90
    Seafood, Creamed Savoy Cabbage
        for, 180
    Seafood Sausage, *154,* 155
Döner kebab, 22
Dressing, Russian, 117
Dried herbs, 37
Dried mustard greens (mei cai), 94
Drop lids, 12
Duck
    breast, searing, 50
    Stew, Duck Leg, 70
    Stew, Potato Gnocchi with, 68, *69*
Dumplings, Cilantro and Pork, Pan-Steamed,
    308, 309–310

E

East and South Asia, 10–18
    China, 12–13
    common tools of, 12
    Japan, 14
    Korea, 15, 16
    street food meals in, 4–5
    Thailand, 16, 18
    vegetarian/vegan cultures in, 186
    Vietnam, 16, 18
Eastern Mediterranean and North
    Africa, 18–22
    common tools of, 19
    cultural influences in, 18
    Greece, 19
    Middle East, 20–21
    North Africa, 21
    Turkey, 19–20
East Mediterranean Grilled Cheese, with
    Tomatoes, *242,* 243
Eggs
    Coddled, Grilled Toast with Coconut Jam
        and, 312
    in Curry, 208, *209*
    Spanish Potato Omelet, 240, *241*
Eggplant
    Parmesan, 190
    Relish, Bruschetta with Ricotta Salata
        Cheese and, 303
    Roasted, Purée with Yogurt and Walnuts, 201
    Spicy Stir-Fried, 200
Egypt, 20, 22
Empanadas, Tuna and Goat Cheese,
    156, *157*
Escabeche, Aromatic Fish, *172, 173*
Europe, 22–30. See also individual countries
    common tools of, 25
    communal village cooking places in, 5
    France, 27–28
    fruits as gifts in, 187
    globalization and migration patterns, 24
    Italy, 28
    northeastern Europe, 30
    Spain, 25, 27

F

Falafel, 22, *316,* 317
Fat(s)
    for frying, 49
    ghee, 89
    poaching in, 52
Fermented Tofu
    red, 93
    Sauce, Braised Pork Belly with Dried
        Mustard Greens and Lily Buds in, *92,* 93
Feta, Baked Phyllo Pocket with Spinach and,
    244
Finfish, 124–128
Finger foods, 9
Fish
    Bouillabaisse, *130,* 131
    braising, 51
    Brandade of Salt Cod, 161
    Cakes, Fried, with Cucumber Salad,
        136, *137*
    and Chips, 143
    Cioppino, 132
    classifying, 123
    Colombian Ceviche with Coconut Milk, 148
    cooking methods, 123–126
    Escabeche, Aromatic, *172, 173*
    Green Mexican Ceviche, *146,* 147
    Grilled, Tacos, *158, 159*
    Grilled, with Tapenade, *138, 139*
    Grilled Swordfish Skewer with Roasted
        Potato Salad, 169
    marinated *vs.* raw, 49
    in Mild Coconut Milk, 144
    Paste, Grilled Spiced, 167
    poached or steamed, 52
    purchase and storage of, 122–123
    Salt Cod Fish Fritters, 160
    sautéing, 50
    Spicy Fried, 166
    Stock, for Bouillabaisse, 174
    Swordfish Kebob, Braised, in Sweet and
        Savory Sauce, 150, *151*
    Tuna and Goat Cheese Empanadas, 156, *157*
Flaky Bread (Roti Prata), 110
Flatbread
    Chickpea, 323
    Stir-Fried Shredded, 290–291
Flatfish, 123
Flattop griddles, 50
Flautas (taquitos), 99
    Chicken, 99
Flavor principles. *See* International flavor
    principles
Flavor profiles, 41
Fleur de sel, 340
Florida, 31
Flower Rolls, Steamed, Peanut Butter-Stuffed,
    318, 319
Food safety practices, 7
Food-safety regulations, 5
Forbidden rice, 343
France, 24, 27–28
    regional cuisines in, 27
French Fries, 177
Fried Bananas in Manioc Crust, 357
Fried chicken, 49
Fried Chinese Crullers, 278–279
Fried Fish, Spicy, 166
Fried Fish Cakes with Cucumber Salad, 136, *137*
Fritters
    Cilantro and Chickpea, 315
    Onion, 235

Plantain, *236, 237*–238
Quark, 360
Ricotta, 357
Salt Cod Fish, 160
Frozen Almond Ricotta, 363
Frozen Mint Limeade, *364, 365*
Fruit(s), 186–187, 330. *See also specific types
    of fruits*
    Salad, Sweet and Spicy, 340
Fries
    French, 177
    Manioc, 234
Frying, 49–50
Funnel Cake Sandwich with Ice Cream and
    Maple Syrup, 344, *345*

G

Garam masala, 89, 208
Garlic and Saffron Mayonnaise, 175
Garlic Bread, Grilled, 248
German Bratwurts, Currywurst, 54
Germany, 24
Ghee, 89
Ginger, Carrot-Apple Smoothie with, 374
Glass Noodles, Stir-Fried, 297
Goat, Curry, with Green Papaya Slaw, *100, 101*
Goat Cheese Empanadas, Tuna and, 156, *157*
Gochujang, 64
Grains, 8, 254–260, 266. *See also specific
    grains; specific types*
    characteristics and applications, 254–257
    cooking methods for, 257–260
    couscous, 19
    grain pilafs, 259–260
    market forms of, 257–259
Grain pilafs, 259–260
Graters, ceramic, 12
Greece, 19, 22
Green Chili Sauce, 85
    Beef Skewers with, 85
Green Mexican Ceviche, *146,* 147
Green Onions, Bruschetta with Roasted
    Tomatoes, Pecorino Cheese, and, 302
Green Papaya Slaw, 118
    Curry Goat with, *100,* 101
Green pea(s), 274
    Split, Stew, 274
Green Peppercorns, Grilled Pineapple with
    Orange and, 332
Griddles, flattop, 50
Grills, 8
    kebob, 19
    satay, 8, 80
Grilled Corn on the Cob, 212
Grilled East Mediterranean Cheese with
    Tomatoes, *242,* 243
Grilled Fish
    Tacos, *158, 159*
    with Tapenade, *138, 139*
Grilled Garlic Bread, 248
Grilled Lamb Kebobs with Walnut-Herb Sauce,
    86, 87
Grilled Pork Skewers, 78
Grilled Shrimp Cake on Sugarcane,
    Vietnamese, 152–153
Grilled Spiced Fish Paste, 167
Grilled Sweet Potatoes, 204
Grilled Swordfish Skewer with Roasted Potato
    Salad, 169
Grilled Toast with Coconut Jam and Coddled
    Eggs, 312

INDEX   395

Grilled Vegetables, Romesco Sauce with, *196, 197*
Grilled Zucchini Kebob, *210,* 211
Grilling, 47, 49
Guyanese Filling, Caribbean Roti Bread with, 102
Gypsum, 281
Gyros, 98

H

Hainanese Chicken Rice, 60, *61*
Haloumi cheese, 243
Ham
    and Cheese Stacked Quesadillas, 95
    Serrano, and Manchego Croquettes, 104
Harissa, 324
Hawaiian cuisine, Spam in, 4
Hawker centers, 5, 7
Hazelnuts Picada, 183
Herbs, 37
    Caribbean cuisine, 34
    Chinese cuisine, 13
    common herbs and their uses, 37–39
    French cuisine, 27
    Greek or Turkish cuisine, 19
    Italian cuisine, 28
    Japanese cuisine, 14
    Korean cuisine, 15
    Mexican cuisine, 37
    Middle Eastern cuisine, 21
    Midwestern U.S. cuisine, 32
    North African cuisine, 21
    northeastern European cuisine, 30
    Northeastern U.S. cuisine, 32
    Northwestern U.S. cuisine, 33
    Southern U.S. cuisine, 32
    Southwestern U.S. cuisine, 33
    Spanish cuisine, 25
    Thai or Vietnamese cuisine, 18
Herbed Tapenade, 249
Hoisin-Peanut Sauce, 177
Hominy, 289
    Red, and Meat Stew, 55
    Stew, BBQ, *288,* 289
Honey
    Roti Prata with Bananas and, 350–351
    -Tomato-Almond Chutney, 250
Hot and Sour Soup, Thai, 134
Hot Chocolate with Masa, 375
Hot dishes, 7
Hot Dog
    Seafood, Creamed Savoy Cabbage for, 180
    Seafood Sausage, *154,* 155
Hot holding, 7
    braised or stewed food, 51
    sautéed items, 50
Hot or Iced Mint Tea, 374
Hot Tea Punch, 378, *379*
Huitlacoche, 219
Huitlacoche Filling, 219
    Pan-Fried Quesadillas, 217
Hummus, 322

I

Ice Cream
    Funnel Cake Sandwich with Maple Syrup
        and, 344, *345*
    Pistachio, 362
    Sandwiches, Mint-Lime with Coconut
        Meringue, *354,* 355

Immersion thermocirculators, 52
Indian tandoors, 12
Ingredients
    Brazilian, 34–35
    Caribbean, 34
    Chinese, 13
    European, 22
    French, 27
    Greek, 19
    impact of, 4
    Italian, 28
    Japanese, 14
    Korean, 15
    Mexican, 37
    Middle Eastern, 21
    Midwestern United States, 32
    North African, 21
    northeastern European, 30
    Northeastern United States, 32
    Northwestern United States, 33
    Southern United States, 32
    Southwestern United States, 33
    Spanish, 25
    Thai, 18
    Turkish, 19
    Vietnamese, 18
International flavor principles, 10–43
    Central and South America, 33–37
    East and South Asia, 10–18
    eastern Mediterranean and North Africa,
        18–22
    Europe, 22–30
    herbs, 37–39
    spice blends, 41–43
    spices, 39–41
    United States, 30–33
Iraq, 20
Israel, 20
Italian Sausage Dog, 90
Italy, 28
    regional cuisines in, 28
    Trajan's Market, 5

J

Jaggery, 333
Jam, Coconut, Grilled Toast with Coddled
    Eggs and, 312
Jamaican Beef Patties, 94
Japan, 12, 14
Japanese seven-spice, 14, 82
Jerk, 81
    Chicken Skewers, 81
Jordan, 20

K

Kabob/kebob grills, 8, 19
Kebob. *See also* Skewers
    Braised Swordfish, in Sweet and Savory
        Sauce, 150, *151*
    Caribbean Vegetable, 213
    Chicken Köfte, 79
    Döner, 22
    Grilled Lamb, with Walnut-Herb Sauce,
        86, 87
    Grilled Zucchini, *210,* 211
    Turkish Shish Kebob, 88
Ketchup, Tomato, 114
Khorma, Vegetable, 199

Kimchi, 15, 63
    Chickpea Stew with, in Pita Bread, 311
    Stew, Spicy, with Pork, *62,* 63
Knives, Japanese, 12
Koju jiang (gochujang), 15
Korea, 15, 16
Korean hot pepper paste, 64

L

Lamb
    Braised, Ravioli in Yogurt Sauce, *282,*
        283–284
    Breads, Tomato and, 230, *231*
    cooking methods for, 48
    Kebobs, Grilled, with Walnut-Herb Sauce,
        86, 87
    Turkish Shish Kebob, 88
Languedoc cuisine, 27
Latin America. *See* Central and South America
Lebanon, 20
Leche de tigre, 34
Leek Quiche, *224,* 225
Legumes, 260–263, 266. *See also specific*
    types
    Caribbean cuisine, 34
    Chinese cuisine, 13
    French cuisine, 27
    Greek or Turkish cuisine, 19
    Italian cuisine, 28
    Japanese cuisine, 14
    Korean cuisine, 15
    Mexican cuisine, 37
    Middle Eastern cuisine, 21
    Midwestern U.S. cuisine, 32
    North African cuisine, 21
    northeastern European cuisine, 30
    Northeastern U.S. cuisine, 32
    Northwestern U.S. cuisine, 33
    Southern U.S. cuisine, 32
    Southwestern U.S. cuisine, 33
    Spanish cuisine, 25
    Thai or Vietnamese cuisine, 18
Lemons, preserved, 211
Levant, 20. *See also* Middle East
Licenses, 7
Lily buds, 93
    Braised Pork Belly with Dried Mustard Greens
        and, in Fermented Tofu Sauce, *92, 93*
Lime
    Agua Fresca, with Chia Seeds, 370, *371*
    -Flavored Sour Cream, 181
Limeade, Frozen Mint, *364,* 365
Liquids, in moist-heat cooking, 52
Liquid nitrogen, freezing with, 331
London, 24
Lotus buns, steamed, 94
Louisiana, 31

M

Mac and Cheese with Bacon, 285
Maillard reaction, 47
Ma-La, 13
Malaysian Chicken Satay, 80
Malaysian Shrimp Paste Sambal, 183
Malaysian Stir-Fried Rice Noodles, *292, 293*
Manchego (Cheese)
    Croquettes, Serrano Ham and, 104
    Vegetable Sandwich with, 222, *223*

Mango
Dried, Black Rice Pudding with Coconut Milk and, *342, 343*
Lassi, 365
Manioc
Crust, Fried Bananas in, 357
Fries, 234
Manioc starch, 314
Marinade(s)
Beef Cured with Lime and Onions, 67
Charmoula, 211
Grilled Fish Tacos, 159
Grilled Pork Skewers, 78
for grilling meat and poultry, 47, 49
Malaysian Chicken Satay, 80
Mixed Vegetables and Beef with Rice, 64
Turkish Shish Kebob, 88
Marinated Tomatoes, 245
Masa, 217
Hot Chocolate with, 375
Mayonnaise, Garlic and Saffron, 175
Meat, 46–53. *See also* Poultry; *specific types of meats*
cookery and cooking methods, 47–53
Corn Dog, 103
marinating, 47, 49
Menudo, 71
preparation and consumption history, 46
tenderizing, 49
Meat tenderizers, 49
Mediterranean
eastern (*see* Eastern Mediterranean and North Africa)
southern, 22
Mei cai (dried mustard greens), 94
Melons in Basil-Lime Syrup, 366
Mexican Cream, 119
Mexico, 35, 37
taco al pastor, 4
taco Árabe, 4
tortilla presses, 31
Mexico City, Mexico, 37
Microplanes, 12
Middle East, 20–21
common tools in, 19
cooking methods in, 22
gastronomic influences in, 18
Midwestern United States, 32
Mint
Chutney, 326
Limeade, Frozen, *364,* 365
-Lime Ice Cream Sandwiches with Coconut Meringue, *354,* 355
Syrup, Crispy Chocolate Waffles with Whipped Cream and, *334,* 335
tea, 374
Tea, Hot or Iced, 374
Mixed Vegetables and Beef with Rice (Bibimbap), 64, *65*
Mobile catering, 6
Moist-heat cooking, 52–53
Molinillo, 375
Mollusks, 122–124
characteristics and cooking methods, 128
Mongolia, 13
Mung bean(s)
noodles, 12
and Rice Crêpes, Chinese, 306, *307*
and Scallion Pancakes, 320, *321*
Mushrooms
Chilaquiles with, 286, *287*

Portobello Sandwich with Madeira-Glazed Onions and Brie, 229
Spicy Tofu with, 202, *203*
Mussels
Cioppino, 132
with Olives, *164,* 165
Steamed, with Spanish Chorizo, 135
Mustard Greens
Bruschetta with Parmesan Cheese and, 304
Dried, Braised Pork Belly with Lily Buds and, in Fermented Tofu Sauce, *92, 93*

N

Native American cooking techniques, 31
New York City, 31
Nixtamalization, 35, 289
Non-bony fish, 123
Noodles, 263–265. *See also specific types*
Chinese, 12
Curry Udon, 294, *295*
Glass, Stir-Fried, 297
Japanese, 14
Korean, 15
Rice, Malaysian Stir-Fried, *292, 293*
Savory Pork Sauce with Corn Pancakes or, 270, *271*
Thai, 18
Nopales, 220
Nopales Filling, 220
Pan-Fried Quesadillas, 217
North Africa, 18–19, 21. *See also* Eastern Mediterranean and North Africa
common tools in, 19
cooking methods in, 22
Northeastern Europe, 30
Northeastern United States, 32
Northern Italian cuisine, 28
Northwestern United States, 33
Nuoc cham, 178

O

Oats, 254
Octopus, "Fairground-Style," 149
Oils, for frying, 49
Olive(s)
Green, Chicken Thighs with, *76, 77*
Herbed Tapenade, 249
Mussels with, *164,* 165
Spread, Tomato, Garlic, and, 251
Tapenade, 176
Omelet, Spanish Potato, 240, *241*
Onion(s)
Beef Cured with Lime and, *66,* 67
Cake, *232, 233*
Fritters, 235
Portobello Sandwich with Madeira-Glazed Brie and, 229
Red, Relish, 113
Orange
-Glazed Chicken Wings, 108, *109*
Grilled Pineapple with Green Peppercorns and, 332
Ovens, 12, 25

P

Paella, 296
Valenciana, 296
Pakora Fried Vegetable Skewer, 214, *215*

Pancake(s)
Baked Cherry, *348,* 349
Corn, 322
Mung Bean and Scallion, 320, *321*
Shredded Caramelized, *336,* 337
Shrimp, 162, *163*
Pandan, 312
Panela cheese, 221
Pan-Fried Quesadillas, *216,* 217–220
Pan-frying, 49
Pan-Steamed Cilantro and Pork Dumplings, *308,* 309–310
Papaya Slaw, Green, Curry Goat with, *100,* 101
Parathas, Potato, 305
Parmesan Cheese, Bruschetta with Mustard Greens and, 304
Pasta. *See also* Noodles
Whole Wheat, with Sharp Pesto, 298, *299*
Pastry chefs, 25
Peanut
-Hoisin Sauce, 177
Sauce for Satays, 113
Peanut Butter-Stuffed Steamed Flower Rolls, *318,* 319
Pecorino Cheese, Bruschetta with Roasted Tomatoes, Green Onions, and, 302
Pequin chiles, 212
Permits, 7
Peru, 34
Pesto, Sharp, Whole Wheat Pasta with, 298, *299*
Philadelphia, Pennsylvania, 31
Phyllo Pocket, Baked, with Spinach and Feta, 244
Picada, 183
Pickles, Vegetable, Southeast Asian, 246, *247*
Pilafs, grain, 259–260
Pineapple, Grilled, with Green Peppercorns and Orange, 332
Pistachio Ice Cream, 362
Pita bread, 111, 266
Chickpea Stew with Kimchi in, 311
Falafel, *316,* 317
Plain Soy Milk, 275
Plantain Fritters, *236,* 237–238
Poaching, 52–53
Poblano (Peppers)
Coulis, 250
in Cream, Tacos with, 221
Political movements, collective kitchens/ canteens for, 6
Pomegranate molasses, 204
Pork
Belly, Braised, with Dried Mustard Greens and Lily Buds in Fermented Tofu Sauce, *92, 93*
Belly, Red Cooked, *56,* 57
cooking methods for, 48
Chinese Crispy Spring Rolls, 106
Cracklings, Radish Salad with, *192, 193*
Currywurst, 54
Dumplings, Pan-Steamed Cilantro and, *308,* 309–310
Gyros, 98
Knuckle, Braised, Bun, 91
Red Hominy and Meat Stew, 55
Sauce, Savory, with Noodles or Corn Pancakes, 270, *271*
Schaschlik, 84
Skewers, Grilled, 78
Spicy Kimchi Stew with, *62,* 63
Vietnamese Crispy Spring Rolls, 105
Portland, Oregon, 31

INDEX 397

Portobello Sandwich with Madeira-Glazed Onions and Brie, 229
Potato(es)
Balls, Deep-Fried, 239
French Fries, 177
Gnocchi with Duck Stew, 68, *69*
Omelet, Spanish, 240, *241*
Parathas, 305
Roasted, Salad, 179
Roasted, Salad, Grilled Swordfish Skewer with, 169
Spread, Garlic, Olive and, 251
storage of, 186–187
Pot rooms (European), 25
Poultry, 46–53. *See also specific types of poultry*
cookery and cooking methods, 47–53
marinating, 47, 49
preparation and consumption history, 46
roasting, 51
Preserved lemons, 211
Privacy, 5
Produce. *See also* Fruit(s); Sea vegetables/vegetation; Vegetable(s)
Caribbean cuisine, 34
Chinese cuisine, 13
French cuisine, 27
Greek or Turkish cuisine, 19
Italian cuisine, 28
Japanese cuisine, 14
Korean cuisine, 15
Mexican cuisine, 37
Middle Eastern cuisine, 21
Midwestern U.S. cuisine, 32
North African cuisine, 21
northeastern European cuisine, 30
Northeastern U.S. cuisine, 32
Northwestern U.S. cuisine, 33
Southern U.S. cuisine, 32
Southwestern U.S. cuisine, 33
Spanish cuisine, 25
Thai or Vietnamese cuisine, 18
Protein. *See also* Eggs; Fish; Meat; Poultry; Seafood
Caribbean cuisine, 34
Chinese cuisine, 13
French cuisine, 27
Greek or Turkish cuisine, 19
Italian cuisine, 28
Japanese cuisine, 14
Korean cuisine, 15
Mexican cuisine, 37
Middle Eastern cuisine, 21
Midwestern U.S. cuisine, 32
North African cuisine, 21
northeastern European cuisine, 30
Northeastern U.S. cuisine, 32
Northwestern U.S. cuisine, 33
Southern U.S. cuisine, 32
Southwestern U.S. cuisine, 33
Spanish cuisine, 25
Thai or Vietnamese cuisine, 18
Prosciutto, Bruschetta with Cauliflower and, *300,* 301
Provence cuisine, 27
Pudding
Black Rice, with Coconut Milk and Dried Mango, *342, 343*
Red Berry, with Vanilla Sauce, 338, *339*
Puerto Rico, 31
Pulses. *See* Legumes
Punch, Hot Tea, 378, *379*

Purée, Roasted Eggplant, with Yogurt and Walnuts, 201
Purple corn, 373
Drink, *372, 373*

Q

Quality standards, 10
Quark, 360
Fritters, 360
Quesadillas
Ham and Cheese Stacked, 95
Pan-Fried, *216,* 217–220
Queso Chihuahua, 220
Queso cotija, 212
Queso panela, 221
Quiche, Leek, *224, 225*

R

Radish Salad with Pork Cracklings, *192,* 193
Raisin powder, 340
Raita, Cucumber, 326
Ravioli, Braised Lamb, in Yogurt Sauce, *282,* 283–284
Raw Tomatillo and Avocado Salsa, 118
Red Berry Pudding with Vanilla Sauce, 338, *339*
Red Cooked Pork Belly, *56, 57*
Red Hominy and Meat Stew, 55
Red Onion Relish, 113
Regulations, 5, 7
Relish, Red Onion, 113
Rempah, 73–75, *74*
Rendang, 73
Resinous herbs, 37
Reuben Sandwich, *96, 97*
Sauerkraut for, 117
Reusable serving ware, 7–8
Reverse searing, 52
Revolutionary Cuisine (China), 6
Rice, 254
Cardamom-Flavored Cream of, with Saffron, 333
Creamy Citrus, 341
Hainanese Chicken, 60, *61*
Mixed Vegetables and Beef with (Bibimbap), 64, *65*
and Mung Bean Crêpes, Chinese, 306, *307*
Noodles, Malaysian Stir-Fried, *292, 293*
preparation tools for, 12
Pudding, Black, with Coconut Milk and Dried Mango, *342, 343*
Ricotta Fritters, 357
Ricotta Salata Cheese, Bruschetta with Eggplant Relish and, 303
Roasted Eggplant Purée with Yogurt and Walnuts, 201
Roasted Potato Salad, 179
Grilled Swordfish Skewer with, 169
Roasting, 50–51
Romesco Sauce, 198
with Grilled Vegetables, *196, 197*
Roti Prata/Bread (Flaky Bread), 102, 110
with Bananas and Honey, 350–351
Caribbean, with Guyanese Filling, 102
Rotisserie, 51
Roundfish, 123
Rum Babas, 353
Russian Dressing, 117
Rutabaga Stew, *206, 207*
Rye, 254

S

Saffron
Cardamom-Flavored Cream of Rice with, 333
Mayonnaise, Garlic and, 175
Salad
of Bean Starch Sheets, *268,* 269
Cucumber, Fried Fish Cakes with, 136, *137*
Cucumber, Spicy Thai, 175
Fruit, Sweet and Spicy, 340
Radish, with Pork Cracklings, *192,* 193
Roasted Potato, 179
Roasted Potato, Grilled Swordfish Skewer with, 169
Salgadinhos, 35
Salsa
Cooked Tomatillo, 325
Raw Tomatillo and Avocado, 118
Verde, 248
Salt Cod
Brandade of, 161
Fish Fritters, 160
Salted Yogurt Drink, *376,* 377
Samfaina, 195
Samosas, *226,* 227–228
Sandwich(es), 8–9
Portobello, with Madeira-Glazed Onions and Brie, 229
Reuben, *96, 97*
Vegetable, with Manchego Cheese, 222, *223*
Sansho pepper, 82
Sashimi, 49
Satays, 80
Peanut Sauce for, 113
Satay grills, 8, 80
Sauce. *See also* Dipping Sauce
Black Ink, Squid in, 168
Fermented Tofu, Braised Pork Belly with Dried Mustard Greens and Lily Buds in, *92, 93*
Green Chili, 85
Green Chili, Beef Skewers with, 85
Hoisin-Peanut, 177
Peanut, for Satays, 113
Romesco, 198
Romesco, with Grilled Vegetables, *196, 197*
Savory Pork, with Noodles or Corn Pancakes, 270, *271*
Sweet and Savory, Braised Swordfish Kebob in, 150, *151*
Tomato, 191
Vanilla, 361
Vanilla, Red Berry Pudding with, 338, *339*
Walnut-Herb, 114
Walnut-Herb, Grilled Lamb Kebobs with, *86, 87*
Yakitori, 82
Yogurt, Braised Lamb Ravioli in, *282,* 283–284
Saudi Arabia, 20
Sauerkraut for Reuben Sandwich, 117
Sausage
Dog, Italian, 90
Seafood, Hot Dog, *154, 155*
Sautéing, 50
Savory Pork Sauce with Noodles or Corn Pancakes, 270, *271*
Savoy Cabbage, Creamed, for Seafood Hot Dog, 180
Scallion and Mung Bean Pancakes, 320, *321*
Scandinavia, 30
Schaschlik, 84
Seafood, 122–129. *See also* Fish
Chili Crab, 140, *141*

398 INDEX

Coconut Seafood Chowder, 133
cooking methods, 123–124, 128–129
Mussels with Olives, *164,* 165
Octopus "Fairground-Style," 149
poached or steamed, 52
purchase and storage of, 122–123
risks of, 122
sautéing, 50
Shrimp in Garlic, 170, *171*
Shrimp Pancakes, 162, *163*
Squid in Black Ink Sauce, 168
Steamed Mussels with Spanish
     Chorizo, 135
Stuffed Baked Squid, 142
Thai Hot and Sour Soup, 134
Vietnamese Grilled Shrimp Cake on
     Sugarcane, 152–153
Seafood Hot Dog
     Creamed Savoy Cabbage for, 180
     Sausage, *154,* 155
Searing, 50, 51
     reverse, 52
Sea scallops, Cioppino, 132
Seasoning. *See also* Herbs; International flavor
     principles; Spice blends; Spices
     to enhance Maillard reaction, 47
     of moist-heat-cooked meat and poultry, 52
Sea vegetables/vegetation, 122
     characteristics and cooking methods, 129
Serrano Ham and Manchego Croquettes, 104
Shallots, Crispy Fried, 181
Shanghai, 13
Shaoxing wine, 57
Shichimi togarashi, 14, 82
Shish Kebob, Turkish, 88
Shortenings, for frying, 49
Shredded Caramelized Pancake, *336,* 337
Shrimp
     Bouillabaisse, *130,* 131
     Cake, Vietnamese Grilled, on Sugarcane,
          152–153
     Cioppino, 132
     in Garlic, 170, *171*
     Pancakes, 162, *163*
Shrimp Paste Sambal, Malaysian, 183
Shwarma, 22
Sichuan cuisine, 13
Sichuan flavor profile, 202
Simmering, 52–53
Singapore, street food hawker centers in, 4–5
Skewers. *See also* Kebob
     Beef, with Green Chili Sauce, 85
     Grilled Pork, 78
     Grilled Swordfish, with Roasted Potato
          Salad, 169
     Jerk Chicken, 81
     Pakora Fried Vegetable, 214, *215*
     types of, 8
Skewered foods, 8
Slaw
     Green Papaya, 118
     Green Papaya, Curry Goat with, *100,* 101
     Southwestern, 182
Slow roasting, 50–51
Smoothie
     Açai and Banana, 368
     Avocado-Apple, 368
     Carrot-Apple, with Ginger, 374
Soup
     Black Bean, 267
     Bouillabaisse, *130,* 131
     Bouillabaisse, Fish Stock for, 174

Coconut Seafood Chowder, 133
Curdled Soy Milk with Fried Crullers,
     276–277
Spicy Chickpea, 272, *273*
Thai Hot and Sour, 134
Sour Cream, Lime-Flavored, 181
Sous vide cooking, 52–53
South America. *See* Central and South America
South Asia. *See* East and South Asia
Southeast Asia, vegetarian/vegan cultures
     in, 186
Southeast Asian Iced Bubble Tea, *380,* 381
Southeast Asian Vegetable Pickles, 246, *247*
Southern Italian cuisine, 28
Southern Mediterranean, 22
Southern United States, 31, 32
Southwestern Slaw, 182
Southwestern United States, 31, 33
Soybeans, 260–261
Soy Dipping Sauce, 107
Soy Milk
     Curdled, with Fried Crullers, 276–277
     Plain, 275
Spain, 25, 27
Spam, 4
Spanish Chorizo, Beef Cheeks and Tripe with,
     58, 59
Spanish Potato Omelet, 240, *241*
Spices, 39
     Caribbean cuisine, 34
     Chinese cuisine, 13
     common spices and their uses, 39–41
     French cuisine, 27
     Greek or Turkish cuisine, 19
     Italian cuisine, 28
     Japanese cuisine, 14
     Korean cuisine, 15
     Mexican cuisine, 37
     Middle Eastern cuisine, 21
     Midwestern U.S. cuisine, 32
     North African cuisine, 21
     northeastern European cuisine, 30
     Northeastern U.S. cuisine, 32
     Northwestern U.S. cuisine, 33
     Southern U.S. cuisine, 32
     Southwestern U.S. cuisine, 33
     Spanish cuisine, 25
     Thai or Vietnamese cuisine, 18
Spice blends, 41–43
     garam masala, 89
Spiced Fish Paste, Grilled, 167
Spicy Chickpea Soup, 272, *273*
Spicy Cucumbers, 325
Spicy Fried Fish, 166
Spicy Kimchi Stew with Pork, *62,* 63
Spicy or Sweet Soft Tofu, 280–281
Spicy Stir-Fried Eggplant, 200
Spicy Thai Cucumber Salad, 175
Spicy Tofu with Mushrooms, 202, *203*
Spinach, Baked Phyllo Pocket with Feta and, 244
Spit roasting, 51
Split Green Pea Stew, 274
Spread(s)
     Hummus, 322
     Potato, Garlic, and Olive, 251
Spring Rolls
     Chinese Crispy, 106
     Vietnamese Crispy, 105
Squid
     in Black Ink Sauce, 168
     Stuffed Baked, 142

Starches. *See also specific kinds of starches,*
     e.g.: Rice
     Caribbean cuisine, 34
     Chinese cuisine, 13
     French cuisine, 27
     Greek or Turkish cuisine, 19
     Italian cuisine, 28
     Japanese cuisine, 14
     Korean cuisine, 15
     Mexican cuisine, 37
     Middle Eastern cuisine, 21
     Midwestern U.S. cuisine, 32
     North African cuisine, 21
     northeastern European cuisine, 30
     Northeastern U.S. cuisine, 32
     Northwestern U.S. cuisine, 33
     Southern U.S. cuisine, 32
     Southwestern U.S. cuisine, 33
     Spanish cuisine, 25
     Thai or Vietnamese cuisine, 18
Steamed Flower Rolls, Peanut Butter-Stuffed,
     318, 319
Steamed lotus buns, 94
Steamed Mussels with Spanish Chorizo, 135
Steamers, bamboo, 12
Steaming, 52–53
Stew
     BBQ Hominy, *288,* 289
     Bouillabaisse, *130,* 131
     Bouillabaisse, Fish Stock for, 174
     Chickpea, with Kimchi in Pita Bread, 311
     Cioppino, 132
     Duck, Potato Gnocchi with, 68, *69*
     Duck Leg, 70
     Red Hominy and Meat, 55
     Rutabaga, *206,* 207
     Spicy Kimchi, with Pork, *62,* 63
     Split Green Pea, 274
Stewing, 51
Stick, foods on, 8
Stir-Fried Eggplant, Spicy, 200
Stir-Fried Glass Noodles, 297
Stir-Fried Rice Noodles, Malaysian,
     292, 293
Stir-Fried Shredded Flatbread, 290–291
Stir-frying, 50
Stock, Fish, for Bouillabaisse, 174
Street food, 4–43
     as career choice, 6
     categories of, 7–9
     Central and South America, 33–37
     defined, 4
     East and South Asia, 10–18
     eastern Mediterranean and North Africa,
          18–22
     Europe, 22–30
     herbs and their uses, 37–39
     history of, 5–6
     international spice blends, 41–43
     preparing, transporting, and serving, 6–7
     spices and their uses, 39–41
     the United States, 30–33
Stuffed Baked Squid, 142
Stuffed foods, 8–9
Sweating, 51
Sweets, 9, 330–331
     Apple Compote, 361
     Baked Cherry Pancake, *348,* 349
     Baklava, 347
     Bananas in Cardamom Syrup, 366
     Beignets, 358, *359*

INDEX   399

Sweets *(continued)*
　　Black Rice Pudding with Coconut Milk and Dried Mango, *342,* 343
　　Buckwheat Crêpes, 352
　　Cardamom-Flavored Cream of Rice with Saffron, 333
　　Churros, 356
　　Creamy Citrus Rice, 341
　　Crispy Chocolate Waffles with Mint Syrup and Whipped Cream, *334,* 335
　　Fried Bananas in Manioc Crust, 357
　　Frozen Almond Ricotta, 363
　　Funnel Cake Sandwich with Ice Cream and Maple Syrup, 344, *345*
　　Grilled Pineapple with Green Peppercorns and Orange, 332
　　Melons in Basil-Lime Syrup, 366
　　Mint-Lime Ice Cream Sandwiches with Coconut Meringue, *354,* 355
　　Pistachio Ice Cream, 362
　　Quark Fritters, 360
　　Red Berry Pudding with Vanilla Sauce, 338, *339*
　　Ricotta Fritters, 357
　　Roti Prata with Bananas and Honey, 350–351
　　Rum Babas, 353
　　Shredded Caramelized Pancake, *336,* 337
　　on a stick, 8
　　Sweet and Spicy Fruit Salad, 340
　　Sweet Tamales, 346
　　Vanilla Sauce, 361
Sweet and Savory Sauce, Braised Swordfish Kebob in, 150, *151*
Sweet and Sour Zucchini, 324
Sweet and Spicy Fruit Salad, 340
Sweet or Spicy Soft Tofu, 280–281
Sweet Potatoes, Grilled, 204
Sweet Tamales, 346
Swordfish
　　Grilled, Skewer with Roasted Potato Salad, 169
　　Kebob, Braised, in Sweet and Savory Sauce, 150, *151*
Syria, 20
Syrup
　　Basil-Lime, Melons in, 366
　　Cardamom, Bananas in, 366
　　Mint, Crispy Chocolate Waffles with Whipped Cream and, *334,* 335

T

Tabbouleh, 327
Tacmiyya, 22
Tacos
　　Grilled Fish, *158,* 159
　　with Poblano Peppers in Cream, 221
Taco al pastor, 4
Taco Árabe, 4
Tagines, 19
Tamales, 346
　　Sweet, 346
Tandoor, 12
Tapas, 25–27
Tapenade, 176, 249
　　Grilled Fish with, *138,* 139
　　Herbed, 249

Tapioca
　　in bubble tea, 381
　　Cheese Bread, 314
Taquitos, 99
Tea
　　Bubble, Southeast Asian Iced, *380,* 381
　　Hot or Iced Mint, 374
　　Punch, Hot, 378, *379*
Temperature
　　for frying meat and poultry, 49
　　for poaching, 52
Terroir, 47
Texas, 31
Tex-Mex cuisine, 31
Thai Hot and Sour Soup, 134
Thailand, 16, 18
　　bamboo steamers, 12
　　regional cuisines, 16, 18
Tiger lily buds, 93
Tiradito, 34
Tofu
　　knots, 57
　　red fermented, 93
　　Sauce, Fermented, Braised Pork Belly with Dried Mustard Greens and Lily Buds in, *92,* 93
　　silken, 202
　　Soft, Spicy or Sweet, 280–281
　　Spicy, with Mushrooms, 202, *203*
Tomatillo
　　Raw, and Avocado Salsa, 118
　　Salsa, Cooked, 325
Tomato(es)
　　-Braised Cauliflower, 194
　　Breads, Lamb and, 230, *231*
　　Grilled East Mediterranean Cheese with, *242, 243*
　　-Honey-Almond Chutney, 250
　　Ketchup, 114
　　Marinated, 245
　　Roasted, Bruschetta with Green Onions, Pecorino Cheese, and, 302
　　Sauce, 191
Tools. *See* Culinary tools
Tortillas, Corn, 279
Tortilla presses, 31
Tostonera, 31
"Trailer parks," 5
Trajan's Market, 5
Tripe
　　Beef Cheeks and, with Spanish Chorizo, *58, 59*
　　Menudo, 71
Tuna
　　Ceviche, Chilean, 145
　　Empanadas, Goat Cheese and, 156, *157*
Turkey, 19–20
Turkish Shish Kebob, 88
Turkish Water Börek, 284
Tzatziki, or Caçık, 112

U

Udon noodles, 294
　　Curry, 294, *295*
United States, 30–33
　　common tools of, 31

Midwestern, 32
Northeastern, 32
Northwestern, 33
Southern, 32
Southwestern, 33
Unleavened breads, 8

V

Vanilla Sauce, 361
　　Red Berry Pudding with, 338, *339*
Vegan dishes, 186
Vegetable(s), 186–189. *See also specific vegetables*
　　cooking methods, 188–189
　　Grilled, Romesco Sauce with, *196,* 197
　　Kebob, Caribbean, 213
　　Khorma, 199
　　Mixed, and Beef with Rice (Bibimbap), 64, *65*
　　Pickles, Southeast Asian, 246, *247*
　　preparation of, 187
　　roasting, 51
　　Samfaina, 195
　　Sandwich, with Manchego Cheese, 222, *223*
　　sautéed, 50
　　Skewer, Pakora Fried, 214, *215*
　　in Spicy Coconut Milk, 205
　　storage of, 186–187
Vegetarian dishes, 16, 186
Verjus, 340
Vietnam, 16, 18
　　regional cuisines, 16
Vietnamese Crispy Spring Rolls, 105
Vietnamese Dipping Sauce, 178
Vietnamese Grilled Shrimp Cake on Sugarcane, 152–153

W

Waffles, Crispy Chocolate, with Mint Syrup and Whipped Cream, *334,* 335
Walnut-Herb Sauce, 114
　　Grilled Lamb Kebobs with, *86,* 87
West Coast cuisine (United States), 31
Wheat, in China, 12–13
Whole Wheat Pasta with Sharp Pesto, 298, *299*
Wine, Shaoxing, 57
Woks, 12

Y

Yakitori Sauce, 82
Yogurt
　　Drink, Salted, *376,* 377
　　Mango Lassi, 365
　　Sauce, Braised Lamb Ravioli in, *282,* 283–284
　　Tzatziki, or Caçık, 112

Z

Zoning rules, 7
Zucchini
　　Kebob, Grilled, *210,* 211
　　Sweet and Sour, 324